Currently Away is a rare combination of practical Great Loop information, an engaging tale of one boat's Great Loop journey, and an emotional look at personal and societal issues. Bruce Tate is a talented storyteller, able to seamlessly weave a dose of humor into his narrative while also tackling weighty topics and current events. As Bruce and Maggie emerge from Covid isolation worse for the wear, they set out on their Great Loop in hopes of rediscovering their adventuresome spirits. *Currently Away* is a candid look at the challenges and triumphs they experience along the way. The book shares the Tates' joy in reconnecting with nature and socializing with family and friends. It also shares their emotions as they deal with profound loss along the way. If you are curious about the Great Loop, or are seeking your own healing journey, *Currently Away* is a great read.

➤ **Kim Russo**
    Director, America's Great Loop Cruisers' Association

Bruce's introspection and analysis throughout *Currently Away* capture the essence of the journey around America's Great Loop. Throughout *Currently Away*, Bruce explains the challenges he's faced in the past two years as a high-risk patient for Covid, the learning curve to operating and maintaining a boat, and the deep desire to integrate his friends and family into this adventure.

➤ **Jenn and Elliot, Gold Loopers,** *Pivot*
    Adventure Travelers and Producers, Scho and Jo, YouTube Channel

Let's face it: things are really messed up. Covid, divisiveness, climate, the list seems endless. It's no wonder there seems to be a general feeling of despair in the world. Most of us hunker down and hope for things to get better. Maggie and Bruce took a different path. They bought a boat, and with no real boating experience set out to complete the Great Loop, a six-thousand-mile circuit around the eastern United States. It was a brave, counterintuitive move. And, fortunately for us, they documented their journey: Bruce's words and Maggie's pictures. The result is a wonderful travel diary, full of interesting places and people, and accidents (both good and bad). More importantly, during their nine months on the water they discovered that if you peel away the news and the social media, the real world is still there; people are, in general, good and kind, the world is interesting, and the journey is worth it.

Read this book, then go looking for yourself.

➤ **Dave Thomas**
Founder, Pragmatic Programmers, LLC

Currently Away is a smart, funny, heartfelt glimpse into a little known American boating adventure, the Great Loop. I laughed out loud, cried, and celebrated along with Maggie and Bruce as they found their skills as captains and refound themselves and each other on their year-long odyssey through the rivers, lakes, oceans, and locks that make up the Great Loop.

➤ **Carol Keith**
Avid traveler, reader, adventurer

Currently Away describes a courageously revealing personal journey on an already daring voyage on a very small boat.

➤ **Sebastien Leclercq**
Project Manager, Atelier Fine Art Services

This memoir of the Great American Loop describes with great humor and humility the steep learning curve of a couple's experience piloting a boat through six thousand miles of rivers, lakes, and coastline. It also honestly details the challenges of traveling while dealing with grief and sickness and balancing those hardships with the profound joy of a newfound community and discovering truths about one's own country, marriage, and self.

➤ **Tasha Doremus, Gold Looper,** *Kittiwake*
Artist

Currently Away

How Two Disenchanted People
Traveled the Great Loop for
Nine Months and Returned to
the Start, Energized and Optimistic

Bruce Tate

The Pragmatic Bookshelf

Dallas, Texas

Pragmatic Bookshelf

For our complete catalog of hands-on, practical, and Pragmatic content for software developers, please visit *https://pragprog.com*.

Contact *support@pragprog.com* for sales, volume licensing, and support; contact *rights@pragprog.com* for international rights.

ISBN-13: 979-8-88865-027-1
Book version: P1.0—December, 2023

The team that produced this book includes:

Publisher:	Dave Thomas
COO:	Janet Furlow
Managing Editor:	Tammy Coron
Development Editor:	Michael Swaine
Copy Editor:	L. Sakhi MacMillan

Part I — Preparations

Part II — To the Gulf

Part III — Florida

Part IV — Atlantic

Part V — Canada

Part VI — Lake Michigan
and the Rivers

Foreword

Currently Away is anything but away. Bruce shares the story of himself and his wife who, after two difficult years, untie the lines and leave the dock for the unknown. During their nine-month journey, they'd challenge their boating skills in ways they didn't expect and be forced to grow as individuals and in their relationship. They'd experience meaningful connections that would reshape their definition of community.

We first met Bruce and his wife, Maggie, in one of our favorite small towns along the Great Loop in Oriental, North Carolina. Bruce, Maggie, and motor vessel (MV) *Currently* had preceded themselves, as we heard about them through the looper grapevine. Loopers talk, and when a young, friendly couple made their way through docktails and sundowners, pretty soon everyone knew about *Currently*. I knew we would hit it off. We met them at a local restaurant and enjoyed a meal while getting to know them personally. I knew we'd connect with their adventurous personalities. We also learned about their diet. On their Instagram @currentlytheboat, we discovered that one unique part of their loop was that, due to dietary restrictions, they cooked vegan food in their small galley. I saw these boaters who had a specific diet, which meant they had to be creative with the lack of resources and space. That's something I admire and appreciate in others. Our friendship would be more than standard meat and potatoes and instead would be full of flavor, variety, and originality. I knew we would like them even before we met.

The Great Loop is a six-thousand-mile boating journey that is most popular with retirees, so anyone who is not a traditional American retired age stands out. Being the "kids" on the loop (we're both thirty-one years old at the time this is written), we instantly hit it off with the "young loopers," who we deemed were people who had kids our age but no grandkids yet. Bruce and Maggie fit into this group, not just in age but also in spirit. Bruce and Maggie were the brave parents who ventured off on this grand adventure like we did. Throughout our Great Loop experience, many of the "young loopers" would be our anchors, providing us with friendships that we continue to value today.

The Great Loop has this ability to connect people like no other community we've experienced. A white, sometimes yellow or gray flag, called a burgee, with the America's Great Loop Cruiser's Association logo on a boat's bow is an instant connection. We share miles, relate experiences, and have similar trials and tribulations that challenge us all in unique but similar ways. *Currently Away* depicts the challenges of buying a new boat, learning how to maneuver it, the fear behind untying the lines for the very first time, and knowing that you won't be returning for about twelve months and six thousand miles. Many "loopers," as we're termed, understand what it's like to cruise day after day in unknown waters. To be miles away from your home port and have to problem-solve boat issues that arise is challenging and scary, yet it's something that unites us as loopers. As someone who has cruised on days we should have stayed put, or has learned the hard lesson of putting all of your trust in your captain or first mate, we understand the value of Bruce's vulnerability in *Currently Away* as he shares the challenges he faced on the Great Loop.

All loopers are looking for something: an adventure in retirement, a healing process after a traumatic event, or a challenge to complete a journey rarer than summitting

Everest. Loopers are not content, because otherwise they would never leave the dock. This desire for something more, something that we strive for in our travels, connects us with each other. We all have our "pre-loop" story that explains what led us to this grand adventure. We then make our "loop stories," which are the experiences that changed us as boaters, travelers, and people. Later we go into our "post-loop life," where many of us crave the daily adventure we experienced traveling on the Great Loop—where problem-solving, planning routes in new territories, learning new skills such as mechanics or reading the weather, enjoying new places, and sharing these waterways with comrades was part of our daily life. Once people cross their wake and complete their loop, this motif is frequently shared. This search for more is what Bruce shares in *Currently Away*.

Bruce's introspection and analysis throughout *Currently Away* capture the essence of the journey around America's Great Loop. Throughout *Currently Away*, Bruce explains the challenges he's faced in the past two years as a high-risk patient for Covid, the learning curve to operating and maintaining a boat, and the deep desire to integrate his friends and family into this adventure. Elliot and I also tell the story of every day on the loop through our YouTube channel and reinforce how this adventure is more about the journey than the destination. This trip is full of highs and lows, and you can't appreciate the highs without taking stock of the lows. This interest in sharing our personal experiences with others is something we share in common with Bruce.

Throughout the book, you quickly understand the heart Bruce has to share this adventure with others. Before their adventure began, they opted to postpone their departure so they could spend more time with their kids, putting them in the back of the "looper pack." Throughout the book, they welcome various guests aboard, disregarding the "never have a schedule on a boat" mentality for the value community and close companionship bring them. A schedule brings significant trade-offs, and because of their choice to schedule, we gain insight into who Bruce is; it's heartwarming to read about Bruce's passion for community and the journey that led him to better understand his world, country, and the challenges that strengthened his relationships. Bruce went from a period of being lost and uncertain to opening his heart as he set out a welcome mat to his modest boat to anyone around them. Bruce is vulnerable in ways that loopers and boaters can commiserate on encountering nasty weather, making less-than-ideal decisions, and telling the stories of being scared at times. He shares the "life" that goes on while embarking on this journey through the losses of a sibling and a beloved family member. Reading *Currently Away*, we felt as if we were along for the ride, reliving much of our own loop experience but through the lens of *Currently*.

Seven months after meeting Bruce and Maggie in North Carolina, we reunited with them as we made our way to Chattanooga, on the Tennessee River side trip. We instantly were reintroduced to Bruce's nerdiness and concern for safety and our well-being, and to Maggie's larger-than-life, welcoming, and warm personality. During our two weeks in Chattanooga, we enjoyed dinner with them three times, including Thanksgiving dinner. During that time, Bruce and Maggie welcomed anyone transiting the Tennessee River into their home so they could intentionally share the hospitality, generosity, and connection that they received on the Great Loop. It was clear that in their daily life in Chattanooga they were focused on making changes in their "post-loop" life to incorporate the lessons and takeaways from their six-thousand-mile journey. Maggie's warm personality is the heart of the home, which comes across instantly when you meet her, and Bruce consistently engaged in meaningful and thought-provoking conversations. Each time we left Bruce and Maggie's home, we were blown away by their continued kindness as they treated us like family while also being entranced in deep thought, instilling in us the importance of critical thinking and open-mindedness.

We understood that MV *Currently* and this grand adventure was much more than just deepening their marriage, building confidence as boaters and problem solvers, and strengthening friendships and relationships with their daughters. It's through the tribulations over six thousand miles that they revitalized their deep passion for community and for sharing some of life's best moments both with the people they love and the friends they didn't know they had yet on the loop. *Currently Away* is here to take you on a thought-provoking journey into a once-in-a-lifetime experience.

Jennifer Johnson (and Elliot Schoenfeld)
MV *Pivot*, Gold Looper 2023

Acknowledgments

Most of the tens of thousands of words on the hundreds of pages that make up this book are written for *you*. These few words are a bit different. These next few words are for me, and for the individuals that made this book possible. I hope to provide enough gems in this section to keep you reading.

Notice that I'll focus these acknowledgments on the book, not the trip the book is about. I'm not thanking all of the people who made this *trip* possible, because I can't. Over the course of the roughly seven thousand miles of preparation and our Great Loop, we were offered immeasurable amounts of critical wisdom, shelter, hospitality, logistical support, and more. All loopers learn to rely on the need of a near endless stream of help. In response, we tried to live a life of thanks. We tried to tip well, be gracious, and be patient.

We bought presents for those who helped us in our voyage—metal mugs that said "Currently Crew". We gave them to lockmasters, mechanics, guides, and critical companions. You'll read about them throughout the book. Still, we could never carry enough of them to match our reliance on the goodwill all around us. It's wholly inadequate, but you know who you are. Maggie and I are deeply appreciative of what you offered to our voyage. You changed the way we see ourselves and made possible one of the defining moments of our lives. Thank you.

Now, please bear with me as I awkwardly draw lines to delineate *Currently's* Great Loop voyage, and *Currently Away*, the book. I am going to get this wrong and leave out some people who deserve our thanks. Please accept that this oversight is not intentional. I *do* want to call out the initial sparks for this combined project. These people dared our family to dream and helped to break us out of some dark places. First, Avery and Christy turned us on to the book *What Is to What If*. Our families make time to dream together for exactly moments like these. That book was just what we needed because it was a powerful invitation reminding us to look at the world through the lens of possibility rather than restriction. Maggie and I can't state enough how much that book shaped our thinking. And where would we be without our dear friends Pat Diviney and Steve Garrison? Steve is no longer with us but was able to greet us at the dock with his quiet smile and encouragement. It was Pat who told us to "go right away," while our life circumstances supported such a trip, and it was Steve's strengths and encouragement that prodded me to write this book. And thanks to Eddy Johnson who modeled service and hospitality through his own writing. At critical junctures, you all made our voyage and, by extension, this book possible.

Maggie took most of the pictures in the book, and they are stunning. Thanks also to Jim Rossman, who provided the iconic cover photo. Other photos came from: Arleen Mauger (*Arion*), Beth Darrow (*Amy Marie*), Jennifer Matchey and Brian Wicks (*YOLO*), Jerry Jones (*Titan*), Jim Rossman (*No Agenda*), Kayla Tate (*Currently*), and Tina Osborne (*Two T's Aweigh*). Thank you all.

Thanks to Tyler Young and the folks at Felt.com, who provided support for us as we plopped *Currently's* XML file into the platform and it spat out a working map. Thanks to Ranger Tugs, who provided the photos of the 2014 R29.

Thanks to the reviewers who helped to sharpen this book. The team at the Prags, Tasha Doremus, Steve Garrison, Holly Hobart, Jen Genovesi, Carol Keith, Sebastien Leclerq, Kayla Tate, and Maggie Tate were our secret weapons. Some are cruisers, some sailors, some professional editors, some were just people who had important perspectives to share. You were the water that lifted this project to the point that it was viable, and even beautiful. Jen and Elliot, you provided selfless guidance and access to your vast bank of knowledge. You also provided a key spark as fellow content publishers and dreamers. Thanks to you all.

I keep saying this, but the Pragmatic Bookshelf has been a wellspring of support and guidance. Thanks to Dave Rankin and Dave Thomas, who believed in this new kind of book for their platform. I couldn't have been more thrilled with our continuing partnership. Thanks to Michael Swaine, who guided this project like an experienced hand on the helm, and to the professional team that provided all of the critical services for editing and designing this project. Again, you have our gratitude.

I would also like to call out my family to thank. Julia dreamed with us as we talked about this writing project. Her skill as a photographer, wonderful sense of adventure logistics, life experiences, and education made her an invaluable foil as we discussed and refined the stories that would become the core of the book. Maybe unsurprisingly, Kayla, who knows me as well as any other reviewer, became the best reviewer on the whole project. She caught the little mistakes, sure. More critically, she helped me rewrite the stickiest, most controversial pages multiple times, encouraging me to do better, to paint a better picture, to *be* a better man.

Maggie took our whole family onto her shoulders while she did the dreaming for both of us when times were dark and we couldn't see a way out. She encouraged me when I got home to put words to the page. Then she made sure those initial awkward words were right by the time we made it to press and provided the stunningly complicated logistical support by providing notes, communication, outreach, and photographs as we fed the fragile paper dream with time and effort until it had a soul. You are all at once my favorite adventure to inspire me, my magenta line to guide me, and my anchor to hold me fast as the winds of life blow. I've written many books before, but this was the first time the whole family participated in the project. Readers, if you are with me, I wish for you the same opportunity to share something as daunting and beautiful with those you love.

Most of all, to you the reader, thanks for taking a chance and buying a nontechnical book from a technical publisher by a technical author. Thanks for sailing with us through reds and greens, both physical and metaphorical. Though people say writing a book is soul crushing, this one filled mine. You are the reason I write. As one last thanks, I wish for you the courage to be curious, the delight of dockside conversations, a safe harbor in turbulent waters, and the vulnerability to accept the love or service of others. The best ships, after all, are friendships.

Part I

Preparations

America's Great Loop is a nautical adventure. The trip spans about six thousand miles and usually takes about a year. Neither of us had much boating experience. Before leaving, we needed to buy a boat big enough to sleep in, learn how to drive it, and learn how to maintain and service it. The first part of the book outlines the few exciting and terrifying months preceding our departure.

Our physical route would take us down the Tenn-Tom waterway to Mobile Bay, around the Florida Keys, through Lake Champlain, Montreal, Ottawa, and Georgian Bay. Maggie says "we left before we left," and it's true. Months before departure, our hearts were already on the waterways.

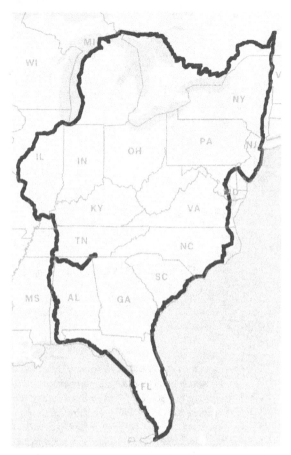

Currently's Great Loop Track

CHAPTER 1

You're Going to Hit the Dock

I can't remember exactly when we lost control. Maybe it was when I tapped the bow thruster, that strange propeller in the side of the hull that moves the nose of the boat sideways instead of forward. Maybe it was when I tried to correct the stern as it drifted further from the wall. Maybe it was the instant we bought *this* boat, or when Maggie plopped the book *From What Is to What If* into her Amazon cart. All I knew is that the boat was spinning, and I didn't want it to be.

Currently wasn't new, but she was new to us; she had plenty of scratches and dents, but few we had added ourselves. All boats have such marks, each capturing some tiny story or platitude. We were in the middle of such a story as we spun in the lock.

But I'm getting ahead of myself. I should tell you how we got here.

Our previous boat, a pontoon, prepared us somewhat for our journey, but not as much as we expected. Pontoon boats and trawlers like *Currently* handle quite differently. Pontoons are generally *outboards*. They have giant engines mounted on a bracket behind the boat that pivot from side to side. An experienced pilot can add both power and direction to perfectly determine the trajectory of the boat. The massive engine dips way down in the water, dampening a boat's tendency to spin. That engine can work like a rudder even when the skipper is not applying power.

None of these things were true of our boat, as I was soon to find out.

The fact is we weren't big boat people. We'd purchased a pontoon boat two years before as a feeble attempt to shake Covid's grip loose. Our old floating couch offered the ability to plan socially distanced outings with those closest to us on the Tennessee River, a beautiful waterway that slithers between mountains and geographical features both dramatic and soothing. *Currently*, it turned out, was a bit different. She's a pocket trawler designed for living aboard and traveling long distances efficiently.

But our boat's next journey, getting her back to our Tennessee home, would be by truck.

After we gave part of our house back to the bank to buy *Currently*, we flew back to Cape Coral to pack up the boat and have a contractor plop it onto a trailer. As we spent our hours in town, we went from West Marine to HomeGoods to begin to provision *Currently* for the Great Loop ahead. We ate more great food and visited more great stores and waved around our leaking wallet until it felt light enough to travel.

We then packed up the boat. First, we looked over the anodes and decided to replace them while the boat was out of the water. I could see the pitted zinc in the protective plates and shields, engineered to be sacrificed so that the permanent metals on the boat could remain whole.

Preparing *Currently* for transport

We taped or tied everything that could wiggle or pivot. We stashed our new provisions into places that felt safe. We pulled off the anchor and packed it in the new pillows and sheets that would warm us over the coming year. Eventually, we were as done as we could be. Steve, our broker, was with us every step of the way. Eventually, we sat in the cockpit, in *our* boat, in a weird cross between a marina and a mall. We waited for the driver.

I had certain *feelings* about this driver. Actually, they were more about his truck. It was not one of the electric ones or the crew cabs more at home in a mall parking lot. His truck had been put to *work*. It had dozens of scratches in the bed, had a well-used, well-stocked toolbox in the back, and had all kinds of attachments and adapters. Trucks like that are all over the Southeast and are usually full of rural folk: simple, kind, and supremely competent workers. He was a seasoned professional pulling an old-school trailer showing more steel than paint. When he caught my nervous look, he eased by mind by saying, "Mr. Tate, this is what I was born to do. *Currently* will be just fine." Having met many such men over the years, I believed him.

In a surreal scene, the marina's staff picked up *Currently* with a forklift and drove the little trawler as she rocked and slipped between the BMWs and Escalades so prominent in the parking lots there. *Currently* seemed to be on the edge of rocking just a touch too far to her doom, but Steve just looked at my rising panic and chuckled. Like an airline passenger taking comfort from a calm attendant, I crammed down my anxiety and tried to enjoy the experience.

The lift lowered our little tug onto the trailer, and she started screaming. Well, the creaks and pops *sounded* like screaming, though the sounds might have been coming from the trailer. Steve successfully distracted Maggie and me while the boat was loaded. We waved goodbye to the driver and made our way to the airport by rental car.

On the way back to the airport, we were both full of the heady mix of anxiety and possibility, as if we'd fired a cannonball recklessly into the future. Would this adventure destroy our business and life savings? Would it wash away our profound sadness? We knew only that we were one step closer to finding out.

We landed in Chattanooga about a day before our smiling driver and his old truck. We met him at a wonderful marina called Island Cove. With great trepidation, we watched as they removed all of the straps holding the boat

Loading *Currently* in Cape Coral

to the trailer and then started driving it toward the lift to put the boat in the water. Our private Little Toot[1] was rocking like a hurricane. I wanted to scream at him to stop, for the love of all things holy and good. Before letting loose, I glanced around to see all of the workers, who had done this countless times before, hoping they'd tell Mr. West Virginia that he'd better put the damned straps back on the damned boat until he got to the lift and he'd best check the drain plug and look at that rocking and slow down…

To the last man, they were attentive enough but thoroughly bored. This madness was apparently normal. Eventually, they picked up the boat with the travel lift, and my baby screamed at me again, and they lowered her gently into the water.

Currently **on the travel lift**

There came a gentle splash, a few light bumps, and blessed silence. I could breathe again. I looked at Maggie and smiled as if I'd always been sure it would all be OK. She was so freaked out that I came across as the calm and unmoving rock she married twenty-five years ago. Or so I told myself.

Then everyone left. Bubba took his trailer and his truck and got back on the road to West Virginia. The dockhands used a boat hook to corral the boat before using our shiny new lines to moor it to the dock and then slipped off to handle the next boat for the next nervous, waiting couple. The crane operator had us sign off and then walked away to the break room, having barely broken a sweat. Maggie and I stared down at the boat, keys in hand, thinking "Now what?"

Back to how we lost control.

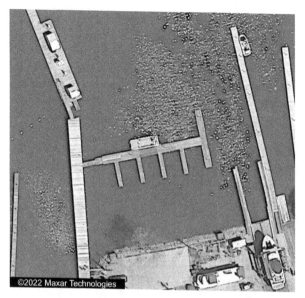

Island Cove from above

Because Island Cove usually loaded the lift from a forklift instead of a trailer, *Currently* was pointed backward toward the lift and the docks. Our first move in *Currently* would be a hard turn in tight quarters. Suddenly, all of the pontoon work seemed wholly inadequate to prepare us for the next great adventure of leaving the dock. I shrugged nonchalantly, pretending all was in hand. We ripped out all of the ties and tape to let all of the things pivot and wiggle again, swiped the fob over the ignition switch, and the right power light came on. The electronics glowed comfortingly. So far so good. Then I pressed the Start button. The starter whirred and nothing happened. I muttered, "Well, that's anticlimactic."

I popped open the engine hatch and then jiggled wires and grunted in a knowing way to hide my ignorance. Every now and then I'd expertly call out, "Try it now." No dice.

Eventually, I remembered a helpful post from an article about moving a boat and smirked triumphantly. I had to prime the diesel! I loosened a whatsit and turned a whosit and pressed a little black button until a stream of bubbly diesel poured into a discarded fast-food cup. The stream of bubbly diesel turned from cloudy to clear, so I turned the whosit in the opposite direction and tightened the whatsit and managed to squeak out a slightly less authoritative "Hit it again." I jumped back as the engine boomed to life, both elbows flying straight up as if I'd been busted.

With luck, I hoped Maggie noticed nothing from the driver's seat but pure competent, oily masculinity, but who was I kidding? Or maybe the diesel engine was kidding me, its hypnotic power sucking me into some stereotypical role. I should have known better.

I closed the hatch, sat at the helm, and confidently barked, "Let's cast off!", leaving the phrase "before it dies again" unspoken. I looked around nervously for any of those marina employees so I could tap into the kinship of the sea. In truth, in chilly October those folks were more likely to be community college kids working over a break. No matter. I'd driven a real *pontoon* and read about what to do on the best sailing guide in the universe, the *internet*. Maggie pushed us off and I pulsed the throttle.

Immediately, I knew I'd made a terrible mistake.

The *internet* said that Ranger Tugs tracked well, but mine was wobbling back and forth like a drunk monkey in a tutu on ice. This elegant dance was taking me right toward the dock in front of us. At this point, several things happened at once.

First, I pulsed the throttle as I'd read about on the *internet*. *Currently* lurched and confirmed that I didn't know where the rudder was pointed. Then Maggie began to help. She told me, "You're going to hit the dock." Her tone was cool, calm, and unlike Maggie at all, which terrified me. Then I could feel the attraction between the dock and the back of my boat as *Currently*'s stern swung around to meet the dock. The harder I turned away from the dock, the more *Currently* rebelled, so I used reverse psychology. I turned *toward* the dock.

At this point, *Currently* knew this dock was not going to be a lifelong relationship. Still, she gently kissed the dock and left a little reminder of the brief rendezvous. The dock gently kissed back and left a little lipstick, and we were free. As I was looking back at the dock, reveling in our hard-fought freedom, my wife's words whipped out at me like the cool voice of a serial killer.

"You're going to hit the boat.

"You're going to hit the yacht.

"If you don't turn right now, you're going to hit the twenty-million-dollar yacht."

Now knowing *Currently*'s "bad girl" propensities, I used my reverse psychology trick again and threw the wheel right toward the "twenty-million-dollar" yacht and pulsed the throttle. We missed it by a foot or two, so that was progress. Plus, the yacht was probably worth ten million, tops.

We limped to a place in the middle of the lake, far away from docks, buoys, and twenty-million-dollar yachts. We looked at each other with wild eyes that said, "We have made a terrible mistake." Our voices simultaneously said, "We have made a terrible mistake." Of course we thought and said those things. That's what the universe was screaming at us.

We weaved around the marina toward our slip and even managed to park *Currently*. Of course, we were in the middle of houseboat row, with slips wide enough to park an aircraft carrier. The boats, in every state of repair, had wildly varied names, and flags reaching to rafters high enough to accommodate a tall ship. If Six Flags Over Fiberglass was a place, we'd found it.

Over our first evening in the boat, we looked back at our situation rationally. We were making mistakes, but we were learning and going slowly when we made them. We were communicating well as a couple. Too, we'd made tremendous progress toward our journey.

Against all odds, we'd found a boat in the time of Covid and come a long way toward outfitting her. I'd learned enough about diesel engines to know there might be air in the fuel lines after a move and what to do about that. We'd successfully transported and splashed the boat.

We'd just need to learn to drive an inboard.

CHAPTER 2

From Perfectly Controlled to Spinning

After our first night on the boat together, the first mate and her less-than-heroic captain gathered their wits. We walked along the docks marveling at the massive seventy-foot-long houseboats and titanic fifty-foot cruisers. Many of the boats cost half a million dollars or more. As we took our voyeuristic stroll down the docks and between the boats, we noticed that one boat, called *Kittiwake*, was shockingly out of place. It was a tiny twenty-two-foot C-Dory with a shiny white flag, called a burgee, waving proudly off of the bow, marking it as a looper. We missed them at that moment, but Maggie had met them online. We made plans to have dinner later.

In the minds of some, the Great Loop can be defined with one word: big. The word *great* underscores the audacity of the massive undertaking, and the route only magnifies that notion. Each individual boat must navigate Great Lakes, the Gulf of Mexico, the Atlantic Ocean, and numerous massive bays and sounds. The loop also has plenty of big boats twice as long as *Currently*. We were keenly aware of that fact as we strolled down houseboat row. We passed row after row of gargantuan sixty-five-foot houseboats that wouldn't even fit in many typical marina slips.

The occasional massive trawler or cruiser just punctuated the scene. The insolent presumption of such a grand adventure in a mere twenty-two-foot C-Dory, with the telltale white burgee mounted to the front, cemented captains Sebastien and Tasha as giants in my mind.

Sebastien and Tasha on *Kittiwake*

Later that day, the crew invited us aboard and we peeked around. They had made excellent use of every square inch of space. There were pull-out shelves, drop-down storage, and added seating to the cockpit in the rear, which Sebastien called the soul of the boat.

The international couple fearlessly piloted that craft across the open Gulf not one night as many boaters do, but three different times to wring every last bit of enjoyment out of the loop. With the short length and tiny draft, they could request small marina slips that would normally go unsold, and they were skilled enough to park it wherever they wanted. They conveniently drove close to shore, where the big dogs never roamed, and were rewarded with sights of gators, snakes, and manatees.

Over a couple of dinners on the patio of a restaurant serving Tennessee's version of Mexican or a local pizza place that couldn't quite manage to get an order right, we got to know them. Sebastien, the French fun-loving lifetime sailor, is good with his hands and knows how to bend a boat to his will. Tasha, the British artist, has a thirst for people, beauty, and travel. Both are first and foremost dreamers. Together, they determined that they would do the loop and found a way to make their dreams real.

Though we didn't know it, Sebastien would be our scout on the rivers and waterways in the weeks to come. If we needed to know what certain weather patterns would do in some locale, Maggie would shoot him a note and the French encyclopedia would quickly respond.

Months later, after we'd completed our loop by "crossing our wake," they came to Chattanooga and we hiked and talked. We learned about their tough political conversations with friends at home. Rather than running away from those interactions, they leaned into the challenge, inviting others who were not like them to have difficult conversations as friends, over dinner or an afternoon out.

Before our first official day on the loop, we were falling in love with the adventure once again—this time, it wasn't the idea of the journey but the people who made up the traveling community. We learned how a tiny white burgee could change everything. The little flag telegraphed our intentions and was a portal into a welcoming community.

After spending a lovely evening with them, we walked them back to their boat in the slip. We passed those empty houseboats with barely a scratch in the paint. So many of those boats were marina queens, mere *symbols* of a life that might be, instead of *action*.

When I grow up, I want to know the soul of *Kittywake*, the C-Dory with custom shelves and various scratches befitting a life at sea. We left Island Cove the very next day, the jarring experience of *Currently*'s splash a distant memory. The lovely captains had replaced those turbulent memories with the promise of waiting possibilities.

Refreshed and confident, we slipped into the main channel of the rolling Tennessee and anticipated our first major obstacle in *Currently*: the Chickamauga Lock. Looking at it from above, facing north, Chickamauga Lock consists of a huge chamber with the downstream door on the left and the upstream door on the right.

Giant concrete chambers like this one serve as elevators on a river. Each one uses gravity, a few strategically placed drains, and doors on either end to float boats up and down, using a system that's been around for more than two thousand years. We had used the locks with great success in the past in our old pontoon boat with few problems, but we'd never been through them in *this* boat. As we'd experienced, the boat is trickier to control, especially at slower speeds.

We called the lock on the radio as we'd done dozens of times before. We didn't have to put out the protective inflated fenders because they were already out. We'd deployed all seven of them before we ever left the marina, marking us as complete noobs. We wouldn't pull them in again until we were good and ready. *You* can make all the jokes about training wheels you want. I wanted to keep that freshly polished look, thank you very much.

I should mention a bit about the VHF. These radios communicate with other boats and waterway infrastructure like locks, bridges, or marinas. Ours had a range of a couple of miles in the river systems or more in wide-open waters. These systems have multiple channels and some rules for communication that were mostly the same within the United States. Those rules varied internationally.

The radio had a fist microphone with a press-to-speak button, an in-dash console, and a connection between them consisting of a coiled wire reminiscent of an old phone's headset and body. Our radio was pretty old, but aside from the tangled and flaking wire, performed pretty well. We'd use channel 16 to initiate a conversation with another boat and then switch to another less-used channel to have a conversation. Marinas, locks, and the like had published channels they'd monitor.

No other traffic was anywhere in sight, and the lockmaster said he'd prepare the chamber for us. That meant he'd need to shut the doors and open valves on the downstream side to fill up the chamber. When he'd done so, the light turned green and a horn sounded. After a shared nervous glance with Maggie, I glanced outside at the fenders. All seven security binkies were out, so we approached the lock and entered the chamber that would lower us some fifty feet in around twenty minutes.

Our initial approach went well, until it was time to actually turn. I slipped the boat over to the side so Maggie could attach *Currently* to the floating metal post, called a bollard. So good, so far. I just needed to nose my bow a little closer. I tapped the bow thruster, a little too hard. Then I goosed the throttle just a little too much, and with the rudder pointed the wrong way. No problem. I corrected with *way* too much throttle, and we were spinning in the lock. I glanced over at Maggie, and her eyes were open wide and her mouth frozen open. No help there, then. I looked back forward as we completed a full rotation as if it had been my plan all along. Miraculously, the boat stopped spinning and we drifted to the other side of the lock.

If you are the lockmaster who didn't publish a YouTube video of the Ranger Tug that went from perfectly controlled to wildly spinning in the span of ten seconds, I thank you.

Sometimes, this whole Great Loop adventure seems like that. The neat spreadsheets and charts that make up our perfectly controlled plans sometimes don't survive the winds, waves, or inexperience life throws our way. One second, we're aiming at a November launch date after a steady drip of delays. Drip...bank loan. Drip...survey. Drip...part shortage. The next minute, fate intervenes to move all of our timelines up by two weeks of unexpected good luck. We're pushed into the current unexpectedly, we tap the mental thruster, goose the throttle a little too hard, over correct, and we're spinning.

But it's all OK. It's a loop after all.

If the adventure teaches us anything, it will be to control the things we can and let go of the things we can't. Truth be told, we're not going to damage a hundred-year-old concrete lock chamber, and our slowly moving boat is surrounded by enough rubber fenders to raise the *Titanic,* so we weren't going to damage *Currently* either. We were always going to come through with nothing but a few new scuffs in our pride.

The rest of the story is as unsurprising as the next sunrise. On the wall, Maggie tied us off like a pro, and the water slowly spilled out of the lock through some unknown pipes and valves. We sank down gently (now under control), let the lessons sink in, and laughed nervously like we'd gotten away with something.

Then we started to pull away. It was cold out, so I passed Maggie the helm and went out to secure the lines and fenders for departure. The lockmaster had mercy on us, so he used the jets of water to wash some stray branches away from *Currently.*

The unexpected jet began to pivot us in the water, and Maggie pulled off of the throttle at the wrong time. No power meant no control. Once again, we were spinning.

And it was all OK.

CHAPTER 3

Our 290-Square-Foot Quarantine

Looking back at our first few days of preparation, it's easy to get wrapped up in the joy of expectation and electricity inherent in an impossible adventure. It's tempting to remember our anticipation and forget the pain that led to our Great Loop in the first place. That would be a mistake. In many ways, the decision to go *is* the story, a tiny sliver of time that transformed bleak subsistence to an inevitable transforming experience. This is how it happened.

My wife, Maggie, is like a plant. Her roots need time to tap into the fertile soil of community and family. Look at all of the faces when she walks into a party, and you'll know the place is alive. They all light up, and she subtly leans toward their light. People are naturally drawn toward her corner of the room for community, and her roots take in what she needs. Sit her out in the sun and feed her, and she's fine.

In 2020, she was not well. After a year and of half of near quarantine conditions, she seemed fine, but Maggie doesn't *do* fine. Most people wouldn't notice the slightest problem, but her friends and family knew differently.

Covid-19 had cut her roots, and the vibrancy that makes Maggie herself was fading.

Like anyone else who had basked in her presence, I could tell Covid-19 was systemically strangling her. As a moderately overweight man with heart symptoms and asthma, I was at high risk for the disease, and that status had successfully isolated us from everything we held dear. In truth, knowing she was broken scared me to death because I was broken too.

I am as far from Maggie as night and day. I'm more puppy than plant, full of curiosity and vitality but helpless on my own. I pull my meaning from the status of important relationships in my life. I take pride in praise for my accomplishments and seek things both shiny and new. I recognize this weakness and stay grounded by providing service and kindness to others.

Our quarantine and my work situation were systemically knocking me down. Covid hit the programming community particularly hard. In 2020, professional relationships I needed were strained and breaking. My circumstances chipped away at my self-image until I was brooding and bitter.

The year 2020 bled into 2021, and Covid kept its hold on the country. Our profound loneliness kept its hold on us. As I worked through these problems, our nation's political situation hovered over us like one more scavenger to pick over our remains. We watched in horror as the events of January 6 unfolded. Part of the country believed the presidential election was stolen, and the other part believed democracy was dying or dead.

All of this mental anguish was happening at once. I couldn't pry myself away from the TV. My availability and attitude suffered. My fragile relationship with my father broke. The political lines of Covid-19 spread through our city and community just as it had in the rest of the world. As a baby boomer, I knew just what to do. I crammed the pain down and moved on the best I could.

On top of this unholy mix of mental anguish, my body chipped in with a healthy dose of heart disease. By the fall of 2021, my widow-maker artery had slowly squeezed to within 95 percent shut in two places, without any symptoms. My diet and emotional problems were officially killing me. After a blessedly minor surgery to implant a couple of stents, the professionals deemed me fixed, but I didn't *feel* fixed. I can't say this strongly enough. I believed to the bottom of my weakened heart that Covid would conspire with my cardiovascular disease and other comorbidities to kill me. I do mean dead as in clinically dead, not dead as in sad inside.

Maggie took on the difficult task of finding a diet that would stem my cardiovascular disease and came up with one that was pretty much the opposite of the one we were following. Our family radically changed our diet to a plant-based one. When Covid *did* release its grip around our throats, our favorite restaurants and meals would remain closed to us. Our diet change stripped away one more source of comfort.

Our feeling of suffocation was different than any other family crisis we'd experienced. In the past, we'd honored an agreement of "one crisis at a time, please." When Maggie suffered, I'd put my troubles aside. Maggie did the same for me. This time, we were too broken to help one another. I don't know how Maggie found the strength to lean once again toward light, away from despair.

Those days, she didn't say much. She read a lot and hid among the folds of the blankets on the gray cushions. One day in particular, I remember coming down the stairs and seeing her reading *From What Is to What If [Hop20]*. The title of the book struck me because it was a book of hope. Seeing her smile helped to crack the blackness around *me*, if only a little bit. The book is about reframing deep-seated thought patterns to imagine solutions rather than restrictions. A tiny word tried to wriggle into my consciousness: hope. Then it was gone. A couple of weeks later, I climbed down the stairs to find her reading, again.

Some moments I remember with clarity: when my mother died, when each plane flew into the World Trade Center, when each of our daughters was born, when Maggie said "Yes"…and when she told me she was reading *The Great Loop Experience [GH14]*, a book about a personal journey by boat. This was her great plan for us, and my smiling plant was once again basking in the sun.

Yes, smiling.

"I guess we're doing this," I said, trying to comprehend the magnitude of her vision.

We both understood exactly what she was saying. Our months of self-focused despair collapsed in an instant, giving way to the beginnings of a stunning plan. We stopped looking backward and shifted our focus to what was to come. This exact moment saved us. I don't know what we would have become, but we would be less than we are now.

At its most conservative, our own Great Loop experience would be something to plan as we worked through our quarantine. At its most extreme, a trip would involve trading a quarantine in our 2,000-square-foot house by the water to a floating quarantine of 290 square feet on the water, and everything would be different. When all was said and done, there would be Maggie, me, our dog, Emmy, and the boat.

We started to plan our trip in broad strokes. We'd need to decide how to finance the trip. Since we both worked remotely, we felt confident that we could make enough money en route to make this trip possible. Since we had a backlog of customers wanting to learn Elixir, the computer programming language I was teaching, we could make most of what we needed by working from the water, as long as we had good internet access. Our business also involved publishing videos and books, an ideal remote profession. When all was said and done, we wouldn't be able to publish and teach quite as much as we needed to. We'd rent out our house to make up the difference. We'd

Maggie, Bruce, and Emmy

use a home equity loan to buy a boat and sell it once our journey was completed.

We also began to sharpen our skills. The trip takes tremendous knowledge and seamanship. Logistically, provisioning a boat was difficult, and we had virtually no experience doing so beyond loading snacks onto our tiny pontoon boat for day trips. We began to read about where to stop, how much food we'd need to take on board, and what equipment the trip would require.

While making preparations, we began to think about when we could actually leave. We initially aimed for departure in 2026, years off, but I soon determined that we could move it up a bit. With a tentative schedule in mind, Maggie went to visit our friends Steve Garrison and Pat Diviney, an adventuring couple we respect tremendously. They were both adventurers and excellent planners.

Maggie didn't get the advice she expected. Steve and Pat told us to go as soon as we possibly could. They advised us to figure out the rest from the water. That night, Maggie and I asked ourselves what was preventing us from going right away. We prepared spreadsheets to lay out the costs and potential incomes, we continued itemizing the provisions we'd need. The logistics were daunting but doable.

We looked at financial income streams. Our ability to work from the water and the rentability of our home were huge benefits. My role as an author and teacher were ideal for working remotely. Finances would be tight, but we could do this.

As the trip became more of a reality, we had to consider the weather. Though the beginning of our journey would be cold, we decided that the best departure month for us would be January. We lived in the south, where rivers didn't freeze over. Most marinas stayed open year-round. We also wanted to be around through the holidays to see our college kids.

With growing excitement, we evaluated whether 2022 or 2023 would make the best departure. We looked to the Great Loop message boards and found several lock closures. We'd need to pass through more than a hundred locks. In 2023, lock repairs would close the Illinois River just below Chicago at a critical time, pointing us toward a 2022 departure. We took a week or so to think about it, and we decided to leave in January 2022, fast approaching.

It was time to buy a boat.

Once we'd decided to go, things began to move rapidly. Our despair slipped off onto the floor like a silk robe, puddled in the last fading pile of doubt. We started looking for our ship, moving from one style to the next, mentally trying them on and casting them aside when they didn't fit.

We discarded some because they were too expensive and others because they were too old. We heard tales of boaters refused insurance because they were too inexperienced and that smaller boats were easier to insure. As our search narrowed, we got comfortable with the idea of living small. We settled on Ranger Tugs. The boat's concept takes a little explaining.

For today's Great Loop, most people decide to make the journey in boats around thirty-five feet long and twelve to fifteen feet wide. Many are bigger. They are literally tiny houses on water. Ranger Tugs are a bit of a counterpoint. They're not real tugboats but take some stylistic cues from traditional tugs. They're skinny enough to fit on a trailer, ranging from eight and a half feet to ten feet wide. Most of the ones that make the Great Loop voyage are from twenty-seven to twenty-nine feet long. They are fuel efficient, shallow enough to go where other boats can't, and quick enough to make a scheduled bridge or lock opening.

The boat we found was a 2014 navy-blue and tan boat powered by a Volvo Penta D4 diesel engine. It crammed the features of a forty-foot yacht into a boat twenty-nine feet long at the waterline and ten feet wide. Even the specs spoke to us:

Waterline Length	29'
Overall Length	33'
Beam	10'
Dry Weight	9250 lbs
Water capacity	70 gallons
Holding Tank Capacity	40 gallons
Fuel Capacity	152 gallons
Hot Water Tank	6 gallons
Propulsion	Single screw inboard
Engine	Volvo Penta D4
Horsepower	260
Hours	214

The amenities provided more than you'd find in a typical boat that size. For navigation, we'd have an aging Garmin chartplotter, GPS, depth sounder, radar, and autopilot. For comfort, we'd have air conditioning and heat. Power systems included a generator, a battery bank with three isolated circuits, and a tiny bit of solar power. Like speedboats, we'd have trim tabs to keep the boat as level as possible.

We'd enter the boat through a door in the cockpit, our open "back porch." On the main level, we'd walk down a narrow aisle on a slight diagonal with the galley on the starboard (right) side and a little dining table to port (left). Continuing forward, we had the helm on the starboard next to a sliding door, and the navigator station to port. Then we'd have another door, followed by the head to port and our V-berth in the bow. On a lower level, there was one more room, if you could call it that. The so-called cuddy cabin was right next to the cockpit door to port, right behind and beneath the dinette. We called it the cave.

The galley had a microwave, a wine fridge, a refrigerator, a double sink, a two-burner stove, an oven, and lots of storage. We would have two staterooms and a dinette table that converted to a bed, so the boat could technically sleep six, but all six really had to like each other. We could shower on board, and we had a toilet powered by the onboard freshwater. These systems consumed more fresh water but didn't tend to smell as bad, especially in saltwater.

We found our boat in Cape Coral, Florida, and were in a car to meet our broker, Steve Hill, to look it over before a sea trial and survey. All that remained was a name. Every ship has a soul, and every boat owner has an innate, perhaps futile, desire to capture the essence of it with a name. The whole process took me back to the birth of our first daughter.

Around three in the morning, Maggie's water broke. Maybe it was the obscene amount of chocolate icing that she took in, or maybe our wildly enthusiastic first child couldn't wait to make her dramatic entrance into this world, so she summoned her inner strength and placed a perfect kick in exactly the right spot to break that dam of amniotic fluid and prematurely start Maggie's delivery countdown.

Sure, we had our meticulous birth plan and we'd chosen the names Megan Elaina for a girl or Michael Allen for a boy. Throughout the day, every single carefully orchestrated moment took us further from our expectations. Nearly

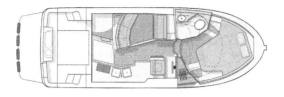

2014 Ranger Tug R-29

twenty-three hours later, the baby was born. Maggie and I looked at each other full of love and wonder. We both knew that this baby girl was more beautiful than we could have possibly imagined, but she wasn't a Megan. She was Kayla Ellen, full of light and life and possibility.

Meeting our boat was like that. We had plenty of possible names set aside for this occasion, but one clear front-runner that we just knew we would choose in the end: Rio Camino. This little bit of broken Spanish means River Walk, and so much more.

As we talked about the idea of taking on the Great Loop, we knew our journey wouldn't be some aimless jaunt around half of our country. It would be more of a pilgrimage. Our daughters had taken their own five-hundred-mile hiking pilgrimage three years prior on the Camino de Santiago, a Catholic pilgrimage in Spain with multiple routes allowing a slow, rambling route that leaves time for intro-spection and self-discovery.

Maggie and I wanted our voyage to take on many of the same characteristics. After establishing a business just prior to the deeply challenging time of Covid, we wanted a time to slow down and enjoy our lives. Rio Camino also captured the idea of a river walk. The river walk in San Antonio has special significance to our whole family. In Christmases past, we'd explored it with international exchange students who lived with us for the short holiday season. We walked the hike-and-bike trail in Austin around Lady Bird Lake. The equity in our home on Chattanooga's river walk would be the very funds we needed to buy the boat. So, Rio Camino seemed to fit.

We arrived in Cape Coral, just south of Fort Myers. Little did we realize that within a year, the town would be devastated by a massive hurricane; the town offered no hint such massive damage could be possible. While we were there, we ate great food and entertained ourselves with the wonderful nautical culture. Steve gave us plenty of time to spend together in the cockpit of a stranger's boat, dreaming happily.

Throughout the few days, we talked with strangers, family, and friends. We couldn't shake the notion that the boat wasn't a Rio Camino. We also tried on other names like Going Remote and Miss Adventure, but none of them truly fit.

Then we considered the name Current Plans, and it felt closer. "Current" represented us as river people, and also the notion of "right now." If nothing else, the trip would be about living the moment. Excited, we riffed on that idea.

Current Plans gave way to the short and sweet *Currently*. The name subtly marked us as river people. One single word captured both whimsical movement and intentional living. The name bubbled and swirled in our imaginations until we couldn't see anything else sketched across the transom.

CHAPTER 4

We Muster the Best Landing We Can

After we introduced *Currently* to her new home, we began to prepare her and ourselves for the arduous journey to come. We signed up with the AGLCA—the America's Great Loop Cruisers Association—to be harbor hosts. That way, we could be there to help boats come in and tie up. We'd have local knowledge about the river and Chattanooga. We'd meet other boaters as they came through and share in their journey.

We met Mike and Beth on *Amy Marie*, another blue-and-tan Ranger Tug. We'd follow the couple's journey on their blog and meet with them several times, culminating in a three-week run down from Chicago to the Tennessee River. On the same dock were Tim and Kate on *Sweet Day*, Sebastien and Tasha on *Kittiwake*, Loren on *Das Boot*, and a few other boats. Some joined us for a walk, and some came over for dinner. We joined the whole crew for docktails, a traditional evening gathering where loopers would sit around a dock, bring drinks, and tell stories together about the loop. We helped a few boaters with a trip to the grocery store here or a ride to the boat store there. Each afternoon over lunch or in the evening after work we offered advice on where to bike, eat, or drink in the area.

We helped *Irish Hurricane* tie up and joined them for drinks, and on the social boater app called Nebo we tracked boats as they came through Chattanooga. We got as much out of the harbor host program as we gave. We learned about the loop and the places on it. We met people and filled up our mental captain's logs with dreams and plans of our own. When the loopers weren't at the docks downtown or on the river, we were with *Currently*.

Since Chattanooga didn't have many options for good marine stores, we spent more time than I care to admit on the Amazon, Defender, and West Marine websites that had the devices and provisions we needed. We began to make a list of the many repairs and modifications *Currently* would need. Some of the items were nautical in nature, like good life jackets and emergency lights. Some were for living, like our folding bikes to get around in port.

Our Zizzo folding bikes

We had much to learn. For two solid weeks, we avoided the toilet because we didn't know how to use the self-serve pump-out device that owners of big boats and RVs know so well. When we finally successfully sucked out our waste with that magnificently disgusting machine, we cheered until we were hoarse.

We also attacked the power systems. We shifted our solar panel to one side of the boat to make room for our dinghy. We pulled out the old batteries and replaced them with six AGM batteries, at around seventy pounds each. Because the marina orientation forced us to haul batteries down three flights of stairs, the hardest part of the exercise was simply moving each of them up the stairs to the car and the new ones down again. We did some disgusting work in the shower bilge with brown water from any or all of the previous owners erupting all over me while my butt was high in the air and my head down deep in the hatch underneath our mattress.

Repairing the shower bilge wiring

We also fixed some broken systems. The most critical one was the stern thruster. That one was critical because boats like ours are hard to steer in reverse or when moving very slowly. With it, we could have avoided the first day's near collisions and the second day's embarrassing spinning episode in Chickamauga Lock. To fix it, we went through a weeks-long arduous troubleshooting process and determined that the motor itself was bad. We ordered a motor, opened up the thruster assembly, and then got all of the tools ready. It was time for some boat yoga.

In my best dead bug pose, I lay down in the engine room face up with my arms overhead and supporting the thruster. I pulled the old motor out and then held the new one in place, shaking with the effort. Maggie offered a hand, twisting in a screw far enough that I could rest a bit. We finished the job and then pressed the rear thruster joystick to the right. We heard a sound like a giant piece of paper tearing, and *Currently's* skinny butt jerked to the right. We punched it to the left, and *Currently* popped it like it's hot.

As the weeks wore on, we agreed on roles, based more on skills than tradition. I familiarized myself with the diesel engine enough to do maintenance. Our bilge pumps were putting out a tiny stream of oil, so we needed to find that leak too. Maggie set herself to bringing the galley to heel so she could cook for our mandatory vegan diets. She tried to find a few simple meals we could cook on a boat.

Mostly, we simply practiced. Because Covid was still in full swing, neither of us were traveling for work, so we could plan our workdays around our boating activities. The river was high and our boat slip was right in the current, so docking was demanding, and our results were…mixed. The rapid current simply overpowered our thrusters, so we'd need to learn to really drive without those two cheating joysticks.

Our marina slip spreads out like a many-fingered hand with the fingertips tickling a pretty aggressive current. When the river is high, docking is a horrendous chore.

Greek salad, a common *Currently* meal

Pulling straight in seems wise but the timing is too difficult. Pulling in from upstream is even worse. We quickly learned to come at it from downstream. The pilot has to slowly creep up against the strong current, let the nose fall away, and then goose the throttle with a hard starboard rudder at just the right time. Most days it felt less like a landing and more like a controlled crash.

Each time we departed, we'd need to quickly untie lines. The mighty current would then shove our delicate little tug toward the jagged teeth on the dock on the downstream side. Occasionally, one of the rubber fenders would do its job, bouncing us into the flow. More often than not, we'd slip neatly into the current and we'd go get gas, or pump out, or just cruise.

We circled around the tiny Maclellan Island, nestled among the four bridges crisscrossing downtown Chattanooga, or peeked up at the Civil War battlefield atop Lookout Mountain, or just drifted downstream.

When we'd tooled around long enough, we would have to do the whole thing in reverse. We'd match the speed of the river, motoring just upstream of our slip. Then we'd turn hard to starboard, let the bow slip into the current, and power the boat into the slip before the river could slam us into the dock. Maggie and I decided that I'd learn to launch and to park first, and then I could teach her how to park it.

Something vaguely familiar was niggling at my consciousness. I'd been in the same situation before. When I found the memory, I laughed like I'd found forgotten money.

Back when our daughters were in elementary school, we moved about five miles across town to downsize. The new home had one feature that stood out to everyone who came to visit: an insanely steep hill with an equally intimidating curve right in the middle. By today's Austin standards, officials couldn't even build that road with that grade today. Indeed, among emergency crews, delivery services, and landscape services, the hill was infamous for lost trailers and cargos.

Riding up the hill for the first time, my girls were in the back seat giggling at the feeling, but we knew these girls would someday learn to drive on this very hill.

When each girl learned to drive, they jammed the brakes so hard the car couldn't even move. After much coaxing, she'd let off the pressure just enough, and the car would lurch forward a couple of inches, and she'd slam on the brakes again. Inch by inch, we'd work our way down until we reached the bottom. Then we'd do the same thing going the other way, with the gas instead of the brakes.

The trauma was pretty bad, but I got over it in time. In truth, after making it through that process, the worst was over. Aside from an occasional late-night call to come rescue a family member in a storm, the hill was not the killer it seemed to be, *as long as you controlled your momentum*. More so, once the girls conquered that hill, learning to drive elsewhere was anticlimactic.

It took me two weeks to master parking and launching in that current. I even left a new scratch or two on the boat. Throughout all of this time, the river was rising and the current was *ripping*. After those two weeks, Maggie said she was ready to park the boat. She pulled up toward the slip, matching the speed of the current.

She smiled and nodded. She let off the throttle but couldn't quite match the speed of the river. We drifted a bit too close to the dock on the approach, and Maggie decided to abandon the approach. She circled around to try again.

The second time, by taking the boat occasionally out of gear, she perfectly matched the speed of the river. Then she turned ever so slightly to starboard, and the bow whipped around, caught by the current. Like me, she had been surprised by the power of the river. She made the right call, and rather than powering through a maneuver, she circled around to try again.

The third time, she matched the current, let the bow slip ever so slightly toward the starboard, and it came around at the perfect speed, so she nudged the throttle toward the slip. We moved into the slip with the perfect timing. Then the current slammed us sideways. Rather than nosing us the rest of the way toward the back of the slip and letting the fenders do their job, she panicked and bailed. We both decided that three times was enough parking practice. Her brain wasn't done working on the problem, though. She dreamt about parking all night long.

At times, our Great Loop preparations felt like that. It was easy to blindly follow life's currents as our circumstances built up a momentum to take us where it would, until we decided with enough conviction to be somewhere else. Then we'd gather our skills to control the momentum and try to muster the best landing we could. Sometimes, the river was just too much.

But sometimes, by practicing and watching long enough, we would nudge, oh so smoothly, out of the channel. The very next day, Maggie docked the boat and never even brushed so much as a fender against the dock. And it felt *good*.

As we crept toward the end of November, the fall colors were remarkable. We took several overnight trips, including to one of our favorites, Shellmound Park. Here we loved hanging out on the lonely dock at night with the wind rustling through the trees.

Evening at Shellmound

It was a quaint little cove that offered great opportunities for checking our overnight systems. We had to cook, make sure our power worked, sleep on board. The two of us would wake up, sip some fresh coffee, and the dreams would blow through and around us, making a whispering sound like sooooooon.

CHAPTER 5

A Wild Prehistoric Trill

Over the next month and a half, we spent all of our free time in the boat. Our marina neighbors who lived on the river would typically put fifty to a hundred hours on a boat in a given year. We put one hundred hours on our boat in *two months*.

Over those two months in the late fall, the river had its usual occasional barge traffic but almost no pleasure boats. *Currently* was there, though. We took her up through Chickamauga Lock and back. We found our rhythm and settled into roles. We switched from time to time, but usually Maggie would drive into the locks and I would work the lines. We learned our hand gestures and settled into a routine as we communicated with the lockmasters. We learned when to call for more information and when to remain silent.

We cruised around Williams Island near Baylor High School, a place we affectionately called Hogwarts because of all of the towers and walls the impressive campus showed. We learned where we could count on our charts and where the river channels might move over time.

We circled Maclellan Island and honked at waving the pedestrians next to Walnut Street Bridge. We slid smoothly and silently down the gorge, affectionately (and maybe a little hyperbolically) called the Grand Canyon of the South. We saw eagles and hawks slicing across the open water and picked out other wildlife on the shore. As barge trains poked their way into view, we learned the lingo for communicating with local traffic and generally what tow captains would want us to do.

We cruised past the Sequoia nuclear reactors on Chickamauga. We learned how *Currently* behaved on both slow cruise and fast cruise. We gathered experience and data on how quickly we could expect to burn fuel and on speeds that were completely inefficient. We also learned at what speed our wake grew to uncomfortable levels for docks on the riverbanks or passing vessels. After handling day trips well, we were ready to take some overnight trips.

About this time, our youngest daughter, Julia, was home from vet school. We thought it would be nice to visit a place called Blue Water Resort in Dayton, Tennessee. We'd provisioned *Currently* just fine as a motorboat. Now it was time to get her ready to cruise.

When we left for our overnight trip, the weather was brisk in the evening but quite comfortable in the day. We cruised all day toward Dayton and spent the afternoon there. As the park was winding down their season, there wasn't much to do. We decided to take out our new dinghy, a stiff inflatable kayak four feet wide and twelve feet long. We'd read about Dayton and anticipated a great pizza joint with lovely shops.

As I was shopping for the dinghy, I chuckled disdainfully at the price of electric motors. I'd been around enough bass boats to know that trolling motors were cheap. I bought the cheapest, strongest one I could find, and a massive lithium battery to use with it, and I'd even tested it with Julia.

Julia in *Currently*'s dinghy

Julia, Maggie, and I overloaded ourselves into the dinghy built for two, put the battery in the case, and connected the trolling motor to the boat. I chuckled condescendingly at the two crappy oars snapped to the side tubes, wondering who would buy such a pristine boat to merely *row*. Then I smiled my best dramatic smile and twisted the throttle.

Damned dyslexia. We shot backward, ruining my moment. Then I twisted the throttle the other way. We shot forward, like—how can I describe it?

Remember that gold-medal-winning Olympic track star Michael Johnson? We shot forward like his grandmother pulling a golf cart. In the mud. We were moving, though. Two miles to Dayton. We were smiling, and the promise of hot chocolate was calling. I glanced down and saw the surprisingly detailed gauge with ten bright blue dots glowing, signifying a full battery and steeling our confidence.

As the creek grudgingly gave way to our little overloaded boat, the little blue dots winked out slowly, leading us to believe the massive lithium battery was more than enough to get us there and back.

The first disappointment of the day was that there wasn't a great way to access town where there might have been. No bother. Onward and upward. Seven blue lights was plenty to get home. Our next little problem was hitting the bottom. The motor threatened to leave us stranded, but it sprang back to life, no worse for the wear. Then it became clear that we wouldn't be going to town at all, as the last possible access point for the town was high and dry. We couldn't get there without wading through an ocean of mud. We glanced down to see light six wink out, leaving five to get home.

Those lights lied to us. The lights went dark and the motor quit just as we turned around to head back. I guess I should have paid more attention to the reviews that said the motor was *mostly* compatible with lithium batteries. We paddled home two miles in complete misery. I'd like to say I learned my lesson, but no. Cheap gear still has a siren song that's hard for me to resist.

The next day was one of our most magical in the whole run-up to the loop. Near Dayton, the Tennessee flows out of the northeast toward Chattanooga, southwest of there. The Hiawassee River dumps into the Tennessee from the southeast, forming a tiny delta.

Every year, more than fourteen thousand sandhill cranes come to nest there. These birds have a wingspan over six feet. The shifting sands and muddy bottom make this particular spot on the river a treacherous spot, but one made for our tiny Ranger Tug with a draft of just under two and a half feet.

We woke up early, with Julia getting in a few more minutes of blissful sleep. Maggie and I cast off and came out to one of the most remarkable sunrises I can remember.

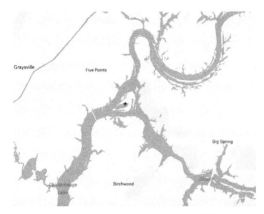

Hiawassee Delta, winter home to sandhill cranes

Sunrise over the Hiawassee Delta

We came around the delta, cut the engines, took the thruster remote out with us onto the bow, and just drifted. We saw dozens of white pelicans, their wings edged with black. As they banked one way or another, we'd see a rippling black flash; then they'd disappear.

Mixed in with the pelicans were a few red-tailed hawks or bald eagles, presenting white golf-ball-shaped flashes in the leafless trees. The stars of the show were the cranes. They would fly in a perfect V formation with the tip of the V occasionally circling around to the back of the formation in an ancient dance. Sometimes the birds came close enough for us to see individual birds powerfully stroking against the resistance of the wind. The numbers were almost over-whelming, with hundreds of birds visible at a time and many more trilling on the ground in the distance.

The result was like something right out of *The Lion King*. All of our senses were tingling. We could see wave after wave of birds flying in a V formation going right over our boat. We could smell the fertile river mud and feel the cold prick at our skin. Mostly, we could hear the warble of the cranes. These birds make this wild, prehistoric trill that's at once haunting and beautiful. The birds on the banks and in the grasslands beyond amplified the sound to something hauntingly beautiful.

Sandhill cranes on the bank

As the fossil records dating back more than ten million years could attest, the cranes are a connection to a distant past. The Great Loop we'd experience in the coming year would remind us twice that our ecosystem in Tennessee was connected to a larger one. We noticed the crane's habitat in both Canada and Florida and marveled at the distances the birds would fly for migration season.

I've had plenty of time to reflect on what makes the cranes special to me. I still can't capture the experience with a word or a picture. The best I can do is this. They are a connection, a tether, yes. They bind me to a specific place, but that magic is not exclusively tied to that one tiny island.

In a sense, we are nothing more than the sum of our memories. Some of my most vivid ones are of those fantastical creatures. On the bow with my family, drifting and smiling, these gray nomads are reminders of those intense moments that make up who I am. Moments like these are anchors to what's important. I suppose everyone has such tethers to their souls. They are why we travel, why we explore.

Watching those cranes, I thought back to our recent past. The years 2020 and 2021 had been a time of suffocating pandemic, without any exploration, but we were beginning to break free. The last few months of 2021 gave us the tiniest taste of what the loop might be like. We wanted more. It was time to go.

Part II

To the Gulf

The first segment of the loop for us meant getting from Chattanooga to the Gulf of Mexico. Since we left in winter, we needed to make the trip quickly. The route took us across the Tennessee River, down the Tenn-Tom waterway, through lower Alabama via river, and to the Gulf of Mexico.

Because of winter storms and near-flood conditions at the start of our loop, we didn't have much of a chance to break in slowly, as some loopers do, and we faced many of these dangers alone. Our breakthrough to the warmer, protected waters of the Intracoastal Waterway boosted our confidence and lifted our spirits.

Tennessee River from Chattanooga

Tennessee to the Gulf

CHAPTER 6

We Were Off

Conventional wisdom says the Great Loop is built as a one-year trip. Generally, loopers winter in Florida or neighboring islands. Then they leave Florida before the approach of hurricane season, make their way up the eastern coastal waterways as spring-like temperatures creep up the beaches in the east. Sojourners then make a decision to stay in the United States on the Erie Canal or pivot north into Canada. Either way, they spend a mild summer in the Great Lakes area. Finally, they head down the river system in the fall, waiting for the final passage of hurricane season in November to enter the Gulf of Mexico.

Early in our preparations, we came to the ugly realization that we'd have to make a difficult choice. We could either head south toward the Gulf with the loopers in late fall or get familiar with *Currently* on the river we knew well and spend Thanksgiving and Christmas with our kids at home. This would make for a long, frigid trip down the southern rivers a few months behind the wave of loopers. We each leaned in different directions, but coming between my wife and our kids was a good way to end our adventure before it even started. We opted for the cold, lonely path down the river so we could see our kids a few more times.

Kayla and Julia are two busy graduate students, each pursuing their dreams through higher education. Kayla is pursuing a PhD at Penn State in Nutrition, hopefully to change public policy around food, especially refined sugar. Julia is in vet school at Mississippi State. We were able to make the most of the holiday season, dreaming with each of them.

Julia and I paired up on some woodworking projects, building cutting boards. Over the next nine months, Maggie and I would carry one of them with us on *Currently* to remind us of that project. Kayla, an ardent traveler herself, scrutinized every inch of the routes we'd take, planning opportunities to join us along the way.

Mom and daughters took their usual trips to their favorite Chattanooga places. They visited the Hot Chocolatier, a candy store with our family favorite hottie hot chocolate. They went to Rock City, a stunningly beautiful outdoor attraction. In the holiday season, Rock City decorates the various trees, boulders, and bridges with one of the most amazing lighting displays I have ever seen.

The girls visited the Whisky Thief, a rooftop bar with the best view in the city. It overlooked the pedestrian bridge and had an especially beautiful view of the structure lit with snowflakes over the holidays. They hiked and walked and did the things college girls do.

As the holidays ended, the girls left. They were the sweet part of the bargain we made with the river. We mustered our resolve to deal with the cold side of the bargain and began to roll the last of our gear to *Currently*. We outfitted the boat one Amazon or West Marine package at a time until every nook was full.

We packed food, including enough dried goods to get us through the off season in the South since provisions would be hard to come by. Our plant-based diet was particularly demanding for the loop. The southern rivers would have poor options for specialized diets like ours. As if vegan looping wasn't enough, Maggie also had soy and gluten allergies to accommodate. Still, we found options and bought what dried goods we could and began to experiment with them out on the river. Beans, rice, lentils, and plant protein were the order of the day. These items were light, dry, and compact.

Because spare parts were hard to come by, we carried what we could with us, including enough oil and parts for several two-hundred-hour services. We carried enough tools to do all but one service; the thousand-hour service we'd likely have to do at the Great Lakes. Depending on a service on the loop was risky because of the shortage of parts and the overabundance of boats looping in 2022, but we thought we'd be able to handle that challenge.

We packed a couple of folding bikes, a dinghy for three, enough laundry for six, and food for our dog, Emmy. Since she was old, with a failing pancreas, we cooked for her. We packed an Instant Pot and a Vitamix blender to handle the plant-based cooking underway, especially in the winter. As we packed, we came to appreciate our little tug even more. It's a clown car for storage.

As we approached the middle of January, the packing wound down. We slowly made the rounds through our friends: our neighbors, our church, our professional contacts. We said goodbye many different times in many different ways. We were leaving deep relationships in our community for a long time, with no guarantees they would be there when we got back home.

In a couple of days, we'd strike out down the Tennessee River, cold and alone. The solitude we could handle. All of our boating career was on this river entirely alone. In truth, we didn't plan for the cold. Normally, weather in the southeastern United States is best characterized as chilly but comfortable. Up to a week before our departure, the winter had been unseasonably warm. If our luck held, once we got to Columbus, Mississippi, we'd see pretty reasonable temperatures, like cold spring days from our neck of the woods. Worst case, once we got to Demopolis, Alabama, we'd start to creep into warmer coastal climates, unless we were badly mistaken.

We were badly mistaken. Old man winter rudely introduced us to the reality that winters are cold, and sometimes very cold. The day before we left, we saw a string of forecasts two weeks long. If the weatherman was right, none of our first two weeks would have lows above freezing. More than half of the days would have lows below twenty, and only a third of the days would have lows above twenty-five.

The weather reports came out, and we knew we'd at least a week's worth of hard freezes. We'd spend most of that time through Nickajack, Guntersville, Wheeler, and Wilson dams on the Tennessee River. Looking at the map, it formed a V pointing south and flowed from east to west.

We always knew that regardless of the posted schedules in guidebooks and the recommendations of friends, we'd never be able to do someone else's loop. No matter what guidebooks or schedules said, we'd have to build our loop to match our boat, life, and dreams. We needed to make the trip our own. After spending our last night in Chattanooga on *Currently*, we woke up to the gently rocking rhythm of the river.

On departure day, looking at the placid river, only our quick check of the Chickamauga Dam release schedule hinted to the violence just beneath the surface of the river. Sixty thousand cubic feet per second probably means nothing to most people, but we knew exactly what it would mean. Remembering that our inboard had almost no steering in reverse, the amount of current would alone determine the amount of time it would take for the river to slam our pocket trawler into the opposite end of the slip. We'd even tested our skills against the angry river two days prior to pump out waste, fill up water, and top off our diesel tanks. We'd popped a fender and scratched our gel coat. Our boat's marks marked us as currently too inexperienced to loop.

Currently's route down the Tennessee River

On departure day, we tried a different approach. We untied all of the lines but one and rigged it so that Maggie could untie it from within the cockpit and retrieve the line from the river with a boat hook after we backed out. We positioned our friend Richard at the end of the docks and posted his mom, Diedre, as a lookout to scan for river debris or the numerous bass boats that screamed by our marina without warning. We started our engines, said our good-byes, and Maggie untied the line. I slammed the Volvo Penta diesel into reverse, and it was a race.

The Tennessee River sought to reunite our boat and the dock on the downstream side, and none too gently. Before that could happen, I raced to make it out to the main channel. Our bow and stern thrusters would normally protect us somewhat, but against that much current they were worthless.

As the boat, no longer constrained by the twenty-foot dock lines, gained speed and moved across the slip, it scooted sideways downstream as if it were the most normal thing in the world. Richard gave our boat a little nudge, and we were free, officially looping.

I had an exciting realization that we were leaving home and would not see this place again for nine months. I glanced back to Maggie to smile. She…wasn't smiling back. She couldn't find the boat hook.

Which meant I couldn't put the boat into forward gear without a risk of the prop getting tangled in our lines. Which meant we were adrift, spinning down the river with the remainder of the docks a mere twenty feet away. Stunningly, I realized once again that we were looping.

Earlier in the day, I had read about the many waves and wakes we'd encounter on the loop. I decided to move our boat hook to a more secure location and tie it down. Maggie, of course, didn't know this because I hadn't told her. I risked a short burst of the engines to keep us off of the docks. Then Maggie found the hook, retrieved the line, and we were off with hearts pumping from fresh adrenaline.

We saw our neighbors in the riverside community. Some were on platforms overlooking the river, some waving their lit phones like fans at a teenage concert. Others were taking pictures, and our phones beeped with the inbound flood of beautiful grainy pictures in the predawn light. Some, wrapped in blankets and holding coffee, were on their second-story decks. Some were running along the river path, smiling and laughing. We felt the welcome mix of melancholy departure with the euphoria of new adventure.

Neighbors catch *Currently*'s departure

We would travel eighty-five miles that day in our first of several hundred mini-voyages that form the adventure of the Great Loop. We didn't know what was in store, but we were already accumulating memories.

Like the time Bruce cleaned the boat and moved the boat hook.

CHAPTER 7

A Magic Portal

Our first day's run took us further down the Tennessee River than we'd ever been before. The crimson streaks of the sunrise lit our way for the first twenty minutes, painting an impossibly beautiful winter vignette. This morning, there were smiles, laughs, and even a few tears as the reality of life away from our home and friends sank in.

Barely two miles downstream, we passed the abandoned Alstom crane, one of the largest on the Tennessee River. The crane once moved nuclear reactor turbines for power generation to the various plants dotted around the river system. Reactors are often on rivers for cooling capacity. The turbines are massive, more than thirty feet long and well north of a hundred tons. Moving them from one river location to another by boat makes all the sense in the world.

Then a massive earthquake led to the Fukushima reactor disaster, and the world lost its appetite for nuclear power. Soon after, the plant shuttered its doors, but the crane still looms over Chattanooga's river landscape, a short one-mile hike down the riverwalk from home.

As we glided quietly across the morning, we'd chase noisy blue herons off of their roost as they sailed angrily away, often downstream to be displaced a few scant minutes later. Within an hour or so, we reached one of the most beautiful places on the Great Loop—the Tennessee River Gorge. Several ridges and mountains stood at attention, Lookout Mountain on our port and Signal Point on our starboard. Through the last five years, we'd hiked at the top, boated at the bottom, and seen many of the places in between. The winter stillness, with the massive current of the river, presented more of a rugged wilderness. We weren't surprised. This river has many faces, and no one would ever live to see them all.

We opened up the Volvo diesel and ran fast for a bit. Through the high water, even fully laden, our tiny trawler reached nineteen miles an hour for small periods of time, making it possible for us to complete our day's run of eighty-six miles plus a lock in ten short hours of daylight.

We approached a massive structure, a building stretching halfway across the river and sweeping across the land as well. From past experience, we knew it was what it appeared to be. Built from 1905 to 1913, Hales Bar Lock and Dam was a marvel in its time. It smoothed the navigation through the once treacherous Tennessee River Gorge, but it was prone to leaks.

In reality, it's still a spooky place. When I'm walking in or around Chattanooga, one game sometimes creeps into my mind unbidden. The rules are simple. I ask myself, "Is this a good place to make a zombie movie?"

Once the TVA assumed control of the project in advance of taming a wider stretch of the Tennessee, they decided to replace the lock rather than rebuild it. Thus, we motored easily around it and headed six more miles downstream to Nickajack Lock.

A couple of hours passed, and we approached the lock. We called the lockmaster, a few miles upstream, and it was a pretty quiet day. He said he'd prepare the chamber for us. Once we arrived, we noticed the lock was set in our favor. The chamber was full and the doors were open. We sailed right in with very little wait—a welcome happenstance on this day with brisk winds and fast current.

I've mentioned a bit about the Chickamauga Lock, but I should take a few minutes to describe locks in general. The Great Loop surrounds nearly half of the USA with thousands of miles of river and coastline. This terrain is not flat, so there are locks to tie together two bodies of water at different altitudes. The world's great rivers flow downward over great distances, and violent rapids mark any great drops in altitude. The best way to manage this problem is by letting the river rise behind dams, much like stairs in a house ease the transition from one floor to the next.

All that remains is a system that lets boats navigate through dams. Engineers can't put a single door in a dam. That would be crazy; all of the water would just spill out, creating a waterfall. Instead, they put a chamber next to a dam, like an elevator shaft. In these elevators, the customers are boats, and the doors are on opposite sides of the shaft. Water won't spill out because only one door is open at a time.

To finish the job, dams need at least two valves. One at the bottom of the lock lets the water spill out. Another at the top of the lock lets the water spill in.

When boats approach from above and the lock is empty, the lockmaster closes both doors and opens the top valve to let the lock fill up. Then they open the doors and let the boat come in. Somehow, the boat is secured to the side. Locks use many different devices for this purpose. We'll talk more about this later. When all boats are secure, the lockmaster drains the lock with the lower valve and, finally, opens the doors.

On this day, because we'd negotiated the opening in advance, a green signal light shone brightly, shimmering against the haze rising up from the warm river on the cold day. The chambers are not all the same, but Nickajack is big enough to accept rafts of twelve barges. Maggie pulled in, and I signaled her to approach a floating tie on a sliding track, called a bollard. She moved us into position expertly, contentedly warmed by the diesel-powered bus heater, like a cat snuggled into a quilt. As the cold soaked through my dry gloves, I tied us in and signaled her that we were secure. She replied in a confident staccato, "*Currently* secure" into our radio to let the TVA lockmaster know we were ready.

With creaks and groans, the massive doors slowly closed, finishing with an echoing metallic THROM. The doors formed a point like a crudely sharpened pencil. The design takes advantage of the current and water pressure. The faster the current, the harder the doors press against one another and the more tightly they close. Once closed, a siren downstream warns any traffic that the lock will release water. Then, valves opened, unseen pipes at the bottom of the lock drain water that came from Nickajack Lake above to the waiting Lake Guntersville below.

Because the doors don't perfectly close, there is leakage. The boiling, hissing water is an ominous reminder that thousands of gallons of water are moving from one pool to another in a short time. The bollards, plastered with stickers of other vessels, groan and creak in their giant metal tracks, smoothed by squeaking wheels. The smells of river water life, obviously alive but decidedly fresh, filled the chamber.

As the boat fell forty feet or so over twenty minutes, Maggie and I used boat hooks to keep the boat in position, making sure neither bow nor stern hit the wall as strong currents flowed through the lock from upstream to down.

Eventually, the river level started to stabilize and the bollard came to a stop. I didn't even notice when the doors started to slip open, a magic portal slowly revealing another world to explore. Maggie fired the Volvo, with *Currently* stretching at her tethers. The lockmaster blew the horn, and we were off.

Departing from Guntersville Lock after the horn

To those who appreciate the role American rivers have played in this country's development, the experience seems impossibly grand, but there's a darker side too. Boats can sink and people can drown. Over the months to come, we'd hear about both happening. We'd see the discordant sight of a boat docked in a lock's paved parking lot. It had sunk just a week ago. We'd also hear about stories of bollards that hung up, forcing crew to cut lines, or worse, and deal with the consequences of doing so.

Today the lock was gentle and the crew kind. With places to be and no time to waste, we motored off downstream. We called on the radio to thank the Nickajack staff. The boom of the closing doors was a sharp reminder that we were *gone*.

CHAPTER 8

Four-Foot Waves
Grew to Six

Beneath Nickajack Lock, we turned southwest. The Tennessee River narrows and tips down into Alabama. The river remains pretty but not as stunningly beautiful as the sections within the gorge. We didn't care. It was cold and we wanted to get moving, so we opened up the engine to head downriver fast.

We spied the occasional lonely heron or eagle on the riverbanks, celebrated it, and kept moving quickly. Soon enough, we reached Goose Pond Marina, a lovely little spot just a few miles from the town of Guntersville. Happy with the day's progress, we hailed the marina on the VHF to let them know we were near. We promptly got lost and waded into the wrong channel with deep weeds on either side. The depth finder sounded a reading of two feet, then one, then several inches, and finally zero, but we never felt the telltale drag of the mud.

With the last light slipping away, we could see the marina across a very small spit of land. We stopped, backed out, and turned around. We pulled back into the river, headed upstream, and found the channel we'd missed. The helpful staff caught lines, and we were tied up for our first night on the loop. We took advantage of warm showers and power, relying on *Currently*'s reverse-cycle air conditioning to keep us warm. The AC unit knew how to move heat. The clever circuits didn't mind whether the heat moved from boat to water or the other way around. With temperatures reaching down below twenty-five degrees and winds over fifteen miles per hour, we were happy to have whatever heat the boat would provide. While we stayed toasty, we did have to watch the external plumbing on the back of the boat closely. As long as we could keep it dry, the rags we taped on from the outside seemed to keep the pipes warm well enough.

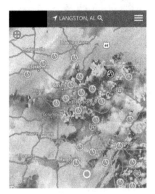

The medium winds from the day before were slightly stronger—a sustained ten to fifteen miles per hour. A winter storm was blowing in. Maggie took a quick screenshot on her phone to commemorate the experience.

As river people, we generally didn't pay much attention to wind. I didn't like to dock in a lot of wind, but wind-driven waves were generally very small whitecaps in our boating experience in Chattanooga. The clouds were gray, but it wouldn't rain. It was too cold. We'd get a healthy dusting of snow all day long. We set out early, planning to go all the way to Huntsville.

The various docks that occasionally occupied the banks were all empty. We kept a safe distance from the bank to minimize wake damage and got up on plane. While planing, a boat surfs its own wave, enabling higher speeds than would otherwise be possible. *Currently* could barely climb up to plane, but once she did, she'd reach speeds over twenty miles per hour at wide-open throttle. We didn't run that fast though. Still, with the fast current, we regularly topped out near a healthy eighteen miles per hour.

Later in the day, with Christmas music blaring, we locked through Guntersville in the snow. We had another big day behind the helm, putting lots of miles behind us and one lock to boot. We pulled over at Ditto Landing. Other than Maggie taking a nasty spill in the dark parking lot as we were taking the dog out, the evening was uneventful. Once again, we made a hot dinner, cranked the heat, watched some streamed TV, and got to bed for another early start.

In the morning, our weather reports told us to expect constant winds of ten to fourteen miles per hour throughout the day, with higher gusts up to thirty. With the winding path of the river, and trees or cliffs to protect us, we didn't pay attention to anything short of a wide-open storm. During earlier voyages, *Currently* had seen higher winds and we'd never failed to handle them.

Here's the thing. Both wind speed and direction matter, as well as geography, boat speed, and direction of travel. All of these things impact one another significantly, but we were river people, and inexperienced ones at that. According to "common knowledge," captains needed to be concerned with currents, debris, and big boats pushing barges around skinny bends. Winds and waves were easily manageable in our experience.

We were missing something important: fetch. Sustained winds blowing straight down a waterway give waves the chance to build over time. That day, the wind came out of the northwest, lined up perfectly along a several-mile-long, straight stretch of river that flowed southeast to northwest near Decatur, Alabama. We approached a town known for loud music and big rapids—the infamous Muscle Shoals.

We pulled out of Ditto Landing and into the current. We saw two-foot wind-driven waves hitting us right on the nose. Maggie and I looked at each other and smiled. Our little tug was *built* for this. The bow would slice right through. We saw a railroad bridge and confirmed through the binoculars that we wouldn't fit through.

Huh. That was a first. Later, Maggie mentioned that she'd read something about that. We found the phone number for the bridge, called ahead, and they opened to let us through. We were chuckling at the waves that would rock us briskly, hitting us right on the nose and evaporating with a hiss. The spray actually slapped on the windshield and then beaded neatly.

The normally placid Tennessee was agitated by a little commercial traffic, the uneven river bottom, high river levels, and some strong winds. Two-foot waves turned to four-foot waves in a blink. *Currently* playfully cut through them with a *woosh*. Maggie was filming the occasion and laughing out loud. I was cultivating the same streak of adventure. This was *fun*.

Five minutes later, the four-foot waves grew to *six*. Our bow buried hard, then popped up, and the waves shot *over* our windshield. The thunder of the dinghy boomed at us. It struck me that the *river* was playing the drum atop *Currently* in the famously musical Muscle Shoals. Then it occurred to me that I could die unless I kept my focus.

Shoving such useless trivia out of my head, I looked at the Garmin and saw nine commercial vessels, tiny triangles on our AIS system that Kayla's boyfriend (now husband!) had helped install. I mean, I assumed that they were commercial. No one else in their right mind would be out there. I couldn't actually *see* any of them because the waves were too high and the water poured off of the roof, coating the windshield.

Coffee cups spilled, and dishes popped off of their hooks in the galley and clattered to the floor. Maggie's wide eyes said what I confirmed aloud, saying "We've got to get off of this river."

A quick glance at our Garmin told us a marina called Pirate's Chest was close by. We could barely make out the barest tips of tiny buoys marking the skinny channel as the waves broke over and around them. I couldn't turn in from upstream. The current and waves would take us right into the side of the channel, grounding us in the mud or smashing us against whatever a muscle shoal was. I would need to turn around, match the speed of the current, and then cut between the buoys. Looking at the gargantuan waves slapping an endless staccato rhythm on our hull, I was not excited about the move.

Not seeing a better option, I waited a second or two for the break between waves and then slammed the wheel hard to port. At this point, you need to know something about Maggie. When she's scared, she's loud, and not just a little bit. She makes her opinion *known*. That's not what she did this day. She calmly turned to me and asked in a voice as calmly as if she were asking the day of the week, "Are we going to die?"

I gave my least convincing smile ever and executed the move of my life. Stealing some knowledge from my white-water kayaking days, I timed our initial turn at the very crest of a wave. I used the face of the next wave to help us carve a perfect turn on the face of a wave, as if I were on the professional surfing circuit. Now pointed back upstream, I slid the boat ever so gently upstream toward the side of the river where the Garmin suggested the shallow water lived. Our two-and-a-half-foot draft should handle any typical marina.

Once again, the river gremlins of the unknown threw a trick into our path. Lake Wheeler is a constant-level river with summer levels and winter levels. Pirate's Chest turned out to be Jay's Landing. Jay, it turns out, is a summer marina man, and his marina is usually available only in high summer levels, even when the dam releases are high.

As we pulled into the marina channel, we felt the boat slow as if it were stuck in molasses. Or river silt, as it turns out. Without us backing off of the throttle, the Garmin ticked through 6 mph, then 5, then 4, and then 3. I nosed up the throttle, desperate to avoid getting stuck in the mud and hammered by waves. Eventually, the river decided to let us go with one last thunk as we kissed a stump on the bottom of the river.

We limped into the protected channel at Jay's, a facility still recovering from a fire and a wreck on the dock. A pontoon not so different from our previous boat had taken out the supports of one of the most prominent docks, and a bit of the rotting structure was tipped into the waves. One of the staff came up to meet us and greeted us with a disconcerting message. We'd be free to stay the night, but we probably wouldn't be able to leave until late in the spring due to shallow conditions, long after the weather window for the Great Loop closed.

We looked at the dockhand, looked at the river, back at the dockhand, and back at the Tennessee. With an exasperated sigh, we gave in to the inevitable. We could not go back out there, so we tried to make peace with the fact that our loop might be over.

The marina hand turned out to be the captain of the Tow US service. He told us the river was scheduled to come down about a foot. As a point of reference, he pointed to a spot on a wall next to a boat ramp. We could see the river covering the mud next to that spot. He told us when the river receded next to the spot, we'd be trapped for the winter, two-foot-six draft be damned. We had our point of no return, so to speak.

The marina owners told us to be patient and take heart. Based on years of experience and the pattern of rains we'd seen, she expected the river to rise. We made a hot meal, watched a few episodes of *Modern Family*, and turned out the lights to pretend to sleep.

The unspoken question in our minds was not whether our loop *could* continue. Rather, each in our own way, we thought about whether the loop *should* continue. The six-foot waves shook our confidence in our preparations and in ourselves. We postponed a difficult conversation about walking away from the hopes and dreams, from the places and from the people, from the promise of shelter from different storms of depression and Covid. We danced around the conversation, each deciding how best to avoid it in our own way.

I didn't sleep all night, but I stayed in bed until the first rays of light crept over the horizon. The pink glow tickling the soft edges of bare hardwoods grew until the light slowly oozed toward the boat ramp. I jerked upright. The river didn't just stop falling. She *rose*.

We pulled out to the bay that led to Jay's Landing. The giant herons silently slipped off the bank, gliding barely inches over the surface of the water, with the slowly flapping reflections reflected right back at us. Then we pulled into the main channel, the heat of the smokestacks colliding with chilled winter air to build white towers in the sky. The reflection made an incongruously beautiful mix of industry and peace.

The Tennessee River the day after the waves

We never had that conversation about whether to proceed. We didn't need to. The taste and the smell of the morning coffee was strong. The beautiful sight of a shiny smooth Tennessee River was welcome. Our mental reflections from the previous day's adventure contrasted against our reflections on the river and bombarded our senses. This beautiful morning, we navigated a path from what might have been to what would be in the months to come.

CHAPTER 9

Friday Night Lights

Leaving Jay's Landing was a beautiful, moving experience. Still, bodies, minds, and souls need rest. As we ran down the river, I passed off the helm to Maggie to take care of my morning routines. My haggard face was no surprise because the events of the day before had rattled me. We pride ourselves on making safe decisions based on our abilities, but the results were irrefutable. We'd found ourselves unexpectedly in over our heads because we'd made real mistakes.

We'd misread the weather report, or worse. The river had brutally taught us about the power of winds to build growing waves over long distances. Even now, sometimes my memories mock me to the rhythm of the waves, whispering "Fetch…Fetch…Fetch."

We'd disregarded the power of fetch because, in the past, it had always been safe to do so. River people typically don't take the shape of the river into weather calculations because, normally, it doesn't matter. After all, the Tennessee isn't a straight river most of the time. If we wanted to continue to loop, we'd need to do a better job of reading the expected conditions for the day, even on the rivers. Once we reached the Gulf of Mexico, we'd have to heighten our vigilance.

We would also need to do a better job of establishing backup plans, especially when conditions were marginal. We nearly grounded the boat because we knew nothing about Jay's Landing. In truth, we were perfectly capable of adequate planning. We just needed to do it. I shifted my thoughts to the positive end of the spectrum.

Our boat had marvelously devoured every task we'd given her. The tug carved up the bigger waves that hit us on the nose, and we'd done OK taking one hit on the beam, though I wouldn't want to make a whole day of it. The tiny draft and extra power had already proven invaluable. We were warm and dry. With a few minor tweaks of some mugs questionably mounted on tiny plastic hooks, everything stayed where we stored it.

The river's mirror-like reflections of dawn's first glow were stunningly beautiful, providing a much-needed reminder of why we were doing this. Wheeler Lake presented a vastly different experience, with good weather and nice conditions. We ran nice and slow, letting our Volvo engines purr deeply in appreciation for the respite from yesterday's adventures. We glided effortlessly along the surface, passing beautiful limestone cliffs and amazing mansions on the riverbanks. We saw American white pelicans wintering from some colder climate and a few proud specimens of the omnipresent herons that glided from bank to bank. Around noon, we reached Wheeler Lock, passed through uneventfully, and called ahead to check the status of Wilson Lock, two hours downstream.

Scanning ahead on our Garmin, we could see a vivid collection of green triangles representing other traffic. This time of year, they would be commercial push boats that muscle the barges up and down the waterways of the Southeast. We counted seven vessels crowding around the next lock, and that could mean only one thing. We'd have to wait.

TVA prioritizes the types of boats that arrive for lockage. Military boats are first. The Tennessee River has few of those, so we didn't have to worry about them. Next are the commercial craft. On our river, the commercial craft are mostly the barge trains that move cargo to and from the cities that dot the river.

Indeed, improving navigation for these barge trains was one of the top priorities for the construction of the nine locks and dams along the river. Three were above Chattanooga: Chickamauga, Watts Bar, and Fort Loudoun. We'd gone through three beneath Chattanooga so far, including Nickajack, Guntersville, and Wheeler. We'd navigate Wilson next, before turning south toward the Gulf of Mexico via the Tenn-Tom waterway. We'd do two more, Pickwick and Kentucky, when we completed our loop in the fall.

Big barge trains flowed up and down the river, hauling many different materials. We'd seen agricultural commodities, concrete materials, scrap metals, and petroleum products. Each barge measures 195 by 35 feet and goes roughly ten feet deep. River transport costs about half as much as rail transport and a mere fraction of highway transport.

The locks we encountered were all optimized for barge trains. With all of the tows in front of us, we wouldn't be getting through Wilson Lock for a good long while. As the lock came into view, we could see several long barge trains dotting the banks off our starboard side, so we decided to cut across the lake to explore the other side while we waited.

We were decidedly nervous about all of the current passing through the lake, pouring over Wilson Dam's gates and into the rocks of Lake Pickwick below. Staying well above the dam, we turned *Currently* and slowly moved upstream to see what the lake's southern bank had to offer. As we cut across the lake, we gaped slack-jawed at the scenery and massive dam, impressive even from the upstream side.

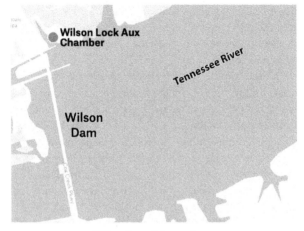

Wilson's Lock from above

Wilson Lock is one of the crowning achievements of the Tennessee Valley Authority. Its 100-foot vertical lift feet is the highest east of the Mississippi. The 137-foot structure was built from 1918 to 1924 to help tame Muscle Shoals.

Originally, the Cherokees identified the place as a shallow bottom that was a fertile bed for mussels, a staple for the local tribes. Over time, as the European influence won out, the same idea with the wrong spelling took hold: Muscle Shoals instead of Mussel Shoals. I'm secretly grateful, because it's better to be beaten to within an inch of my life at the hands of powerful, bulging muscles than dirty, little mussels.

Wilson and Wheeler pacified the endemic flooding and dramatic swings in river navigability, and the shoals sank far beneath the waves. Muscle Shoals, the name, would not die, because the Alabama town of the same name conjured a different kind of fame. Two famous recording studios gave rise to *Muscle Shoals*, the movie, a documentary with an amazing collection of recording artists; some of the biggest names in soul and early rock and roll. The list of soul artists included the icons Percy Sledge, Aretha Franklin, and Otis Redding. The folksy rock list included a staggering slate of Bob Dylan, Paul Simon, Rod Stewart, the Rolling Stones, the Allman Brothers, and more.

After consulting the map, we decided to tie up at Steenson Hollow Marina, where we encountered a picturesque slough cutting deeply into the Wilson Valley. With depths of fifty feet or more on the approach, we could relax, so we tied up the trawler and chatted with the manager for a while. We made arrangements to stay for the night.

The little marina was a quaint, quiet respite from the activity of the few days before. Nestled in the huge Alabama hills and dotted with huge hardwoods, the marina had a little store, a small crane for haul outs, and a few dozen slips. In January, it was also dead quiet, and that suited us just fine. The summer season would bring concerts and parties common in Muscle Shoals. We soaked in the little sun that we could and let our dog, Emmy, stretch her legs. Then we called Wilson Lock to get the situation for the following day.

Wilson confirmed their busy day but gave us some unexpectedly welcome news. They told us if we could get to the staging area by 4:00 p.m., we had a chance to lock through and tie up in Florence, a scant mile or two downstream. We hung out for a couple of hours at Steenson Hollow before heading out to the lock. Though we'd already paid for the slip, the family marina reversed the charge without us even asking them to do so. We made plans to come back.

Heading across the river, once again we gave the dam and the high currents around it plenty of respect, maybe too much if I'm being honest. We headed nearly a mile upriver before crossing to the other side and headed downstream. We found a little creek with enough room for us to maneuver began to circle as the barges juggled into position and locked through, one by one. I found the whole thing stressful, but Maggie didn't mind. She just drew hearts or letters in the GPS tracks and marked the time contentedly.

In commercial lock operations, high-river conditions, tight schedules, and crowding lead to snags. Today while tying up, a barge train drifted sideways in the lock and wedged itself in tightly. As 4:00 turned to 5:00, we wondered what the status might be. The last thing we wanted to do was bother the helpful TVA staff, who at this point had their hands full with the last commercial locking of the day, without having to worry about tiny, little *Currently*.

After nightfall, we called, and the lockmaster had bad news. "Plans have changed. A barge went sideways on us. We won't be able to get you through until maybe nine."

He went on to explain that tomorrow would likely be worse. We told him we were nervous about operating at night, and he graciously gave us the option of tying up to a massive Army Corps of Engineers barge in their auxiliary chamber for commercial traffic to lock through in the last dark hours of the night. He explained how an early-morning lock-through might work.

While the surrounding river was dark, the locking infrastructure was well lit. Tows don't usually start operations until daylight. Our goal would be to tie up in the chamber using Wilson's lights and lock through just before the sun rose. Then we could exit the lock right at sunrise. Because we wouldn't be on the river until dawn broke, we gratefully accepted the offer. We pulled into the auxiliary chamber and tied up to a barge.

After watching tows operate from the distance of our Chattanooga house and tiny pontoon boat, we had a front-row seat to commercial operations on an industrial river. We shared a chamber with other riverboats. We tied up our tiny lines to the massive cleats used to secure up to 1,500-ton loads. We watched the lights and heard the deep rumbling diesels of the boats that move over half of the grains our country's farms produce. The infrastructure TVA uses to maintain riverbanks was also on full display. *Currently* shared the space with tows and maintenance barges.

Tying up in Wilson Lock

We settled down with the intent to get in a few hours of sleep, and mostly we did, but the staff asked us to keep our radios on in case we had to move. Throughout the night, we heard the staff get the last two barge trains safely through and even heard a random pleasure boat go through around 3:00 a.m. Eventually, we drifted off to a short but surprisingly refreshing sleep. Around 5:00, we woke up to give the morning staff a call. TVA confirmed our plan. The morning crew asked us to keep the radio on and to be at the gate by 5:45.

We finished our morning work, checking the engines and making coffee. We pulled out right on schedule and were met with a wall of light brighter than any *Friday Night Lights* episode. Every inch of the operation was lit. Our chamber, the approach, and the main chamber all had lights.

They locked us through their secondary chamber. The gates worked a little differently from the others we had used, and the water moved a little faster. Otherwise, the experience was exactly the same as we'd seen elsewhere. I put on gloves because the twenty-degree weather demanded them. I sat in the cabin, warmed by the bus heater, and gripped the tight rope that snaked out the side door, around the bollard, and then to the boat.

Over about thirty minutes, Wilson Lock dropped *Currently* in a fast ride down almost one hundred feet. The horn

Commotion in the Wilson Lock aux chamber

sounded one short blast, and I released the line from the shiny, yellow bollard. The heat from the bus heater met my frozen fingers and I winced in pain. I noticed the dimming lights. Then I smiled because I was mistaken. The lock lights weren't dim. They were just a bit harder to see against morning's first glow.

Alone in Wilson Lock before sunrise

We headed down into Pickwick Lake, and I laughed out loud. Maggie smiled too. Our "misfortune" turned into a lifetime opportunity to get a small glimpse of life on a working river. Wilson—no, Pickwick—gurgled below as if to say, "Welcome to the Great Loop."

CHAPTER 10

Our Dog Let It Rain

Looking back, it's tempting to present the loop as obnoxiously perfect, or big, or beautiful. Much of the time, it was exactly that. But in truth, some of the time we traded a messy, boring slog through Covid quarantine in a big house for a messy, boring slog through Covid quarantine in a tiny house, but one on water. A *windy, cold* quarantine over water.

As we slipped through Lake Pickwick, the winds that plagued us continued, out of the north some days but out of the west today. The winding banks of the river gave way to bigger, wider Pickwick Lake. Waves grew to a constant foot high, with occasional swells higher, but nothing like what we'd seen in Decatur, Alabama, near Jay's Landing. We also knew what to do. Where we could, we slipped into the lee of the southern cliffs over the lake. Though the wind was out of the west, we had tiny slivers of calm water near the shore.

The temperatures stayed cold, below freezing for pretty much the whole day, outside of an hour or two. We hoped that it would be enough time to refill our fresh-water tank. To this point, the marinas had done a good job of making services available to the few people foolish enough to travel. The few pleasure craft we did encounter were captains moving boats from one place to another. We'd seen no loopers yet.

It struck me that we'd not yet been on the Great Loop proper. True, the Tennessee River to Chattanooga was listed in almost every guidebook as a worthwhile side trip, but side trips were not part of the overall circuit. We'd have to retrace our steps exactly to get home. Today, we'd mark the beginning of the published Great Loop.

We'd stop for a night at a town called Iuka, Mississippi, a tiny town where Tennessee, Alabama, and Mississippi meet. Strangely, two massive marinas were there. The guidebooks sang the praises of Grand Harbor, but we'd heard tales of service slipping in recent years. Based on a good diesel price and a discount on the slip, we reserved a spot there.

From Pickwick, we'd turn south, following the Tenn-Tom waterway named for its connection of the Tennessee and Tombigbee rivers. The two-billion-dollar project connects the Tennessee River to the Gulf of Mexico and provides an alternative means of commercial navigation to the Mississippi River. Once derided as wasteful, the waterway became essential in 1988, when a drought closed the Mississippi to commercial navigation.

We would navigate the whole 234-mile course, passing through ten different locks. Our plan was to blow through the canal system quickly, if we got lucky enough for all of the locks to let us through. We'd heard rumors of some lock closures and river flooding.

From the Tenn-Tom, we'd move to the Tombigbee for a few days before weaving through the various tributaries that feed into the turbulent Mobile Bay. We pulled out the spreadsheets and planned, making wild guesses of how many locks and river miles we could cover from one day to the next. We cooked in our Instant Pot underway, a hot meal of beans and rice, with Emmy watching from the floor, right next to the heater.

We braved the uncomfortable but harmless waves where they were the highest, the fetch from the eighteen-miles-per-hour west-bound winds in lake straightaways. Before the lake could build to something dangerous, the channel would turn, offering some welcome protection. Most of the day was tedious like that, save the minor bright spots like the picture Maggie took of the GPS that showed us in three states at once.

Eventually, we rounded the corner to the bay that would narrow to our canal. We had previously made a reservation and hailed the marina on VHF but got no response. After all, no one was out on the lake in this cold. We called on the phone, and the person answering at the fuel dock said they'd have someone to catch our lines, a welcome bit of assistance on such a windy day.

Predictably, the wind gusted just as we approached the dock. Maggie steered us in, and I threw the dockhand our line. With twenty-mile-per-hour gusts blowing us off the docks, the tiny girl just stood there, line in hand. She made no move to tie it to the dock. In swirling, gusting winds, Maggie struggled to nudge *Currently* close enough for me to get off onto the dock, but the disinterested employee still held the line limply. I leaned to grab a second line from the bow so we could pull the boat in together. The wind gusted harder, blowing the boat off the dock. Satisfied that I had a line in hand, our helper dropped her line, put her cold hands into her pockets, and strolled inside.

Huh.

I circled a cleat to add some friction and, between gusts, dragged the boat an inch or two closer at a time until I could secure one cleat and then two, just as the dockhand should have done. I was glad the marina knew we were coming and that we'd be able to fill up our diesel tanks and pump out waste, even if water wasn't available. Unfortunately, we were told upon arrival that the staff had shut down the water and pump out early due to the dropping temperatures. We'd have to find service elsewhere, later.

Grand Harbor fuel dock, home for a night

In fairness, it was a huge facility, and they had many fixtures to prepare, with no customers coming in.

We walked *Currently* farther down the fuel dock to a transient spot for the evening. Emmy hadn't peed in more than twenty-four hours because we'd tied up on the barge the night before. Though we'd prepared a warm thermos of water to rinse off a spot should Emmy pee, she wouldn't go on our swim step or on the Army Corps of Engineers barge. So we walked the dog down beautiful concrete docks to a green spot with a huge No Dogs sign.

Emmy looked longingly at the grassy spot, and I looked frantically for a place in the pet-friendly marina for her to pee, seeing dozens of grassy areas. We walked past the entrance. More grass, more No Dogs signs. Amidst this sadistic game of Where's Waldo, Emmy saw the giant field of grass in front of the marina office. I was horrified.

Emmy got the best of me. She faked left and bolted right, making a beeline to the pristine winter sod before I ever saw the No Dogs Allowed sign. Instants later, I saw the marina manager, and a tiny spark of shame and panic in me started to bloom to full flame. On the warm, dry side of the glass, the big blue-haired boss looked up and saw us too, surprised that anyone would be out here. Her quick, mechanical expression froze before full smile as the scene played out before her.

In slow motion, the timid smile transformed to full scowl as the thirty-hour drought ended and our dog let it rain. I saw the manager see Emmy assault the dormant winter turf with a furious stream of straight chemical toxicity. Instinctively, I knew there was just no stopping our piddly pooch. I briefly considered dropping the leash to run back to the boat, but alas, it was too far; they'd track me down. Then I resolved to drag Emmy off the grass, midstream, but I knew my dog, and she wasn't anywhere close to done. She'd keep peeing, and nothing would stop her. So I sheepishly smiled and profusely pantomimed all of the apologetic gestures I could think of as I waited.

And waited.

And withered beneath the glare of the poodle-piddle police. Eventually, I think she actually shook her finger at the dog and me. Knowing we didn't want to get thrown out of the marina into the wind, I kept my frustration sheathed and mouthed a final, shameful "sorry." Looking around the marina, we eventually found the tiny pets area, tucked into a little corner next to the kids' playground.

Huh.

For the rest of the day, we did those final things we had to do before entering the isolated Tenn-Tom. We had to get groceries, and that meant checking out the courtesy car at the management office. I again apologized, and the very same manager politely and distantly accepted. We signed the paperwork in silence, tiptoed to the car parking lot, full of surprisingly modern courtesy cars. We hopped into the Acadia, blasted the heat, and went about our business.

On our first night on Pickwick in Grand Harbor, we buttoned up for the night, cranked the reverse-cycle heat, and made peace with the cold the best way we could. To keep my cold-hating wife warm, I took Emmy out twice more and checked the engines. Maggie managed the galley, and soon we were eating well, as we always did. We had pasta with a cashew-based vegan cream sauce, with sprinkles of some kind of protein that had a surprising resemblance to ground turkey.

We woke up and decided the winds would climb too high for us to run far. We didn't want to lock through in high winds, but we could steal an hour of serviceable weather to head across one mile to Aqua Yachts. Our strong feelings about leaving were strange to us. This was the famous Grand Harbor all  of the old looper guidebooks raved about, and one we'd circled from early in our research. True, the buildings were nice and the docks were immaculate, but we were frustrated and more than a little ashamed. We also needed to get some water on board in advance of more winter weather before we reached the run of smaller marinas on the Tenn-Tom. Aqua Yachts agreed to do their best to help us do so.

I should mention now that we had a second experience at Grand Harbor. I don't know what changed. Maybe they just had a bad day the first time or a good day the second. Maybe ownership changed, and priorities with them. Whatever happened, our second stay was absolutely excellent.

In any case, leaving Grand Harbor was weird. Our interactions had rattled us a bit. It made us think about ourselves, notions of hospitality, and our unrealistic expectations. I also thought about our current realities for a bit. We were boating with an old dog. Sometimes, the experience would be a messy one. Looking down at the golden pool of love and fur on the floor, I knew bringing her along was worth it. She was a great boat dog. This creature who had brought us so much joy for so long was too old to run half-marathons, as she had when she was younger, but she could walk around in port cities just fine. She didn't complain, was great with people, and had great bladder control, as she had proven. She could enjoy our company, and we hers. Resolved, we started to get *Currently* ready for departure.

CHAPTER 11

An Arctic, Aquatic Groundhog Day

We cast off our lines and made our shortest cruise of the loop. The winds were beastly, but manageable. Shielded by the trees on the shore, our approach and mooring went without a hitch. There, we found the support and the facilities we'd missed at Grand Harbor.

The staff expertly helped us tie up and worked to make the pump out work for us in the brief hours that the temperatures snuck above freezing. They had a dedicated water line we could use that was protected against the cold. They even had laundry. Maggie decided to take advantage of those facilities, and I took Emmy for a good long walk. She was downright frisky in the cold.

As Emmy and I returned from our walk, with the cold sneaking through the many layers of clothes and assaulting my cheeks, I heard a strange conversation emanating from one of the quaint buildings near the docks. It took me a while to realize that the sounds were strange because they were both women. It took me way too long for logic to blow away the cobwebs. Someone else was doing laundry—in a marina with pleasure boats. This marina didn't cater to liveaboards, so they were cruising and were probably as crazy as we were. It was too late to be simply moving a boat, so she could only be a looper.

As I walked into the laundry room, I saw Jennifer. She would have been easy to spot even in a room full of random boaters. She was the one in the Great Loop smile and the Great Loop cap with ARGO on the back in big, bold letters. Her husband, Robert, was on board, sweating out the last bit of food poisoning.

We settled into a conversation over the clanking, tumbling laundry and a chilled stroll along the transient dock. Maggie stared in admiration at their forty-eight-foot Defever. Jennifer, in turn, looked over our little twenty-nine-foot tug. Two different vessels were different solutions for making the same journey.

As the conversation unfolded, I heard Maggie tell our story—scared business owners escaping Covid and isolation through the miracles of vaccination and a Great Loop quarantine. Jennifer talked about her Great Loop dreams and their plans to move their boat down to Florida. Their Great Loop would look different than ours. They'd travel in short segments, when they could break away from their tree-trimming business.

Jennifer also talked about her experience with Covid. Both she and her husband Robert had had it. Her case had been mild, and Robert had a case that got better only after she obtained "Hydroxi" for her husband after ten days. I saw Maggie's eyes flicker with concern. Jennifer was one of *them*.

In previous months, these few facts spoken aloud in a moment of weakness would have laid out our preordained roles in the conversation. We'd play our parts, drifting toward inevitable conflict or toward awkward, isolating silence. After all, the country was broken and *we* were broken.

Then something magical happened, or perhaps I should say didn't happen. The explosive words tossed into the mix shrank and mixed with the other words, becoming mundane and as powerless as idle chatter about hair color or ice cream flavors. I gaped in wonder. What was happening? As I joined in, or maybe was drawn in, I too forgot what divided us and focused on other things. Throughout the rest of the day, as Robert recovered, we celebrated our newfound friendship and talked about our businesses, our wildly successful kids, and mostly the coming journey. We dreamed together and did the things that the most promising of new friends do.

Evening turned to morning, and we left early in what would become routine for a week or so. *Argo* would be our buddy boat through the entire Tenn-Tom voyage. It was a small convoy but important for me. We would offer each other a small measure of safety. In the evenings, we'd have companionship and dreams of warmer times to come.

That first full day on the loop, we did three locks, including the spectacularly moist Whitten Lock, which we jokingly dubbed Whitten Leak. Braving the manmade rain even in suitable rain gear is no fun in temperatures near freezing. Following were Montgomery and Rankin locks. Throw in fifty-six river miles, and it was a full day.

True, the conditions were tough. Half of our running hours were in freezing temperatures and unsteady winds. Sustained winds were only of eight miles per hour, but frequent gusts were up to nineteen. The winds drove down miles of the canal unimpeded, the fetch sometimes leading to waves of a foot or two in the chambers. With the security blanket of our buddy boat, we felt prepared and ready.

As we looked into the channel to stop for the evening, we could see a field of stumps, called the Midway Minefield, poking just above the surface beside the entrance of the marina. We easily poked our way through the sometimes-troublesome hazards. We were glad to make it in safely.

Argo **locking through on the Tenn-Tom**

The stumps of the Midway Minefield

We stayed the evening at Midway Marina, where we met Brad and his friend, who were bringing a new boat down to Florida after hitting a stump or a rock on the bottom of the river and having to stop for repairs. That day, Brad was carrying space heaters into his boat. I told him about the reverse-cycle heat on *Currently*, and he mentioned that his boat had the same feature. They just didn't know how it worked or whether it would be safe to operate in temperatures below twenty degrees. I knew exactly what he meant.

I didn't know exactly how much protection my outdoor plumbing systems would need. All of the literature and support videos from the manufacturer had people pulling their boats in cold weather or fully winterizing them. We couldn't do that because we needed the water, so we winterized the raw water faucet the best we could and occasionally ran some heater tape around the exposed outdoor faucets. When it got especially cold, I would wake up to make sure the system wouldn't freeze hard and break the fixtures.

On our next leg, we left Midway and we locked through at Fulton, Glover Wilkins, Thad Cochran, and Aberdeen. We pulled off the river less than a mile above John C. Stennis. There we met my daughter Julia, her now fiancé, Reid, and her friend Becca. They brought us some packages we had mailed to them, some engine filters to keep the diesel purring, and the vegan creamer to fuel the coffee addiction that keeps the people purring. The pile of packages was massive. Maggie asked Julia to bring quarters from the bank for laundry because we neglected to bring any. Being grad students, no one had time to run extra errands, but they rounded up all the quarters in their house and car for us. It was a wonderful gift.

The relatively mild and calm conditions in the country in November and December that made our loop preparations so pleasant had given way to a wave of winter storms across the whole country, even in the deep south. Though we had dodged a predominance of the winter precipitation that hammered everything north of the Tennessee border, we had to contend with day after day of cold temperatures and high winds. I did most of the nightly errands, setting up power or walking the dog, as Maggie managed the tasks in the relative warmth of the cabin.

Argo and *Currently* at Columbus, Mississippi

Our brisk visit with Julia reminded us of her milder October visit, but let's be real for a bit. The windy, cold conditions we encountered in the southern rivers for weeks on end were *hard*. They relentlessly hammered at us like an arctic, aquatic ground hog day.[1]

The storms north of us also brought water, so we dealt with high waters just a notch below flooding. Rising river currents scoured the banks, washing all sizes of branches, logs, and even tree trunks into the main channel. Even on the Tenn-Tom, we had massive amounts of flotsam and jetsam to dodge from the helm. Robert would bark out, "Dead head off your port" or "We're slowing down until these branches thin out a bit." In particularly bad periods or when the sun was in our face, we needed four eyes on the river. It became harder to work between driving shifts because, often, all eyes were needed at the front of the boat to spot mostly submerged wood, called dead heads.

---

1   https://www.imdb.com/title/tt0107048/

To the south, no loopers were moving because of a closed lock and river flooding. We hoped that river levels would drop to safe levels by the time we got down to Demopolis, Alabama, in three or four days. By then, the southern latitudes would welcome higher temperatures, which would raise our spirits in turn.

Here's what a typical day might look like in the *Groundhog Day* movie, where the same day played out over and over. Our version of the flick featured the beautiful Maggie Tate and her sidekick Bruce. We would wake up in time for Bruce to feed and walk Emmy and check the engine. Maggie would make coffee and lay out a cold breakfast. When the boat was deemed safe, Bruce would unhook the power cords and store them while Maggie called the lock to check for commercial traffic.

We would cast off with Maggie at the helm and Bruce managing lines. Then Bruce would get up to the front of the boat for the first lock of the day. *Argo* would tie up on the starboard, leaving us to the port side. Bruce would put out fenders to keep *Currently* off of the walls. Then Maggie would drive in, and Bruce would tie off.

We'd then run until the next lock, switching drivers more often when there's more flotsam to handle. We'd grab our own snacks or drinks, and lock through again, or get lunch when it was time. In the evening, we'd come in. Bruce would prepare the boat with power and check the engine room while Maggie made dinner. Bruce would lay out all of the protections against the cold we thought we might need, and then the alarm would sound, and we'd do it all again.

You've doubtlessly noticed that these roles have Bruce out in the cold and Maggie in the warm cabin. This is by design because she hates to be cold. HATES it. We've adopted roles that let her stay warm and happy through the loop. After all, it's ground hog day. If we're going to do something more than once, we'll choose to do it with a smile on our face.

CHAPTER 12

One Too Many
Mississippi Mud Pies

We slowly clawed our way down the Tenn-Tom lock by lock, stop by stop. From Columbus, we left Julia to her studies and went immediately through John C. Stennis lock with *Argo*. We then spent our third night on the Tenn-Tom at anchor, or "on the hook" as the captains liked to say. We were tied up in deep waters with only tiny ripples on the surface, but the current was swift. Loopers tell stories of anchors breaking free from the bottom and waking to giant sweeping spotlights tows use to find the bank. Losing confidence in the anchor systems leads to uncertainty, which in turn leads to sleepless nights, and ultimately mistakes.

We slept like babies because we were prepared. Rather than figure out how to do all of this work on our own, we relied on experienced captains to show us the ropes, so to speak. We read articles, talked to loopers, and watched many hours of videos. Being harbor hosts as dozens of loopers poured through Chattanooga was invaluable to our preparations. Loopers helped us choose hardware, refine our approach, and even gave us demos of the various anchors and mooring approaches.

Our twenty-two-pound Rocna Vulcan anchor is on the large side for a boat. Loopers who anchored often told us that anchors couldn't be too big or too heavy, so we bought the biggest one that would fit on *Currently*'s bow. We also worked out a system that would better secure the rode—the chain, rope, and connections that connect the anchor to the vessel—to a cleat once the anchor was deployed. Our rode included fifty feet of chain and two hundred feet of rope. Chain is heavier, stronger, and more expensive, so there's usually less of that. Rope is lighter and cheaper.

As we prepared for our loop, I slowly built repeatable procedures to deploy and retrieve the anchor, and it was time to put my research into practice. We first let our buddy boat pull into the anchorage. The first job was to work with *Argo* to pick an acceptable anchorage. Since we were working from the same guidebooks, it was easy. Because of the time of year, we'd be alone. We chose a stranded little paperclip-shaped channel, long since abandoned by the canal, in favor of a shorter, straighter channel. It made a good anchorage because access to it was relatively shallow, but the cut was deep. There would be no barge traffic, and we were protected from wind and current.

After a long day of running, *Argo* slid in first. We preferred to anchor in eight to ten feet of water, but *this* water was twenty feet deep. I took the tug to a spot fifty feet or so from *Argo* and pointed the boat into the current since it was stronger than the wind. Next, I released about five times the rode that it would take to reach the bottom, about 125 feet in all.

Our boat had buttons we could use to operate the windlass from the helm, but I used another set of foot operated buttons on the bow, instead, to see exactly what was happening. The windlass clanged as it paid out chain, and the red tape that marked each section of twenty-five feet of rode slid over the bow roller and then beneath the muddy waters of the canal. *Currently* slid slowly backward until we tied off the rode. Maggie pulled us sharply in

Lower Cooks anchorage on the Tenn-Tom

reverse, the boat snapped back against the Rocna, and the hook was set. For an evening, we'd be protected from runaway barges or tows, and even surprisingly big winds or waves. We didn't expect any of those things.

Robert graciously came by to look our anchor setup over and gave us a thumbs up. Then he motored his dinghy back to *Argo*, picked it up by crane, and climbed back aboard for an evening cocktail. Maggie and I would sleep better for that extra bit of confidence.

We splashed our tiny dinghy and its massive battery and motored the dog to shore. Predictably, the shore was slick and muddy, and Emmy wanted no part of it. Eventually, we coaxed her out. When we returned to *Currently*, we looked like we'd tried to deliver one too many Mississippi mud pies to Jay's Landing on the wrong day. We both shed clothes on the back of the boat and put them aside into trash bags for another day's laundry, just in time to catch the setting sun. It was a pleasant, peaceful moment, made so by our confidence in *Argo*.

Then we turned on our generator. At the time, we thought our generator had problems. In truth, we just didn't know how to use it. Four switches had to be set exactly the right way to make it work. Today, we had things set correctly, so Maggie was able to cook a hot dinner—lentils with rice and vegetables in a nice curry sauce.

We brought out cushions to the bow to lay back to see stars and then used a tiny bit of hot water the engines heated up throughout the day to take a warm shower. We crashed for the night and slept like babies, the result of good hardware, a good anchor set, and sound research.

In the morning, we turned on the radio and made a quick breakfast. *Argo* called, and we were ready to go. Maggie took the helm, and once the diesel was warm, we crept upstream with me on the bow, using the boat's power to move forward while I slowly used the windlass to gather up the anchor. It popped straight up without drama, with a nice-sized clod of Alabama mud as a souvenir.

This day of running would take us through the last of the Tenn-Tom canal. Along the way we saw the odd incongruous White Cliffs of Epes, a medium-high chalky formation reminiscent of a smaller White Cliffs of Dover. I vaguely remembered that they were formed around the same time. Though they looked out of place in that muddy winter landscape, our curiosity fired and we each took a turn in the cockpit taking it in.

This day's goal was to reach Demopolis, an obscure spot on our map we had eagerly circled with a bright red marker. Most locals said that town was the place that would signal the beginning of tidal waters and bring warmer weather. Alas, in these historically cold days, we would have to wait a bit for warmth. Lows stayed below freezing, with highs of the day barely over that mark. We pulled into Kingfisher Marina to find a grumbling group of liveaboards. They were itching for a break in the weather. We could tell

Sunset at Lower Cooks on the Tenn-Tom

White Cliffs of Epes

that they were a tight group that liked their home marina. A few lingering loopers were there as well, but generally the group was made up of folks who planned to visit the Bahamas or the Florida Keys. Seven of the boats would head south on the next good-weather day.

One of the couples we met were the Rossmans on *No Agenda*. Jim was nearly legendary among loopers. *No Agenda* flew a gold flag because they'd completed the full loop. Jim had a six-pack captain's license, meaning he could accept six paying customers aboard. The Rossmans were in a thirty-nine-foot Mainship, and we immediately liked them.

The Minnesota couple crossed their wake more than ten years ago and just kept on going. Like many loopers, they were a fun-loving, curious couple. We chatted with them on the docks about their experiences and learned that a group of vessels would be leaving Kingfisher to lock through together.

Lockmasters tend to like it when pleasure boaters travel together so they can be locked through at once. They had called Kingfisher earlier in the week to request coordination of boating groups, and Jim was leading such a group. We'd take a day to rest and let bad weather clear, and we'd leave the following day.

At Kingfisher, we took our extra time to top off fuel and water. I did some engine maintenance and worked a bit with our generator. I didn't know it at the time, but a hidden breaker had blown, and we couldn't figure it out. We'd run the next few days without generator power. Instead, we'd rely on our battery bank, and do our high-power cooking underway.

We also took some time to do laundry, take on provisions, and even get a little bit of work done on our professional website. I recorded a few videos and then worked on the website. I also prepared for the class I'd be teaching in Florida via Zoom.

The weather couldn't quite decide what to do. Some reports said it would kick up and then lay down, and others predicted the opposite. When all was said and done, we tucked into our warm V-berth for the evening and woke up early. One brief weather check later, we decided to go. Our small convoy met right behind the Kingfisher fuel docks and then rolled out onto the river, one by one. Four of the seven boats planning to leave were there. The others decided to sleep in or leave the following day.

For the first time in a week, we were on another river, the Tombigbee, or more precisely, the Black Warrior-Tombigbee. In the distant past, I'd enjoyed the rapids on some small sections of the Locust Fork of the Black Warrior by kayak. Over the next several days, we'd run on the Tombigbee-Black Warrior to the junction with the Alabama, forming the Mobile River. Then we'd follow that river out into Mobile Bay.

Before we could officially close the book on the American winter rivers, we'd need to brave just a few more cold days. After the two locks below us, we'd have no locks between us and the Gulf of Mexico and we'd enter tidal waters. This first segment of our adventure was winding down. We were so close to the Gulf that we could almost taste the salt.

CHAPTER 13

Locks Are Dangerous Places

As the boats negotiated pecking order in the little convoy, we fell in behind *Argo*. We'd sail fourth because lockmasters usually load big boats first. This rule is not to protect status. Big boats are typically harder to secure, and inexperienced captains can react badly in docking situations, especially in tight quarters. The whole loading operation becomes safer when big vessels are tightly secured against the wall as the smaller, more vulnerable vessels enter.

As we watched *Argo* lock down their boat, we thought back to the last lock we'd done with them. When we first met Jen and Robert, they struck us as a strongly independent couple with a hard streak. They ran a tree-trimming business, complete with their own big-crane larger jobs. As we spent more time with them, they talked more about their business. You can learn a lot about a person by the way they treat employees. Robert treated his with love and respect even after he and Jen had been burned by theft, fraud, and more.

We heard another story about the big-hearted captain. He'd seen a man struggling in a canoe on the Mississippi

River. The adventuring paddler was working down the whole river by canoe. Because the river was higher than expected, he was out of energy just to the point that his planned voyage was turning dangerous. Robert convinced him to load his canoe onto *Argo*. They traveled down the river together, and Robert eventually dropped him off in a town, where the youth secured work on a barge.

In fact, the day before we arrived in Kingfisher Bay, *Argo* had a chance to talk to the would-be Huckleberry Finn. From miles away, *Argo* saw the tiny triangle representing the tug on AIS. They recognized the name of the boat as the employer of their brief charge. They called ahead and arranged a conversation, just as we arrived at Demopolis Lock.

As we approached the lock, *Argo* pulled off to the side, letting her bow drift close to the channel. The tug rose up in the lock with her load, and the boats established communication. We switched on our radio, as well, so we'd hear the conversation. As the tug captain passed the radio to his deckhand, the lockmasters and *Currently* all listened to the remarkable reunion. We heard emotionally charged small talk of people who genuinely cared for one another. I confess that I barely held it together.

In a strange moment of discomfort, I looked out the window, somehow embarrassed for my wife to see my emotional response. I don't know why. An accountant would have been moved, mid-audit. These kinds of moments are the very soul of a Great Loop adventure. They transcended the matters of faith and politics that would normally come between us.

Some of the loop's stories are uplifting ones, like that one. Others are a bit more foreboding. Over the months to come, we'd see boaters treating locks pretty casually, but we knew the truth. Locks are dangerous places. We wouldn't have to go too far downstream to get all of the confirmation we would need.

Argo **meets with the barge**

We journeyed toward Coffeeville Lock that day. As we approached the lock, a strange sight awaited us. In the parking lot were four cars and a boat. I had to look twice. The boat looked to be in fine shape, but I'd learned that there was significant damage below the waterline area in spots I couldn't see.

The pleasure craft, called *Pearl River*, had sunk in the lock a couple of weeks ago, locking down the river traffic that wasn't already stopped by hazardous flooding conditions. The boat sat for a bit until a crew worked out a way to extract it. Eventually, they lifted it out by crane amidst the frigid temperatures and flooding waters. There was no damage to the lock and no significant debris left behind. They plopped the boat in the parking lot, where it loomed over us.

All of the loopers on the water knew about that boat because the sunken vessel had shut down the Tombigbee to transit. We didn't know *why* the *Pearl River* sank. Stories swirled around the event like the spinning waters in the chamber. We asked the lockmaster what happened.

He said they didn't know for sure, but the boat had likely hit some debris. I imagined the bilge pumps keeping up while the boat was underway, likely helped along by the suction of the passing water on the hull. Once the boat was stationary and tied up on the lock wall, maybe the

The boat that sank in the lock

inbound jets of water were too much for the onboard pumps to handle. The pilot, who was the only person on board and wearing a life jacket, climbed out safely at the lock ladders.

Commercial craft also have accidents. Earlier in the day, we heard a lockmaster dressing down a tow crew that was a bit too cavalier with their safety. The lockmaster told the story of one young man who had recently slipped on some ice on the deck and fell into the lock. He was able to safely swim to a ladder. The water was cold and he was hypothermic, but he lived to tell the tale.

Not everyone is so lucky. Just two weeks before, a man slipped off a barge in the vicinity of the Sonny Montgomery Lock we'd transited on the Tenn-Tom. He was crushed between a barge and the lock wall. Another man died on the Ohio River after falling off of a barge.[1] Another boat pushing a barge struck a stalled pontoon on the Tennessee near Wilson Lock.

---

1   https://tinyurl.com/loop-article

Contemplating life choices in Coffeeville Lock

Loopers tell hair-raising stories of floating bollards that get stuck, leaving boats hanging in the air off of lock walls. Many others talk about having to cut ropes, and the importance of having knives close by just in case. I haven't verified any of those stories. I've never had the need. Just seeing the power of the current, and boats weighing tens of thousands of pounds getting pushed around by winds, motors, and currents is enough for me. I wear my life jacket, keep a knife near, and mind the ropes carefully. Nearly a year later, I came across a picture of me locking through after seeing the boat. I was without my typical smile; the boat in the parking lot was weighing heavily on me.

After Coffeeville Lock, we had planned to anchor out at Bashee Creek anchorage, but the river levels and conditions there made it a poor choice. We decided to push on.

In the next few hours, the remaining convoy reached a famous looper "marina" called Bobby's Fish Camp. I'd seen a review of the place a couple of weeks ago: "The Name Says It All." I laughed at the time. I was not laughing now.

Bobby's Fish Camp

The marina was little more than a few barges tied together, with a defunct fried-catfish restaurant. Nearly legendary in Great Loop circles, the place struggled significantly when the marina's namesake passed and willed the establishment to his children. We paid nearly two dollars a foot for a few feet of rusty barge, no land-based services, and regular wakes and lights from passing tugs on the working river. Still, many of our party needed to top off their diesel tanks, and the regular anchorages were closed to us because of silting or flooding conditions.

We'd heard about others who stopped at Bobby's in other seasons and had a great time. They raved about partying with the locals and trading stories with real river people. That has a certain appeal. Visiting Bobby's outside of the Great Loop season was a different experience.

After Bobby's Fish Camp, *Argo* would pour on a little speed and slip away. It's tempting to wonder why. Maybe their longer boat made it awkward for us to find a comfortable speed for running together. Maybe their skills for nighttime travel or my coming class on the Florida coast made separation inevitable. We didn't look at our short time together as an inevitable separation. We looked at it as an opportunity to spend some precious time with a couple of spectacular people. We still check in from time to time with Jennifer and Robert. This first parting was both natural and typical of what happens on the loop.

From Bobby's, we ran downriver with the Rossmans. We stayed with them for a couple of nights at an anchorage called the Tensaw River. We pulled into one of the numerous horseshoe bends that sometimes had current and sometimes didn't. Today the river was high, and we slipped in easily. We dropped the hook in about fifteen feet of water.

Maggie had one of her worst few hours of the loop there. I left the boat to help Jim with an engine repair. In truth, Jim is a more capable mechanic than I, but his engine room is tight and requires some uncomfortable acrobatics to service. Maggie stayed behind with the dog. The day was grey and cold and the river fast.

Since Maggie hadn't ever operated our windlass, she felt helpless to react to any emergency, and our lack of a working generator meant she spent most of the time in the quiet. No hot breakfast. No coffee. No cell service. No dinghy due to current speed. Once I returned, Maggie helped me thaw my cold hands and I Maggie's cold spirit.

We got the generator going, and that felt like a huge win. A good hot dinner was a lovely prelude to a beautiful sunset. Then we climbed out to the bow through the side door to watch the stars. We talked about dreams of dolphins, warm nights, beaches, and salt. In one more day, we'd break through to the warm, inviting Gulf Coast.

CHAPTER 14

Mobile Bay
Let Us Off Easy

Our time at Tensaw anchorage came to a close. Over the course of the two days, another couple of boats joined us, but they moored around the corner and we heard nothing from them via radio or otherwise.

When the time came to go, both the Rossmans and we were eager but nervous, each for our own reasons. Jim was nervous for his new alternator belt. In retrospect, it turns out that his concerns were well placed. His alternator problems from a bad serpentine belt were exacerbated with a bit of rust that had built up on one of the pulleys. Over time, each new belt would start to slip and ultimately fail.

Maggie and I were nervous for a different reason. We were new to saltwater and didn't know how to operate in it. Under our ownership, *Currently* had never been tied to anything but a floating dock, but we knew changing tides would require a different skill set. We'd never experienced the wind or fetch we would face on bays and open waters. The six-foot waves on the river were more than enough to scare us silly. We also didn't know how to track through the Intracoastal Waterway. Some of the signs were different than the ones we'd seen before. Also, what we didn't know haunted us like an empty shadow riding along in our flip-down navigator seat.

At the agreed upon time, we raised anchor. Ours was sticky, and the windlass slipped a bit. Irrationally, we saw *No Agenda* slipping away to leave us. We needn't have feared. Jim was nervous too. It was a good day to have a buddy boat.

Argo crossed the Mobile River and bay the previous evening. They said the lit buoys made the exercise a quite pleasant one. We kept up with them on the social media app Nebo, sending them our heartfelt thanks and pictures of our voyage along the way. They kept us informed of conditions and options to anchor or stop for the day.

At the confluence of the Alabama and the Tombigbee, the river grew wide and strong. Constant debris kept us watching. We were also aware of the omnipresent poverty we'd seen, interlaced with bigger houses that signaled wealth. Big agriculture, including King Cotton, had its dark roots buried deeply in the sandy brown fertile mud. Visions of past old-South plantations prodded my imagination.

Sure, certain places were industrial and sad. At most others, the river was a symbol of power going back hundreds of years. The Chattanooga bluffs along both Signal and Lookout Mountain were seats of power and wealth, from Rock City's flowing garden trails to the massive homes on the brow that bordered one of the first memorial parks in the Civil War system.

The small, rural Alabama rivers felt different. We'd see barns and houses melting down the riverbank, the poor structures no match for the erosion of the banks. Old barge ties and abandoned industrial derelicts dotted the banks like hulks of a long-forgotten war. In a way, they *were* victims of a fight against time.

At places, the rivers wound around like ribbon candy. We could sometimes see traffic through the leafless trees coming the other way. I glanced down at the GPS and saw a wild reversing pass with land masses separated by a tenth of a mile. Sebastien on *Kittiwake* called this section the great inefficiency.

As river momentum built toward an ultimate crescendo in Mobile Bay, abandoned infrastructure gave way to active barge operations, the working river system gathering forces to build and feed the growing south. Then we could see it in the distance—Mobile, Alabama.

At just under a quarter million people, Mobile was the largest city we'd encountered, discounting the outskirts of Huntsville we'd seen mostly from a distance. Mobile was different. We'd go right down the barrel of the river and the industrial marine operations. We thought we'd get a reprieve from the typical commercial activity based on the time of year. We were wrong.

Faint industrial scents of oil and sulfur tickled our noses, announcing our approach to the city. The buildings grew, the river picked up speed among the restrictive concrete channels, and the vessels grew too. Gone were the trains of two-hundred-foot barges and the tugs that moved them. What we saw was on a completely different scale. The river tugs built for smaller places gave way to cargo ships a thousand feet long.

We gaped at the titanic cargo ships as we snuck by, some shaded with rust and others brightly painted as billboards, unseen for weeks at a time on the open ocean. Our AIS display exploded with dozens of little triangles, mostly green. The red ones denoted craft on or near a collision course. The tugs, too, were huge, two or three times as long as the ones we'd seen on the rivers. To them, we were mere minnows among so many sharks, too small to even register as a snack.

We crept our way down the river, me driving and Maggie calling out obstacles. Most of our AIS targets stood stagnant along the sides, the electronics announcing a speed over land of zero miles per hour, long before our eyes could accurately categorize the approaching ships as threats or

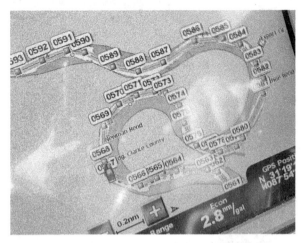

The winding Tombigbee on the Garmin

safe. The rest moved down one side or the other, the puppies leaving the middle of the channel clear for the big dogs, with two tugs in the middle of the channel.

As we got closer to the bay, we saw a problem developing in front of us. Two tugs were coming up the river toward us in a wide formation, cutting off the river on our starboard side from safe passage. Another tug on our port side was setting up to reposition one of the giant container ships. We would potentially be passing this tug's stern when it engaged its engines to drive the container ship closer to port. Those engines would fire, and we could be swallowed in the turbulence behind the boat. Under no circumstances did we want to be anywhere near that tug when it happened.

Jim called on the radio to the two approaching harbor tugs, but got no response. He flipped to channel 13 and hailed again. "*Gasparilla, Gasparilla,* this is *No Agenda.*" He got no answer. Again and again he hailed, only to receive silence. We were simply too small to warrant a response.

Approaching tugs block our intended path

Then we found ourselves the one place we did not want to be. We had to pass behind the port-side tug. We knew we were going to take some prop wash. There was nothing for us to do but give it as much room as we could.

Jim got hit broadside and was blasted clear to the other side of the river. I knew I didn't want to take that prop wash on my stern. That kind of wave could fill up the cockpit of little *Currently* in seconds. I turned my bow to angle into the prop wash and let the powerful push drive me sideways and back. As I fired our engines, the current did indeed push me backward, but the bow sliced through the wave and the Volvo did its job, preventing me from being tossed into *No Agenda* or the approaching tugs. As the pressure subsided, I turned out of the prop wash and pointed my boat downstream, just as I'd done each time I left an eddy in a kayak twenty years ago.

Later we'd learn that Ranger Tugs had in fact been victims of swamping and sinking from large vessels' prop wash. We would need to be more careful in the future. We should have waited for the situation to resolve before working downstream. We also should have been listening on the local commercial traffic channel to better communicate. With our boat intact and still right side up, I heard Jim

The tug that blasted us across the river

give a nervous chuckle and say, "OK then. On we go." Nothing more needed to be said. We'd learn from the experience and do better next time.

The rest of the run down the Mobile River went smoothly. As we passed the occasional commercial traffic, Jim coached me via VHF, setting my expectations for the conditions we could see in the hour to come. Mobile Bay is notorious as a wide, shallow body of water. Tall waves can whip up quickly. Prodigious amounts of commercial traffic flow through, kicking up waves that build to violent proportions if the fetch is bad. Shifting shallow sands ground boats, winds hold them fast, and waves pound the unsuspecting craft—an unholy partnership of mayhem.

As we poked our nose out, we noticed a small grouping of pleasure craft from Kingfisher Marina. They planned to take the same route we did. We'd nibble across to the closest marina, one of several that dotted the Dog River confluence with Mobile Bay. The riverbanks provided a refuge on the western shore of the ominous bay. Maggie asked me to take the helm as the pushy waves out of the north quartered us,

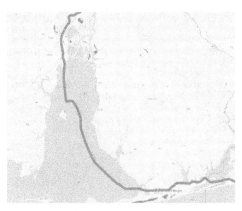

Currently's route through Mobile Bay

our tiny stern washing out in a predictably unsettling dance set to the rhythm of the waves. To Maggie, each time the stern washed out, the butterflies in her gut fired just as they would if her car broke traction in the rain. She wanted no part of this weather.

I was seeing a pretty constant chop of two feet or so, but Jim said the waves were practically nonexistent for this time and place. Lies, Maggie assured me. I tended to agree with my wife, but the other Kingfisher boats saw what Jim did. Seeing a sliver of promised freedom from the month of cold and wind, they decided to angle out across the bay toward the east. After a quick conversation with Jim, we agreed, and made the same choice. We'd skip the west coast and make for the Intracoastal Waterway.

We carefully picked our way along channels through the area marked as spoils on our charts—those underwater mounds of sand and dirt that pile up as dredgers fight the mariner's battle against sand, time, and tide. We watched the depth sounder count down to four, then three feet, and eventually down to two. We listened for the scrape of sand beneath our keel that never came. Then the depth thankfully ticked slowly back up to happier numbers.

At that point, we knew we'd made it. Mobile Bay let us off easy. As the bay gave way to the more settled Intracoastal Waterway, we took stock. We'd taken fourteen days to traverse fifteen locks and five different winter waterways. We'd made it to saltwater. We'd broken through to a warmer place, where new fears, adventures, and friends waited for us.

Part III

Florida

The Florida coastline is a major part of the loop, and many loopers spend a quarter or even a third of their time there through the winter months. We spent a couple of months in Florida. Most loopers cut across the Okeechobee Canal to shave off some time, but we went all the way out to the Keys while the canal was closed for maintenance.

Parts of Florida were physically demanding, like the crossing of Tampa Bay with my dying brother, or psychologically difficult, like the jarring news of the invasion of Ukraine. Even so, we started to find ourselves, maybe for the first time in years. We played with dolphins, invited passengers aboard, found the greater looping community, and connected to the world after years of Covid-19 and isolation.

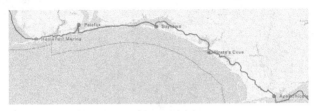

The Florida Panhandle

The Florida Coast

CHAPTER 15

Are We Settlers
or Locusts?

Leaving Mobile Bay behind, *Currently* glided into the Intracoastal Waterway (ICW), and we could immediately see the appeal. Protected from the elements, the businesses on the ICW beckoned small boats and big. Restaurants, marinas, hotels, and condos provided a vastly different feel from the rivers we'd recently traversed. A quick glance down at our Garmin showed a thin strip of water in what we would later recognize as a fairly typical stretch of ICW.

The United States is often protected by a series of barrier islands. The ICW is a waterway that uses them to weave together a passage from Massachusetts to Texas. The man-made river is a godsend for loopers. Over the months to come, we would motor all of the way around Florida and into New York Harbor, braving the unprotected Atlantic only once and the Gulf of Mexico twice. All other times, save a few bay or river crossings, we'd be in safer waters with protection against wind and waves from open waters.

More than just an accident of nature, the ICW is infrastructure made up of many systems that work together. The channels must handle both high and low tides, and key

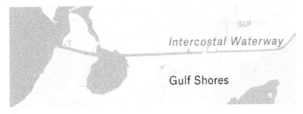

GUF

Intercostal Waterway

Gulf Shores

Leaving Mobile Bay on the ICW

fixtures like bridges must be marked with scales, like white rulers, so captains can definitively tell whether their vessels can pass beneath. Fixed bridges must be high enough for sailboats to pass beneath. Lower bridges must open to allow boaters to pass through. Inlets must let vessels in and out. Channels must be deep enough for vessels to pass through. All of this infrastructure would be worthless without signs.

As we passed our first few signs, Jim, on *No Agenda*, pointed them out. Like the red and green buoys on the rivers, the red triangles and green squares had several different forms. They might be buoys or complex beacons, possibly with sounds. They could be signs mounted on the shore or on posts firmly set on the bottom. On the ICW, buoys were numbered so you could tell exactly which buoy was next in a given sequence.

The premise is mostly simple: go between the reds and greens. For a given stretch, reds would be on one side and greens the other. These buoys are important for two reasons. First, they are regularly maintained. Said another way, the facts a buoy shows about a waterway are assumed to be true. Second, other parties respect and use them. Other vessels navigate with them. Marinas use them to help their customers safely enter their facilities. The Coast Guard communicates to the boating community with such markers, using them to identify safety concerns. Bridge and lock operators funnel traffic to desirable and safe places in the channel.

Jim explained that navigation was nuanced. Sometimes buoys might mark a different channel than the markings on a paper chart or a chartplotter, like our Garmin. Charts must change over time as sands shift and channels move, and they even have mistakes. Dredging, erosion and shoaling impact channel bottoms. Reds and greens are usually more up-to-date as marks set by people on site, such as the Coast Guard. We relied on the tireless workers that put tangible marks on the planet as physical boundaries between safe and unsafe. To Maggie and me, the message was simple. Buoys kept us safe.

As we puttered slowly down the ICW, we took it all in and glanced longingly at the afternoon sun and its promise of warm days to come. Eventually, we approached Gulf Shores, the Alabama coastal community dotted with fishing charters, tourist attractions, and restaurants. Opened by Jimmy Buffet's sister, Lulu's was one such restaurant. Alas, for the duration of our visit it would be closed for renovations over the off-season, so there would be no Margaritaville for us. For our Buffet fix, we'd have to wait for Cabbage Key near Fort Myers, the home of the diner made famous by the song "Cheeseburger in Paradise."

HomePort was a lovely, homely little marina, but a pretty expensive one compared to the rates we'd been paying on the inland rivers. Because of a confluence of Covid boat sales and the increased pace of hurricanes, marinas were all more expensive and harder to find. One fast looping couple on *Baboo* told us they'd had trouble finding space anywhere on the Panhandle. We were fortunate, probably because we were traveling with Jim. He planned well and helped us find space.

As we were tucking ourselves into our slip, Maggie took a nasty spill on the dock and bruised her hand. Only a deathlike grip on the power tower saved her from falling into the water between the boat and dock. These kinds of events happened to loopers from time to time. Most of the time, they left mere bruises. Throughout our loop, we saw broken legs, ribs, arms, and even a hip. Traveling between unfamiliar locations with different cleats and fixtures on docks was just a recipe for accidents. Other than that, our stay in Alabama was nice.

After putting on shorts for a day, I pulled out long pants again, as the weather turned chilly once more. I worked on the Volvo engine's two-hundred-hour service. I used a manual oil extractor to pull out *most* of the warm oil. The rest of it wound up on my pants. Luckily, none of it made it out of the engine compartment and into the marina.

Changing the oil at Homeport Marina

Colorful language rolled like thunder across the marina as I changed the fuel filters. It was hard to get the fuel filters off, but eventually a hammer and screwdriver persuaded them to let go. The filters and most of the diesel inside them joined the oil in my bucket, and the rest joined the oil on my pants. I also replaced the various expensive but necessary air filters on the boat. I struggled to prime the engines, but they eventually sprang to life. By that point, I was angry and messy, so Maggie and I went to have dinner and drinks. And yes, she made me change my pants.

A couple of days later, we were ready to leave. With clean oil in the boat, clean laundry on our shelves, and clean pants on my body, we followed *No Agenda* to Pensacola. We would have to hole up there for a couple of days because the wind, waves, and rain were kicking up. Once again, we stashed our shorts in favor of our jeans.

And puffy jackets.

And rain covers.

Yes, this was the Florida we'd been anticipating for so long. The marina pickings were slim, but we were pretty sure we didn't want to be at anchor through this blow. We finally settled on Palafox Harbor. The sea wall there had been destroyed twice in recent memory. Ivan destroyed it in 2004. Sally, the seventh named storm in a crazy 2020 season, exploited a flaw to destroy the harbor again. In 2022, the marina had yet to be rebuilt, but the wall had a few dozen slips for use.

The intensity of the weather wasn't lost on us. We'd nibbled around the edges of winter storms and experienced day after day of record lows. Throughout our five days there, we'd walk out to the sea wall and watch the waves make their point- 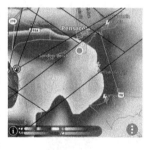 less assaults on the concrete, wondering what kind of forces it would take to overcome this mighty fortress of a wall.

The smell of the winter salt mingled with the freshness of the rain to give us hope, but the cold and gray days stacked up on one another like the little AIS triangles we'd seen approaching Mobile Bay. They just kept coming. I was holding my optimism, but my sun-loving wife was wilting from the cold and the gray.

We spent a good amount of time in the Pensacola museums. The history museum gave us a sense of the people that occupied the place, flying five different flags through its history. The influences of Spain, France, and Great Britain spread throughout the region, bowing over time to the political might and whims of monarchs four thousand miles and an ocean away. All of these places left indelible traces on culture and cuisine, from the architecture to the names of places throughout the town.

We also visited the museums of commerce and industry. We saw exhibit after exhibit showing the virtues of Pensacola's growth. The timber industry went from hardwood to softwood products, including both lumber and resins to protect nautical finishes and fill gaps.

Shocking transitions marked the casual economic shift from one resource to another. Hardwoods gave way to pine, then fish. At different times, Pensacola was known for oysters, shrimp, and snapper.

The museums painted vivid pictures of nearly inexhaustible resources serially exhausted. Some exhibits didn't point to why the stories changed, but it didn't take too much investigation to see that the hardwood and pine forests of the nineteenth century were just gone. In later museums, we'd hear similar stories about the once omnipresent oyster beds and fisheries of the area.

Neither of us were idealists. We understood the price of the luxuries we owned. Still, we couldn't help but be just a little less sure of ourselves in that place. We filed the experience away, just one more in a mounting pile of memories to sift through later.

Throughout the week, a growing brooding feeling snuck in like the miserable damp cold. We were in a place we wanted to *see* but didn't want to *be*, at least for any great length of time. Being storm-bound for days is difficult. The feeling hit Maggie particularly hard. After a frustrating morning of a failed oven, laundry room closure, and no hot water in the marina shower, she was right on the edge of a tearful collapse, when Jim came over for a visit and a chart lesson.

Jim walked us through some anchorages and techniques for navigation. He coached us up on our expected journey through the unfamiliar salty Gulf with all of its peculiar tides, winds, and currents. The conversation was important, but not for the reasons our cheerful neighbor thought. Maybe it helped us reflect on the future, offering belief in weather that would relent in her own time. Maybe it was just the right sort of distraction at the right time. In any case, our moods lightened as we watched our weather, marked our time, and readied boat, pet, and crew to move on. It was our first extended stay in a town. The Rossmans trained us in looper traditions like docktails, where boaters in one place joined one another on a dock, boat, or deck to tell stories about the day. We spent our first few docktails on *No Agenda* or at Jaco's, the nice restaurant at the marina.

In all honesty, I can't say we'll look back on Pensacola as one of our loop's great moments, but I *will* remember it vividly. Life's best journeys allow time for joy and moments so empty they seem frivolous. Our loop would have such moments, but this one was more of a time of discovery and reflection. In particular, two questions popped up.

Jim and Pat Rossman from *No Agenda*

The first was about the weather. It felt unusually windy and cold for the location. At home, our prolific news consumption raised increasingly dire warnings of climate change. In Tennessee, these vague concepts were far away, but in our tiny trawler the direct results were hard to ignore. The gathering evidence wedged in our consciousness like an irritating grain of sand in an oyster. We'd have five thousand more miles to think about these questions.

The second question was one from the museum about identity and purpose. Are we colonists and settlers, transforming our discoveries to a grand and marvelous empire? Or are we locusts, plowing through mountains of plenty time and again until they were no longer enough? Maybe we're both at once; I don't know.

In either case, Pensacola was a singularly important stop. The loop grew in those five days. We were always going to learn more about ourselves, but this small Panhandle town became a place for us to understand more about our communities, our country, our world, and our impact.

CHAPTER 16

A Dolphin Almost Hit Me in the Face

Throughout our six-thousand-mile journey, crews on different buddy boats shared their best and worst with us. We survived the winter storms with *Argo* and *No Agenda* in the southern rivers. We braved Delaware Bay with *Long Recess* and continued through New York and into the Hudson. We picked up a *Stray Cat* in Montreal and *Via Mer* in the Rideau. We ran with *Arion* and *Magnetic North* through the Trent-Severn and Georgian Bay. We sped down the northern rivers with *Amy Marie* and followed *Titan* and *YOLO* on the final stretch home. We would not trade any of those moments, but some of the most remarkable moments on the loop happened while we were alone.

Knowing we'd leave *No Agenda* soon, we poked our nose out of Palafox and into Pensacola Bay with less-than-ideal conditions. The waves were every bit of the three-foot seas our websites predicted.

We made our way around a corner, with big waves hitting us about forty-five degrees off of the stern. Once in the bay, the disconcerting feeling stirred up the butterflies in our guts as the waves repeatedly washed out *Currently's* stern. It wasn't comfortable, but we knew what to expect from our crossing of Mobile Bay a week ago. As expected, the channel settled down and gave way to some of the most beautiful beaches in all of Florida.

Maggie wasn't yet ready to anchor out, so we planned to stay at Baytown Resort in Sandestin. Jim and Pat planned to sneak away to a quiet anchorage they'd encountered on a previous loop, but plans at sea are always tentative. We enjoyed the sprawling resort town tremendously, taking our time to walk the dog along meandering paths with silent herons tucked away in the sea grass.

A heron at Baytown Resort in Sandestin

Then we got a text from *No Agenda*. Still struggling with their alternator, Jim and Pat limped into port. We caught lines for them and made plans for dinner. The Rossmans found a mechanic, and he was able to fix their alternator belt, at least for the moment. We had a nice dinner together and moved on down the ICW the next day without them.

We had plans to meet Kenny, son of my brother, Mike. *No Agenda* went to find a nice anchorage, so we pulled into Pirates Cove alone.

While we were waiting in a busy channel for the marina to contact us and guide us in, we drifted into shallow water and eventually grounded. After a half hour or so, I was able to use my bow thruster with a liberal dose of reverse to back off of the shallow spot ahead of the falling tides. With nothing hurt but our pride, we limped into our slip.

Maggie asked how I was doing. Not one to waste the opportunity of stopping at a real pirate's cove, I started hammering her with the local lingo. " 'Tis true lass, the sea humbles a man." She implored me to give her a more serious response. I ignored her, replying "Avast ye salty dogs; help me set up the pow-aarrrrr." They just kept coming. I invested more and more energy into plank-walking, deck-swabbing, booties, mates, and bottles of rum until she finally cracked a smile.

Yes, we'd been on the bottom for fifteen minutes or so. Yes, the whole marina had watched us make fools of ourselves. We weren't the only ones, though. In our sixteen hours there, we witnessed three different boats running aground, and all of the others had needed help to get off. Sea Tow made a killing that day. The events and weather of our first few weeks started to roll off, slowly.

We had our nice dinner with Kenny. He'd arrived two hours later than planned. The marina restaurant closed while we waited, but we made the best of it, telling him he'd get to experience life on a boat. Kenny handled the plant-based burgers just fine. Go, Dr. Praegers.[1]

We took our time with Kenny, letting him sit at the helm and trace our route on the GPS. We showed him the engine, the sleeping quarters, the galley, and everything else on the boat. It was a heartwarming visit, and he seemed to take to this new environment well. My brother, Mike, had done an

---

1   https://drpraegers.com

Our nephew Kenny visits in Panama City

impressive job encouraging his sons, Kenny and Mikey, who both have autism, to be as independent as possible.

We said our goodbyes, slept like logs, and cast off in the morning, following the markers instead of our GPS tracks. Funny, the markers marking the channel were easy to spot from the marina. We sliced our way across the mouth of St. Andrews Bay. While cruising through a narrow channel, a small warship with a massive wake passed us.

We'd seen bigger wakes, but this one was perfectly symmetrical and it rocked us hard. Maggie was driving often those days to build up her skills to ready us for sharing the load in the rocky bays to come, but the waking was too much. Shaken and frustrated, Maggie gave up the helm.

To settle *Currently* down a bit, I picked up our speed to ten or eleven miles per hour and never really slowed down. It was our least efficient speed but also our most stable. For such a small boat, *Currently* can throw an enormous wake, and we did that day. About a half hour later, we noticed a

The warship's wake rattled us a bit

few dolphins in a pod, peeling out of formation and moving toward our boat. The importance of the moment crashed against me like the wake rolling behind us. I have always been obsessed with dolphins.

Childhood memories are funny things. Some are patchy or fading, like the time my father woke me right around the time a tornado passed over our house, toppling a fifty-foot-high oak tree in Pamela Mirehagen's backyard. Some are vivid, like my memory of my third-grade art contest. I entered a painting with a trainer, wearing a sailor's cap and a red-and-white-striped shirt, feeding a leaping dolphin. I can still see the hard edges and the trainer's bulging nose I couldn't get quite right, my inner critic still front and center after almost fifty years. Too, I could see the pleasing fade from gray to black on the dolphin's body. I recalled my mother's praise of the mix of wet and dry work she'd taught me recently. I could see her standing over me, the curve of her smile beckoning me, the sloping angle of her neck that I somehow saw as endearing rather than the prelude to disease.

Even as a first grader, I could tell you how fast dolphins could swim, that they were mammals instead of fish, that they were among the smartest of the marine species. I could recite the one-liners the dolphin trainer fed me when I was invited to participate in the Liberty Land Theme Park dolphin show. I can still feel the dolphin's skin from that day and remember the nodding signal the trainer passed to the dolphin.

These past experiences built up an unfair importance on the pending encounter, but we don't get to pick our childhood memories or their impact on our adult thought patterns. I saw the dolphins come in and Maggie did too. I left the helm like Forrest Gump, oblivious to the sea around me, running to the back of the boat.

All of the videos we'd seen from Great Loopers hit me, graceful bottlenose jumping and twisting off of a vessel's pressure wave on the bow. The dolphins would come closer from the distance, time their moves, and jet toward the bow. They'd miraculously twist to fall in and surf the bow, oblivious to the crew on the bow of the boat. That's not what happened for us.

Still running at ten or eleven miles per hour, our wake was absolutely huge. Our pressure wave on the bow was tiny as it always was. I noticed the dolphins coming in, and I opened the cabin door at the back of the boat and ran out to our cockpit. I peeked around the corner of the cabin toward the bow, irrationally wanting to avoid scaring off the huge mammals. That's where I knew we'd encounter dolphins. And then...

Nothing.

I waited for a minute, and then two. Finally, I came to grips with reality. The shape of our boat or the temperature of the water or the color of the hull, or something, was wrong, and we'd not see dolphins that day, or maybe ever. In my childish disappointment, I turned around in a huff away from the bow just in time to see a dolphin, suspended in the air, almost hit me in the face less than two feet away.

It did a half-pirouette and fell back into the water just below the waves. I could then see the silver shadow just

Dolphins played in our wake

beneath the surface, slicing back and forth, surfing our wake! Like so many times before, I'd been looking in precisely the worst direction to see what was happening.

I exploded with involuntary laughter. The raw joy of the moment was indescribable. I enjoyed the show for five long minutes, and then ran inside and took the wheel so Maggie could experience the same thing. I *knew* Maggie, so I could read her joy by the way she stood, the shape of the shoulders, the excitement in the movements. Even a quick glance at her back told me what she was experiencing.

The dolphins leapt, spun, surfed, and twirled a mere ten feet behind the boat. Little did I know that this was the warm-up act.

We slowly dialed in the speed and let the dolphins fall in. A full pod of them came in to play with us. Three adults would leap in unison close enough to touch, their noses passing mere inches behind the back of the boat as they disappeared into the turbulence. When they leapt, we saw their blow holes and facial features clearly as they angled one way and twisted to the other.

My feelings were strangely similar to the love I experienced watching my fully grown daughter surfing our wake a year ago on a cheap kneeboard behind our pontoon. The welcome joy and nostalgia piled up moment by moment.

Over the next half hour, the dolphins stayed with us. Maggie and I swapped back and forth to share the love and joy of the moment. The three bigger mammals stayed close, just a foot or two behind the swim platform. Four or five mid-sized ones moved back and forth between the various contours of the waves, jets, and bubbles that made up *Currently*'s wake. Ten or fifteen feet back on the smaller waves skimmed the youngsters of the pod, popping out a foot or two with tentative jumps only seconds apart.

The whole encounter moved me more than I expected it to. I don't know what I imagined or what was real, but looking into the eyes of those beautiful beasts touched my soul in ways that absolutely floored me. I started to film, hesitated, then put down my phone and allowed the joy to slowly seep in.

When it was all done, I sat dumbfounded, Maggie in the back and me at the helm with tears freely streaming down my face. I wiped them off, embarrassed with the show of emotion. The welcome feelings were strange to me. How can I describe them to you?

I just melted. The tension and cold from the past three weeks just thawed and slid away. The Covid isolation and injury from the past two years just cracked and dissolved away to nothing.

For just a few minutes, my inner child broke through. Today, we played with the dolphins. Yes, today, we *played* with the *dolphins*, and I can feel the joy seep in. Wherever you are, thank you.

Dolphins almost close enough to touch

Silver streaks and gray streaks

CHAPTER 17

The Best Crossings
are the Boring Ones

The encounter with the dolphins may have been the most important one of our entire voyage, especially for me. While those silver streaks offered miraculous healing by rekindling joy and wonder, they couldn't solve other problems. They couldn't help us figure out how to buy groceries, fix our stuttering generator, or help us solve the maddening problem of tying up our boat on a fixed saltwater dock. They couldn't validate our internet in advance of the first class I'd teach on the loop.

Most importantly, they couldn't help us cut through the Gulf. As first-time loopers, we had never ventured into the open Gulf of Mexico before, and we'd done precious little cruising at night. Sure, we'd rifled through the pages of various guidebooks until our fingers bled, reading about the various towns and the number of buoys we'd encounter along the way. We heard tales about long nights and big waves, the metaphorical curled scales on the back of the lone giant serpent on the loop.

Conflicting with the comfort of the dolphins, the anxiety of our coming class and the pending crossing scrambled our emotions in the way great adventures usually do. I should take a little time to explain.

Most of the route through the Florida coastline was within the protected confines of the ICW, with one major exception. The tiny corner of coastline where the Florida panhandle meets the western coast is called the Big Bend, and the waters within are notoriously shallow. Loopers must venture deep into the unprotected Gulf for a period of time. This short trip is ominously known as "the crossing." Over the course of the loop, we'd lose sight of land only four times: this Florida crossing, reaching the Florida Keys, a run offshore of New Jersey, and a small fragment of Lake Michigan.

So this first crossing was on our minds as we battled the medium winds and waves through Choctawhatchee Bay and snuck into a skinny, shallow canal that wound its way to Apalachicola. More dolphins greeted us at the head of the canal but peeled off and meandered away as we split the red and green to enter the channel.

As we'd seen in Alabama, many beached and broken sailboats lay high on the banks, remnants of Hurricane Sally's September march across the Panhandle in 2020. Beyond the destroyed boats, the canal had few signs of the opulence we'd seen in the major bays. The canal had its own kind of beauty, winter tones of tans and sepias contrasting with the gray channel reflecting the hazy skies. Occasional beaches speckled with egrets and seabirds were doubtlessly home to gators we never saw.

A swing span bridge greeted us as we neared our destination. Composed of triangles for strength, one bridge span perched atop a turntable. The guidebooks told us that the automated bridge was open except when occasional trains needed to cross. We pulled into the Apalachicola River to the sight of a sleepy commercial fishing town. We passed a free marina, opting for the so-called Icehouse Marina because it was right beneath the Verizon cell tower. We'd have great internet for my coming class. The dock was an extension of commercial docks, so it dwarfed little *Currently*, but it was otherwise perfect.

I should take a moment to describe our expectations. In the past, we'd dabbled in beach real estate in Texas. Most of the tourist beach towns we'd chosen were kitschy towns with gift shops shaped like lighthouses or giant sharks. They catered to tourists. Seafood tended to be fresh but overcooked and under-seasoned. Downtowns were built to *seem* authentic. Businessmen coated such places with buoy lights, nautical signs, fake ships, and boardwalks.

Sure, some beach towns had more marble, concrete, or shining chrome than others. Signs and storefronts might be more professional or costly, but the formula was the same: camouflage all things uncomfortable until the true heritage is all but gone, a blank canvas for profit. Replace what was with what most tourists want to see, Pirates of the Caribbean on a budget. We thought we knew what to expect from this town, but we were wrong.

My friend Boyd told me west of Panama City on the Panhandle, people came to find a party. Pilgrims came to the eastern Panhandle to find rest for a weary soul. East of there, we'd find rest for our soul. We should have listened.

Apalachicola was none of the things we expected. It *was* authentic. We moored the boat on a once commercial dock, mere feet behind a commercial shrimping operation. The dingy white trawlers spread their big wide nets as wings, angels promising the sweet flesh of prawns. In town, we found hand-sized macaroons and authentic café con leche. The fried oysters had the marvelous flavor reminiscent of sea and earth, cooked just to a lovely cookie dough texture—none of the usual coastal overcooked calamari wannabes, please.

Apalachicola's dock dwarfs *Currently*

We found local seafood stores with proprietors kind enough to let a ragged mariner use the trash or have a bag of ice for free. Struggling with the lack of vegan options in rural Florida, we caved. We bought grouper there, as fresh as we've ever had, and cooked it several ways without even a trace of guilt.

And the sunrises, oh the sunrises. We were in a lovely weather pattern for the first time in perhaps our whole loop, and in a sleep pattern that led to waking up before the dawn, as we'd trained ourselves to do. A year later, I can still feel the serenity of the moment at dawn on that dock.

Our bikes on the Apalachicola dock

Still, as the week unfolded, the crossing loomed over our boat like a personal cloud. We'd religiously read *Eddy's Weather WAG*, a playful acronym meaning *wild-ass guess*. If you're a looper, you've probably heard about Eddy Johnson and his beautiful Grand Banks named *Spiritus*. We read his blog as disciples looking for a divine weather window, the serendipitous slice of time when winds slowed down and the waves lay down for just long enough to sneak across the Gulf of Mexico. Eddy, a pilot with some skill at reading weather reports and who had crossed the Gulf many times, says the best crossings are the boring ones with calm seas.

We started reading about our own weather window when we first started planning for our loop and we never stopped. We learned the magic criteria. We'd need to check three websites predicting less than two-foot seas and winds fifteen miles an hour or less. We knew the rules. We hoped to find other loopers to cross with us, someone else who knew the way and wanted a buddy boat. We even fantasized about a close friend to join us for our pending shouting match between *Currently* and the sea.

We had a problem, though. I needed to teach a class to pay for our loop. We planned to run to Apalachicola and then wait for the right window. Our class would run from Tuesday to Friday morning. As we read the blog, Eddy mentioned a weekend window that might open on Saturday, and then he promptly followed that post with a suggestion that the window might close. All the while, the loopers and other crossers gathered over the week in Carrabelle, the traditional starting point of the great sleepless slog across the Gulf.

And then the windows came. Wednesday. Then Wednesday night. We watched the scene play out with horror as our safety net composed of other loopers evaporated, sliding across the Gulf in search of adventure and warmer weather. We'd be going alone, and it felt like we'd waited too long. In weakened moments we could even irrationally see our whole loop slipping away. Then, as I taught my class, Maggie saw a thirty-six-foot Grand Banks pulled up right behind us. She raced out to help them tie out, as all loopers do, and there they were. Linda and Eddy on *Spiritus*.

Linda and Eddy on *Spiritus*

That night they invited us over for drinks, and it was like we had always been friends. We told them about the great impact the *Weather WAG* had on us. The blog gave us the confidence to do the loop safely. Linda talked about the places they had been, the looper culture, and about loopers they'd met along the way. They taught us the Looper Toast:

> There are good ships, and wood ships
> And ships that sail the sea
> But the best ships are friendships
> And may they always be.

Over time, our stories came out, and we felt each other out as new friends do. Linda and Eddy could sense our fear. At some point, Eddy came to a decision. He told us he'd be glad to walk us through the technical details of a safe crossing. He told us if we had enough range, skill, and speed, we could make it across in the coming weekend. We checked off all of the prerequisites, and Eddy agreed to meet me in the morning two hours before the start of my class. Like many seamen, he was an early riser. The following morning, I'd be up again. I snapped a picture or two of yet another spectacular sunrise, with pelicans sweeping across the river, and then slid over to *Spiritus* and self-consciously tapped gently on the hull.

Pelicans at sunrise in Apalachicola

Eddy walked me through the crossing, bit by bit. He told me a story about a friend who had been in the Gulf when his alternator had blown and his electronics failed. His message was clear. We should have a paper record of our progress, and a backup means to communicate with the Coast Guard. He walked us through writing a paper journal with GPS coordinates, hour by hour.

Then he quizzed me about what I knew. He talked about the biggest waves I was comfortable facing and then asked me how much we could take on the beam, at night. He drilled into me the idea that we should have a built-in error margin. He liked the criteria of waves *less* than two feet and winds fifteen miles per hour *or less*. After talking with him, I agreed.

He talked to me about crab pots, about building in a time buffer before and after the trip, about the importance of a stable weather pattern, and more. He walked me through the steps for checking three different weather sources, preferably built from different data sources. He watched me do this successfully several times before he was satisfied.

He told me to set one route, from the first red marker that entered the Gulf to the red marker at the end of our crossing, and to slightly adjust the throttle to arrive precisely on time. Mostly, Eddy told me how to take the informed opinions of others and do my own research, to take the tentative suggestions from others to build solid, safe plans for myself.

We told Linda and Eddy how much the encounter meant to us. We gave them one of our Currently Crew coffee mugs, daily reminders of the common bonds all loopers share. Then our friend Sam told us he thought he was going to try to stitch together an itinerary that fit his budget and our timing. Yes, we would have  to cross the Gulf as all loopers do. We'd do so with help and confidence, thanks to Sam, Eddy, and Linda.

The next Thursday morning, we saw *Spiritus* off, the happy couple waving as they made their way toward Tarpon Springs and their own crossing. His next blog entry left a cryptic note for a Friday night window for "anyone teaching a class," a secret message crossing an ocean of words from friend to friend.

Later, from the Gulf, he was kind to remember us. He sent a few notes about his Thursday crossing and inquired Friday about our crossing. Months later, he would send me the message, "Just finished some coffee in my 'Currently' cup and wondering where y'all might be." He attached a picture of the mug somewhere beautiful.

Eddy and Linda taught us about the procedures for planning a crossing, but other lessons were more important. This great adventure works because people are willing to share their gifts with one another. I hope we'll see their smiling faces again somewhere down the line. The best ships *are* friendships, and may they always be.

CHAPTER **18**

Chum for the Great Sharks

The confusion of opening and closing weather windows started to clear like a slowly lifting fog. It became clear that the traditional crossing from Carrabelle to Tarpon Springs would be off the table. We needed to be in Apalachicola to finish my class. Fortuitously, we met George, the marina's owner and dockmaster, for a brief conversation.

George was a huge fan of crossing from Apalachicola to Clearwater because it saved a ten-mile double-back from Carrabelle to Dog Island. By leaving from our current mooring, we'd save a night at the cost of about twenty miles. In the scheme of things, that extra distance was nothing. We also planned to skip ahead to Clearwater after ducking into protected seas near Tarpon Springs, saving another night. We moved on to the next set of details to consider.

Eddy verified what the guidebooks said. Our route would take us from the red R2 buoy, on the west side of Dog Island, to the R4 buoy, which marks the entrance to Tarpon Springs Harbor. We also knew to expect crab pots upon arrival, those metal cages tied to rope or cable that could tangle up a propeller or even severely damage a boat.

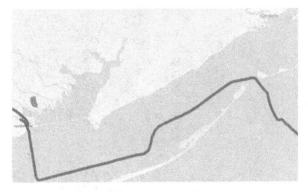

Currently's eventual crossing route

By Thursday afternoon, I'd mostly confirmed most of our crossing plans and tweaked a few others. Now the day was almost upon us. Eddy and Linda were gone, so Maggie and I prepared to serve ourselves up as chum for the great sharks of the warm Gulf. I kid, I kid, but our trepidation was persistent.

Armed with confidence inspired by Eddy's coaching, our fears subsided just a little bit. There wasn't much left to do, but there wasn't much time left to deal with those last-minute details. I would be teaching Friday right up to the moment of our departure. We got the final good news that Sam, our long-time Chattanooga friend, managed to cobble together a checkered itinerary of planes, boats, and automobiles to join us.

For the first time in years Sam was between jobs, with just enough time to join us for a crossing, and he'd found a way to do it frugally. He drove a rental car to Tallahassee, and we sent a private car to bring him to our tiny house on water. From there, he'd ride with us across the Gulf, sharing more than twenty-four hours of consecutive driving to Clearwater. Then he'd pick up an Uber, fly back to Atlanta, and take a shuttle van back home. Before we could blink, he rode up in a bright-green car, bearing a big bag of gifts from home.

Sam arrives by private taxi

The Moores were some of our dearest friends in Chattanooga, and we missed them. We led a small group together at church. Seeing Sam was a bit of a lifeline, and he came with the promise that we'd see Nickole further down the loop.

At this point, I should say that the crossing is not a place to travel with casual acquaintances. Our boating experience was *all* in protected waters, yet the Gulf was unprotected. All but two hours of our experience was in daylight, and our crossing would happen overnight. I'm a person who naps every day and gets my eight hours of sleep, and the crossing would start promptly at nap time and wouldn't end until twenty-something hours later.

The classic crossing route

In all likelihood, Sam would see us at our worst, and he was OK with that. Our families had navigated the sometimes wonderful, sometimes closed Chattanooga culture as outsiders. They'd seen us go through job transitions, sickness, and personal crises. We'd seen the same from them. We *knew* Sam, and when the obnoxiously colored pea-green car pulled up in the marina parking lot, we practically danced with excitement. We felt an almost tangible shift in perspective as the final piece of our crossing team slid into place.

Sam wasn't a sailor. He'd never even driven a boat like ours. He sometimes had balance issues and wasn't the kind of person to walk into a situation with answers to questions we didn't even know to ask. To our team, he was almost everything else. As a trainer and team builder, he had a grace under pressure in new situations. As a missionary used to unfamiliar and uncomfortable situations, he brought a natural problem-solving ability only the perpetually curious can offer. As a gentle optimist, he never complained and was easy to be with.

We spent Thursday evening together, catching up and planning the last few crossing details. The food, words, and places quickly dissolved the time between us, and we laughed as friends do. The weather did its part too, moderating to something downright pleasant. Saving the final preparations for the last day, we spent the time satisfying Sam's insatiable appetite for news of the loop. He brought us gifts, including our favorite hot sauces, and we gave him one of our coveted Currently Crew mugs.

We went to bed, us in the roomy V-berth and Sam in the cozy midberth under the salon table. Surprisingly, we slept well, the uncertainties tamped down enough to give our tired minds some blessed rest. Gloriously the sun rose, bearing yet another Appalachicola sunrise. Stoic shrimp boats silhouetted against vivid oranges and pinks provided dramatic backdrops to dozens of proud pelicans flying in formation, wing tips mere inches above the glassy river. Unseen fish splashed now behind me, now beside me, leaving rings flashing outward, first orange, then midnight blue. Sam snuck out with barely a sound, save the gentle click of his camera; the beauty of the place spoke for itself. Maggie woke too, still robed in pajamas and fleece, greeting us with hot coffee.

Eventually, we broke the silence. The day slowly picked up the natural momentum of pending adventure. We had a hot breakfast, but Sam passed on Maggie's offering in favor of a chance to support one more local business. I reluctantly broke from the rest of the crew to prepare for my class. As my students popped up on the Zoom screen, Sam and Maggie left to do one last bit of provisioning. They spent a few hours in town, finding a surprisingly authentic café con leche, and Maggie buying enough pastries to choke an elephant, or maybe cross the entire Atlantic. They bought fresh fish and came back to the boat to break down the folding bikes, tie down everything that needed securing, and cook some extra grouper tacos for snacks. By this point, we'd given up on a strictly plant-based diet. Finally, they finished those last few tasks just as I finished my first-ever class from a boat. Within a half an hour, we were off.

As we motored toward the Gulf, we converted the dinette to a bed so we'd have two beds available for the pending overnight crossing, so two could sleep while the other drove. We motored three hours slowly toward that final buoy before the open ocean. We filled the boat with nervous chatter, none of us willing to admit to our inner fears.

After completing the full loop, I know now things I didn't know then. The crossing has the reputation as the most demanding segment of the loop, but that's rarely the case. Lake Michigan often has bigger waves with shorter periods. Georgian Bay is arguably as remote and demands more navigation skills. The Jersey coast and Delaware Bay are regularly more dangerous. Why was the crossing such a daunting obstacle? For *Currently*, it was the *first* significant danger we faced. When R2 crept into view, the truth was that we were ready, and we'd done the research to *know* what to expect. The crossing was just another day at sea, but one with no hazards to hit and no steering to do.

I took over to take us through the parting channels behind a shrimp boat. As we left protected waters, the butterflies in our guts fluttered away just as the seabirds thinned with the increasingly changing climates. The depth finder started ticking up slowly, passing ten and twenty feet on its way to sixty. We were alone in the sea. We took a bit of time to enjoy one another's company.

It felt surprisingly good. We initially set the autopilot incorrectly, and it predicted a crossing four hours longer than we'd calculated. After a few perplexing moments, we corrected the problem and the right arrival time began to slowly count down. If all went well, we wouldn't need to touch anything but the throttle, nudging it forward or back,

Bruce on crossing day

until the arrival at R4 in Tarpon Springs—the autopilot said 10:00 a.m. sharp.

As time ticked on, the sea went from gentle to downright flat. Marveling at our good fortune, we prepared our dinner of delicious grouper tacos and homemade black beans. Putting on yet another show, the sun slowly oozed over the horizon, melting into a vivid pool of purples, reds, and oranges. Sam documented the moment well, framing shots to include just enough of *Currently* to tell just the right story. His skills from his past mission work were on full display.

Pinks and oranges faded into grays and deep blues, and later, the black of night. I glanced out to see our red and green navigation lights working as expected, but Maggie looked up to find the navigation light on the top of our mast was out. I passed her the helm and searched our storage

Bruce and Sam on crossing day

bins until I found our backup light. I put together a config-
uration that I could use to clamp the temporary battery
powered light to the top of our mast so other vessels could
see us in the night. Maggie shot me a worried look. I just
shrugged my shoulders, put on my life jacket with an
emergency light, and slid out the cockpit door.

It's hard to climb outside a moving boat at night against
a black sea without imagining falling overboard, but I felt
as safe and prepared as I could be. Surprisingly, the seas
were as smooth as we'd seen since leaving the river systems.
I stepped up once to reach the top of the bow. Then I
grabbed the bottom of the mast and heaved myself up. The
backup light slid on as easy as you please. I climbed back
down and slid back inside without incident. Like the rest
of the crossing, it was surprisingly easy to do.

With calm seas and nothing to do save nudge the
throttle forward or back every hour or two, we settled down
for a broken night's sleep. We covered up the electronics
we couldn't dim, and tailored the ones we could to maintain
our night vision. We turned off the red overnight running
lights and fell into a gentle rhythm of two hours asleep and
one hour at the helm. Ideally, each of us could have gotten
more sleeps, but as the captain in charge, I wanted to keep

Crossing the Gulf in beautiful weather

an eye on things. Every three hours I needed to check details the crew didn't know as well, such as engine metrics, the autopilot settings, and the local charts.

I must say that I fell asleep just about immediately after my first evening driving shift and each one thereafter. My first few shifts driving were uneventful, but memorable just the same. I'd take a turn in front of the faint glow of the electronics, alone with my thoughts for an hour at a time. I listened to music, thought about the ways the loop was changing me, or basked in the silent beauty of midnight blues and gray tones. Maggie sometimes prayed, or even sang softly. I don't really know what Sam did, but he manned his shift perfectly. Every time his shift was over, our arrival time was within minutes of 10:00 a.m.

Once, when I had the sliding door slightly open, I heard a great splash next to me and imagined a great dolphin begging the sleepy sailors to come out and play. Smiling at the thought, I thought about the difference between the imagined and real crossings. Eventually, the early hours crept into a morning glow and a vivid ocean sunrise.

We continued our rotating sleep schedule until Maggie called for help. We saw an ocean full of crab pots, hidden metal cages connected by webs we couldn't see or understand. We laboriously picked our way through the best we could, trying not to cut across a line of pots marked in the same colors.

The morning after crossing

Eventually, we saw a boat pick a spot right between two similar pots, revealing the answer to one last mystery. We looked at each other dumbfounded. We had no idea that such a thing was possible. It turns out that we didn't have to go around each string of pots. If we picked a spot near the middle, we could go right between them. I blurted out in my best Pippin Took voice, *"It comes in pints?"* Snickering, we quickly crossed the last of the Gulf and entered the channel at R4 in Tarpon Springs.

Once back in protected waters, a huge Pursuit fishing boat passed us and tossed us about, today's turbulence of civilization contrasting unexpectedly with the calm of last night's placid sea. Maggie yelled at the driver, but he was long gone. She quietly grumbled something about decency, and something I won't repeat here, so I took up the helm and we motored into Clearwater.

Looking back, our crossing wasn't the one any of us feared it might be. The little things worked. Our autopilot worked, the engine worked, and *Currently*'s hull and bilges performed just fine. We had plenty of gas, plenty of dinner, and plenty of pastries for dessert.

More strikingly, we had no wind and no waves. The sound and fury of our expectations melted into our individual, silent reflections, alone on a moonlit night.

CHAPTER 19

Navy to the Core

Sam, Maggie, and I made our way down the Florida coastline. The compass had tipped, trading the east bearing along the Panhandle to a southern one along the protected western coast. We were thrilled with the passage, grinning ear to ear, but we needed showers after our twenty-hour passage.

Sam, Bruce, and Maggie after crossing the Gulf

With Clearwater came the sun. We finally packed away our winter gear for good and slowed down. Our crossing allowed us to catch the tail of the fat wave of loopers cruising around and through Florida. Truth be told, we didn't *want* to be where the biggest wad of boats was. We thought that peak loop sounded a bit like Water World meets Hunger Games, where we all donned Columbia fishing shirts and battled to the death for a sliver of dock space, a pump out, boat parts, and toilet paper. We *did* want to get around Florida and through the Atlantic in time to take some interesting side trips, especially to Montreal.

Sam, Maggie, and I walked around Clearwater. We met up with some of Sam's family for dinner and dessert. Still in the midst of the pandemic, we ate outside and masked up in the bright tourist shops that dotted Mandalay Avenue, the main drag near the beach. We said our goodbyes, and Sam caught his Uber into Tampa. We picked up another passenger.

Before our departure from home, we invited my brother, Mike, to run with us for a day or so in Florida. We thought he'd never make the trip, because none of the family thought he'd be healthy enough to come.

I had heart issues of my own, but Mike had them in spades. A victim of bad genes, I had two angioplasties to put in stents before I turned fifty-five. I have a good diet, don't drink much, and never smoke. I'm pretty active and live in a three-story house, so I climb stairs throughout every day. I just share my brother's bad genes. I listened to my doctors, and Mike didn't.

I remember someone asking at a doctor's appointment whether he had any comorbidities to put him at risk for Covid. Maggie chuckled, and the nurse looked up with a challenging glance. Then Maggie rattled them off. Congestive heart failure. A seven-way bypass from plain old plaque buildup and the resulting heart attack. Later came a defibrillator and pacemaker from heart arrhythmia. Ongoing diabetes (untreated). Kidney disease. Asthma. The list went on, and the nurse caved and shook her head when she asked Maggie to repeat the last disease on the long list. Even in the midst of all of that bad karma, he was the most optimistic man I have ever known. Maggie and I both marveled at his attitude.

In truth, Mike and I were not as close as I wanted to be. We shared a wanderlust, but that can have a cost. He spent a good amount of time abroad and doing his own thing. Our physical and emotional distance closed a little when he came to Chattanooga so we could help him get his health under control. He'd been very ill for the past five years. He healed up well enough to take one last trip abroad to visit Thailand and Ukraine, before the Russian invasion. Our meeting in Tampa would be the last time we'd ever see him. His passing later in June was somewhat expected, though the timing was a bit jarring. Even though I knew it was coming, I wasn't really ready.

It shouldn't have surprised us that once we got close to Tampa, Mike announced that he would drive over to meet us. We decided on meeting in Clearwater. Mike insisted that he was well enough to boat for a day with us. As the day approached, we thought it would be best for him to drive to our marina, stay with us for a night on the boat, and then decide if he wanted to go out into the surf with us once we saw how the weather in Tampa Bay looked. If it was a go, he'd run with me through Tampa Bay to Sarasota. Maggie would drive his truck over land and meet us.

As the day approached, I showed Mike exactly what the weather would be. We would have one- to two-foot seas for an hour or two. We considered putting off the trip, worrying it would be too much for Mike. These waves would land partially behind us and partially on the beam, making them seriously uncomfortable. I had no doubt that he'd see the occasional three-foot wave right outside the starboard window. I silently wondered if his balance and strength would be enough for the trip. Remember, our skinny boat has a ten-foot beam and a very light draft, so beam seas rock us hard.

Try as we might, we couldn't talk Mike out of the trip. As we got ready to go, I coached Mike through driving the boat for a minute or two, because I'd need to use the head at least twice. In truth, he was barely up to the challenge of driving his *truck*, let alone a boat on one-foot seas or worse. My plan was to get to the most protected place I could find, turn on the autopilot to hold a straight line, put the boat in forward idle so it would max out at three miles per hour, and tell him to put the boat in neutral and drift if anything bad happened. In the meantime, I would pee like the wind. In the middle of a big bay like Tampa on a quiet weekday, we hoped there wouldn't be any trouble.

I glanced over at the little floating Tiki bar in a slip just across from *Currently*. We'd seen dozens of the little pontoons, and they seemed like they operated in just about any conditions. I figured if they could do it, Mike and I could too. After all, he'd been in the Navy for almost ten years, and I was, well, not as green as I had been. Then it was time to get underway.

As Maggie and I discussed in advance, she cast us off and threw our lines onto the bow and into the cockpit. Mike grinned, and I hoped my grimace wasn't too transparent. She started the short drive to Sarasota, and Mike and I pulled out of the marina.

As we approached a quiet straightaway before the bay proper, I took the opportunity to use the restroom and let Mike drive. He had his hands tight on the wheel, and I don't think he even noticed that I had taken it out of gear. When I came back, we were both, um, relieved. Over time, the winds started to build, so I knew the bay would be potentially rough. To give him a job and take his mind off of the growing waves we knew were coming, I gave Mike our new binoculars and asked him to pick out the red or green buoys that marked our passage. He loved this task. Fully

These party pontoons were fearless

engaged, he asked questions, picked out the right buoys, and left me laughing and stunned.

The bay crossing started quietly enough, but as we expected, the wind and waves grew as we crept into Tampa Bay. Our track curved and the waves grew, until we were taking two-footers right on our beam. About halfway across, we started to hear radio chatter on our VHF radio. A small sailboat had capsized near the inlet, ten miles off our starboard side. Our route would take us within four miles of the rescue.

Throughout the rest of the tense crossing, we could hear the Coast Guard but not the vessel in distress:

"What is the nature of your distress?" …

"How many people are on your vessel?" …

"Is everyone wearing a life jacket?" …

This drama would play out, and then the sequence of the same questions would repeat. Throughout the loop, we heard several dramas like this one unfold. This one was particularly tense for me because I could see the waves pushing Mike around in his seat as he held a death grip on his chrome handrail. We heard more radio chatter, idle conversation about mundane details to keep the distressed sailors calm while help was underway. Off the starboard, we saw a helicopter headed for the distressed boat. Later, we saw a Coast Guard cutter pushing rapidly toward the vessel. They were going to be OK.

As the day wore on, I could see Mike struggle more and more with his failing strength and the seating. I didn't want to stare. He kept interacting with me, pointing out buoys and asking questions. He also told me about his time in the Navy, what big seas were like on the *Iowa* and what it felt like when the huge battleship fired a broadside. He also told me about the infamous turret explosion and the subsequent investigation. He smiled and said these conditions were nothing.

Eventually, the radio got quiet and we spotted the channel on the other side. Near the shore, the seas grew to three feet or so. I stole a glance over my shoulder, concerned about the heart patient next to me. Strangely, he had a death grip on two different rails, but he was grinning ear to ear—Navy to the core. That's what I will remember, that smile and optimism. He wasn't in over his head. He wasn't getting beat up by big waves. He was on just another adventure, and loving life.

Our day of adventures was winding down. We picked our way into the skinny water of the protected channels leading from Tampa. True to form, our electronics plotted us a perfect line toward our eventual destination. We'd surprised Maggie by getting in earlier than she expected and got no help from the marina because we arrived an hour after they closed. I told Mike to keep his seat, and I pulled out the thruster remote we rarely used. As *Currently* slid to a stop, I mashed the buttons on the remote to close the distance between the dock and our ship. *Currently* gently kissed the dock, and I mentally did backflips, celebrating my first solo landing. Not showing my excitement, I casually stepped off and tied her off, with Mike beaming and wondering how he could swing the purchase of a Ranger Tug of his own.

Somehow, I knew this would be our last adventure. The loop is like that. I'd see many more firsts and lasts, some of them enormously consequential and others mundane. Though I didn't get to share as much with my brother as I would have liked, we'd shared one more adventure, and the images in my mind would have a tremendous impact on me after his passing. He sank into the seat of his Dodge Ram truck and drove away alone, but with a trademark smile on his face.

Mike. 1963–2022. I'll miss you, brother.

The Great Burgee Hunt

With the last of our visitors behind us for a little while, we relaxed into the rhythm of the loop. We would nibble down the coast a tiny bit at a time and take in Florida. The glorious warm, calm weather was the perfect platform for discovery. The warm weather meant more of the smells of the sea, more people on the streets, and more loopers.

We were keenly aware that leaving Chattanooga on January fifteenth put us behind. We essentially traded relaxed autumn-colored leaves in Alabama for the chaos of our two-week run through winter storms with snowflakes in the locks. Our decidedly isolated run through the Panhandle led to plenty of self-inflicted pain, because all of the looper "bibles" we read, like *The Looper's Companion Guide* [Wri19] and *The Great Loop Experience* [GH14], all have the same general idea. Most loopers build their trips to chase spring for a year.

Loopers generally winter in sunny Florida from January through March and sometimes into April. Head up the eastern coast once it gets warm. Make your way into the Erie Canal when it opens around the beginning of June. Summer in the north in the Great Lakes and Canada. Leave the Great Lakes by September or early October, when the storms tend to kick up. Head down the rivers in the fall, taking a side trip or two to avoid the Gulf Coast until hurricane season ends, around November fifteenth. It's a tried-and-true formula. We needed only to glance down at the Nebo app, which showed the dense constellations marking the galaxy of loopers in Florida, the Keys, and the Bahamas, to reinforce this reality.

When we decided to deviate from that schedule, our logistics got a little tougher, like finding flowing water and a pump out that wasn't frozen solid. We also missed those glorious loopers, the crazies who think selling a house for a depreciating asset in exchange for an adventure is a good idea. The looper community is one of the main reasons people want to take this trip. To Maggie and me, the promise of community in the midst of Covid was a lifeline.

The eccentric group supports all age groups, vastly different economic stations, dissimilar political ideologies, and various levels of experience. Folks ranged from "I've never seen a boat before the loop" to "I pilot one-thousand-ton craft." Boats ranged from jet skis to multimillion-dollar fifty-foot yachts. Ages ranged from thirty-something to eighty-something years old. Regardless of age or means, no boater can take on a six-thousand-mile voyage unsupported, and many times the support comes from other loopers. Our off-schedule departure meant we'd encountered only a small handful of loopers early in our journey. In Florida, that changed.

Mostly, we found loopers in two ways. To find the general location of loopers we used Nebo, a social boating app. We could open it to a map and see the numbers and names of boats in a general area. Then we could zoom in until we could see a boat's exact location. Most of the loopers we encountered were on Nebo.

The other process was the great burgee hunt. A burgee is a flag marking some recreational boating membership, but loopers tend to use a narrower definition. The AGLCA (America's Great Loop Cruiser's Association) burgee is a flag with the telltale red path around the map of eastern

North America. They come in three colors. *No Agenda* sported a gold flag because they'd completed a loop. Eddy and Linda had the platinum flag, signifying the magnificent achievement of two or more times around. Ours was white because we hadn't yet completed our first loop.

The ALGCA Great Loop burgee

To Maggie, the color didn't matter. Any burgee was an inevitable conversation, a potential relationship. I'm not always as forward. I'm a stereotypical programmer, a proud nerd who sometimes feels awkward around people. In those situations, my socially nimble wife is my security blanket, my golden ticket to "the club." We pecked our way down Florida and I followed her through marinas, aisle by aisle, taking each waving white flag as an invitation to say hello. Those who were home couldn't resist Maggie's charm, our master key for opening doors and starting conversations.

We worked our way down the lower coast of western Florida. At Sara Bay Marina, we saw a half dozen loopers. We just barely caught Maggie's aunt in Sarasota. We poked into the quaint Venice Beach in Florida, meeting three loopers before braving our first day traveling in the fog.

Deep fog near Venice Beach

Along the way, a strange thing happened. We began to encounter loopers with less experience than ourselves. Potential cruisers with grand plans asked us if we liked our boat, or how we bought provisions, or how we went about our daily tasks like navigation. Some early loopers, insecure with their inexperience, were looking for companionship and conversation. At this point, we were imposters, but we provided whatever guidance we could. Back at home, no one had expected us to know anything.

I sat back as one such conversation played out as we sat with our dog in our cockpit. Then it struck me, and I giggled, drawing strange looks from our guests. We found others through their white flags, but it never occurred to me that others would find us in the same way!

At each stop, we rapped on hulls, had conversations, and slowly grew accustomed to the vibrant, eclectic communities that were so endearing. As we worked our way south along the ICW, we'd see burgees as we traveled, read the boat's name, and call them on the radio, like the day we first saw *Dog House*.

"*Dog House, Dog House*, this is *Currently*."

"Up one to seventeen?"

"*Currently* on seventeen. We saw your burgee and noticed you're from Texas…."

On the VHF, we talked about common places we'd been in Texas and then our common plans. We were going different places for the moment, but later we'd meet in Savannah for dinner. Strike another win for burgees and Maggie's social vortex.

After Venice Beach, we pulled into Cayo Costa State Park's Pelican Bay. When we arrived, there were already fifteen boats in the anchorage. Throughout the day, the number swelled to fifty boats overall, and ten of them were flying AGLCA burgees. As usual, most were white, but some were gold. Maggie and I got settled and then hopped into the dinghy with our dog and our new Torqeedo electric motor.

We'd taken delivery of this little technical marvel in Sarasota, Florida, and it was incredible. Hauling the inadequate fifty-pound battery in and out of our dinghy was a thing of the past. We silently zipped among other boats, joyously hunting those triangular pendants. Just about everyone answered to a friendly rap on the hull.

Crowded anchorages in many ways are self-selective. These places tend to be beautiful destinations for social types. We experienced none of the awkwardness that we found meeting others in a new town because we were already part of a community of pilgrims on the loop. We'd talk about where we came from and where we were going over the next few weeks. We'd chat about adventures, common friends we'd met along the way, and the Great Loop made greater by the tiny triangular canvas. Sometimes we'd be invited aboard, and sometimes not. It didn't matter either way, because the sea was our front porch—a turquoise invitation to something deeper.

Hunting these fluttering Easter eggs, we met Peg and Craig from Minnesota and hit it off immediately. The chat migrated from dinghy to boat, where Craig made fresh salsa, tantalizingly slicing through fresh cilantro, tomatoes, peppers, and onions with a deliberate slowness that built our appetites. We could smell the faint whiff of oil from the lime rinds. With the burgee as a common bond, we spoke like old friends.

Over the course of a week, we found ourselves visiting them often. One day, we'd brought over fresh banana bread and shared it in the morning sun. They told us about a manatee hole, where we might see one or twelve of the gentle giants. That afternoon, we took our dinghy over to the place they had pointed out. We didn't see any manatees, but we *did* see the biggest gator we saw on the loop. We didn't get the dinghy close enough to get an accurate measurement, but it had to be longer than ten feet.

Back when we'd met *Spiritus*, Eddy Johnson gave me some advice I didn't fully understand until Cayo Costa. He said the trip gets more interesting when you take the time to come off the magenta line that marks the official ICW and leave the guidebooks. In truth, we'd driven right by some points of interest. We heard about Bama Hinge, but we were tired and didn't go. We also skipped on several of the more remote side trips.

In a past life as a mountain biker, I loved getting off the main trail. The best drops, the nicest views, and the most unusual wildlife encounters were all like the roots off the tap root of the main trail. It took *all* of the roots to feed a true adventure.

As we sat in our Ranger Tug on a balmy Sunday, we debated whether to check off another iconic mark from our list, a restaurant on a tiny island called Cabbage Key. As mostly vegans, we wouldn't even eat much of what was on the menu. It was a long holiday weekend, so the place promised plenty of crowds with the wakes, sniffles, and coughs that invariably go with them. We planned to go with a couple we met on a boat called *Wildlife*, but they ran aground over the evening.

We were debating whether to go it alone and take a trip to one more crowded bar in a literal sea of them. True, it was Cabbage Key, made famous by "Cheeseburger in Paradise," but we were just about to call it a day when we got

Craig and Peg in Pelican Bay

a text. Craig had invited us to go way off of the magenta line through swampy shallows and mangrove forests that eventually led to a local hideaway called the Tunnel of Love. With Eddy's advice ringing in our ears, we took the invitation.

Just a few minutes later, Craig and Peg pulled up to our swim platform in a twelve-foot hard-bottomed dinghy with a powerful twenty-horsepower motor on the back. It seems we'd be traveling in style, with the power to rise above the chop of the bay. As we skimmed over the tips of the tiny waves on plane, Craig expertly guided the craft, zipping close to the crab pots, knowing they had to be placed by vessels with a deep draft. The smell of the pungent salty seas was powerful but fresh, as the bright-white sand and deep-green mangroves met the turquoise sea. We passed hunting osprey and playing dolphins in the short trek past Cabbage Key Island and the next island down. Just as it seemed we'd be settling in for a longer trek, Craig smoothly swept the tiller to his left, and the boat slid to the right, pointing right toward a dock.

We had a brief conversation with a couple just on the verge of departure, a family Peg and Craig knew well. After catching up, we again picked up the pace and swept toward a tiny path cut through the mangroves. We'd seen several tunnels like this one before, but none quite so densely packed. Craig brought up the motor until it just tickled the tops of the waves, dialed back the speed, and slid into the tunnel. There, we squeezed between the shallow bottom below, the sharp edges of the freshly cut mangroves on each side, and drooping mangrove branches from above.

The Tunnel of Love through the mangroves

I sat on the bow, working to keep the sharpest branches off of the boat. Craig continued to weave his way through the tiny passage. This tiny tunnel would never show up on a chart, and the only mention in any guidebook would warn tourists to save themselves and their dinghies from puncture damage.

Those books are wrong. After walking a couple dozen steps, we emerged into one of the most beautiful stretches of beaches I have ever encountered. These pristine shores were clearly visited by locals, since long dead hurricane-damaged tree trunks were decorated with patterns of shells, plants, or whatever adornments the sea provided.

The beach was impossibly lovely, the water wonderfully fresh, and the cold splashes felt like bubbling laughter on our skin, washing away the fear that stems from leaving the magenta line. The place made our conversations more vivid, and the vivid colors told stories our words could not.

Decorated tree at the Tunnel of Love

We had one of those beaches we always read about all to ourselves, making the voyage we took to get there all the more significant. We saw little tree trunks decorated with perfect little seashells in geometric patterns and learned that Peg had been building these little easter eggs for years, little treats for passersby to discover.

Eventually, we settled back in the dinghy to head home to tend to our old dog and our appetites. Along the way, we met the loopers from *Wildlife* and stopped in for a drink, the unofficial docktails wiping away some of the frustration from grounding a boat on their second day of the loop.

That day, the burgee gained additional meaning for me. I could imagine Eddy's platinum burgee pointing away from the magenta line. Hundreds, even thousands of tiny adventures split off of the big one. The burgee is an answered invitation, yes, to conversation, but also to adventure.

CHAPTER 21

Someone Else with a Bigger Boat

Full of hope and newfound optimism of community, we made our way down the coast. Gone were the huge bites of grueling seventy-mile runs. Rather than gorge ourselves, we nibbled, running slowly three to six hours each day. At this slow pace, we could take in the architecture, the food, and mostly the people.

We maintained the great burgee hunt, making it a regular challenge to find the loopers in a place and have conversations. We talked about places, weather, families, and even took the occasional dabble into politics. This last topic was new to us. At home, politics didn't have hot-button topics. Politics *was* a hot-button topic. Sadly, that no-man's-land grew over time to absorb one thing after another. We couldn't talk about religion in the most churched city in the United States, or healthcare in the midst of a pandemic, or about a whole host of other topics. Over time, our lack of communication *became* the problem.

Among loopers, it was different. This audacious trip was the biggest thing in our lives, and most other topics became secondary. In nine months of looping, we had only one conversation get so challenging that we decided to exit gracefully. That person was a local Canadian boater (not a looper), and we somehow wandered into Alex Jones[1] territory. In all the other conversations where we had greater identities as loopers, political identity lost its power. Inevitably, any conversation would drift back to all things loop: favorite places, worst docking experience, worst weather, upcoming plans. We assumed each other to be friendly, and we were all curious. We all became known by the name of our boats or dogs.

After leaving Caya Costa, we stayed at Tarpon Point. Up until then, the marina was one of the most opulent places we had ever seen. They don't usually take transient boats, but they took us for a night. The dockmaster gave us a slip number and we drove down fairways so wide you could drive a battleship through them. Looking both left and right, it was easy to see why. The yachts surrounding us were huge. I'm sure that *Currently* was half as long as the smallest boat in the harbor. Some of the dinghies were even longer than us. Eventually, we pulled in between boats of 70 feet and 120 feet. It was the easiest docking job on the loop, but my heart was racing. One nick on either vessel would lead to my indentured servitude for life.

The marina was part of a massive complex of outdoor tiki bars, with live music and great food. We met our broker, Steve, for drinks. We ate on the boat and later dreamily walked through the evening, with gentle breezes blowing, fairy lights twinkling, and "Under the Boardwalk" floating over the water. Despite being obvious interlopers, we enjoyed ourselves immensely, paupers among the gentry in a castle.

The next day we met up with Brad on *Altitude Adjustment* from Colorado. We had met at Midway Marina, on the river in Mississippi. His wife, Kristen, had flown out to join him, and their time in Florida was winding down. They

---

1   https://en.wikipedia.org/wiki/Alex_Jones

Sunset in Tarpon Point among the gentry

generously offered to take us in their rental car to wherever we needed to go. So in true boater fashion, we hauled our laundry bags through the marina hotel lobby and went to the nearest laundromat. We waited out the loads in the adjacent Starbucks. We were delighted to catch up, and get laundry done.

This little sliver of Florida's west coast gave us one affluent stop after another. Fort Myers, Cape Coral, Naples, Marco Island, and the like were all intensely wealthy. At every marina, dazzling white fiberglass and chrome on massive monuments of opulence reflected the blinding Florida sun. These big boats took different forms. Some were the sport fishers with three or four engines, each more powerful than the beefy Volvo on *Currently*, with telescoping rods and high-flying bridges jutting dozens of feet into the air. Others were mega-yachts with many staterooms, swim platforms wider than *Currently*, and bows decorated with shiny stainless anchors jutting proudly toward the sea.

The prices of the marinas ticked up. We'd started the loop paying around a buck a foot, and these days, we were lucky to get prices under three dollars a foot per night. There were always other fees, like electrical hookups and high pump out fees. Naples was a similarly wealthy town, but the marina was just a hair more down-to-earth. We were in the City Marina, with plenty of transient boats full of our kind of people. The marina was clean and well managed, with strict but fair rules. We pulled in right next to Laura and Mark on *Wildlife*.

Naples City Marina

The shops in town were expensive but understated. Everyone was naturally or artificially tan and appeared naturally or artificially fit. We felt like our multipurpose looper clothes were a little too casual for the place, and the side eyes and almost smiles let us know.

From Naples, we made our way down the shifty and shallow waters of the ICW to Marco Island. We watched our markers closely, and *Currently* did fine. Here though, I found a disturbing pattern of rude behavior. To understand what I mean, you need to know about a time-honored tradition among boaters. Since vessels have sailed the seas, there have been big boats and small boats. Mariners throughout the world establish rules and traditions to share the waterways. For example, powerboats tend to give sailers lots of room to operate because a ship under sail's direction of travel depends on the direction of the wind. Big power-boats tend to give smaller craft a wide berth because the larger boats can generate wakes of up to three feet, causing discomfort, damage, or even the sinking of smaller craft. Wakes also usually travel faster than natural waves and have less time between them. This behavior is so pervasive that it has a name: *waking*.

To offer perspective, many loopers tend to stay in port when seas are greater than *two* feet—thus the saying, "Weekends are for wakers; weekdays are for cruisers." These problems are easily avoidable. One way for faster boats to protect smaller or slower craft is to use a marine VHF radio to negotiate a slow pass. Here's how it works:

The driver of the faster vessel hails a slower moving craft and suggests they both slow down. Then, at marginally slower speeds, they pass one another in relative comfort. The slow pass is a time-honored technique, wrapped in kindness and respect for fellow seafarers.

As we worked our way down the Florida coastline, we noticed a disturbing trend. Boaters were no longer concerned with waking their neighbors. Kindness and respect gave way to expediency and indifference. One afternoon, when going from Naples to Marco Island, we navigated more than a dozen wakes of three feet or more, jarring us enough to jettison coffee mugs and anything not tied down, with complete radio silence. Often, captains would turn around and watch the results of their carelessness.

Even commercial operators weren't immune. One frustrated captain chided a weekend warrior, "You have no manners down here." That brief scolding was particularly jarring to us because of the conditions the captain must have seen and the radio discipline commercial operators usually practice. Our experience was similar. Out of dozens of encounters with overtaking boats, we were slow-passed only four times in three days. Dozens of times, other boaters waked us hard, causing big waves that knocked us around. After a time, we got used to it, but we saw reckless or intentional wakes as more than waves that eroded banks and destroyed property by banging around boats. We saw them as deliberate attacks on respectful society. So battered, the bonds between sailors tied by common kindnesses becomes nothing more than loosely coupled loyalties across those with big boats.

The problem is there's always someone else with a bigger boat.

We finished our wake-filled run to Marco Island and pulled into a canal surrounded by homes valuing two to twenty million dollars. We dropped our hook in Smokehouse Bay among a half dozen other boats. Mediterranean red-tiled roofs covered three- and four-story mansions, and the vivid green lawns were punctuated by docks along sea walls.

Among the beauty of Marco Island, we learned the horrible news that Russia had invaded Ukraine. We were absolutely devastated. Maggie and I knew several Ukrainians through our work with the Elixir programming language. As we saw live video feeds on the news of refugees crossing a bridge, we pictured our friends, who had quit posting on their usual accounts.

As we poked our way around town, we fully expected to see the now common iconic sky-blue and gold flags in solidarity for Ukraine. Instead, we were shocked to learn Trump posted on social media that "Putin is a genius." He profusely praised the "savvy" autocrat. It was deeply disturbing and sickening to me.

Though I no longer identify with the GOP, I was a once-proud Republican, a conservative who gathered all of my news from the sanctioned sources. My reasons were sound. Though I generally supported liberal social and environmental policies, I wanted strong national defense, fiscal responsibility, and...it doesn't really matter; I grew up in a conservative culture and adopted that world view, as we tend to do.

Smokehouse Bay at Marco Island

Over time, many of my opinions have changed due to experiences and conversations with people not like me, a middle-aged white male programmer. Now, I tend to think about the *institutions* that must support *any* peaceful and free system of governance over time. When I spend time on such things, my thoughts drift to issues like the value of free press, the peaceful transition of power, the assimilation of legal immigrants with different viewpoints, and the separation of powers. I believe such institutions make us more respectful. More tolerant. More creative.

More.

It pains me to say that I haven't always been tolerant of other political perspectives, but I've worked on getting better. This trip was changing me even more. On the loop, we appreciated one another's differences. We listened to stories together. We ate and drank together. We supported one another through hardship. We protected each other from Covid by taking precautions, whether it was masks, vaccines, distance, or all of the above. We helped one another, regardless of our appearances or viewpoints.

So, consider my state of mind as we anchored in the beautiful turquoise waters of Smokehouse Bay. My friends in Ukraine had been attacked. I was worried about them.

Trump supported Putin, and his support had this strange, rippling impact on the news coverage in Florida. Then the ripples spread as signs in Marco Island came out, saying "Don't Blame Me, I Voted for Trump," "Make America Great Again Again," and "Let's Go Brandon," the battle cry that echoes the syllables of F**k Joe Biden. The last is a virtual secret handshake celebrating incivility.

Truth be told, I can't say for sure that the signs in Smokehouse Bay came out in response to Putin's invasion. We had seen them elsewhere on the loop. I can only say that's what it *felt* like. I could see my friends hunkered down in the growing storm of autocracy, imagining tanks rolling through Ukraine like it was tissue paper.

I thought about my friends and wondered if they were safe. I thought about the war and wondered if Julia's fiancé would be swept up in it. I thought about our friends in Poland and wondered how they would be impacted by the pending flood of refugees. This was a solemn moment for unity and reflection, not politics. It was the worst moment on our entire loop, and it ripped our hearts out.

We were on this grand trip, feeling a profound connection to people from all walks. Suddenly, Ukrainians we knew became refugees, and Trump spoke in a profoundly insensitive way, and the people around me were *celebrating*. It felt like Trump was *waking* us at a singularly vulnerable moment. It was ugly, we were profoundly sad, and we felt helpless. This moment was a conundrum on our loop, one that occupied our minds and conversations as we talked about what life would look like *after* our loop.

That night, the shrimp were nibbling on the hull, making a telltale crackling sound like sparking wires. A gentle breeze, pleasantly cool on my skin, blew through the fore hatch. The warm lights in Smokehouse Bay glowed a soft, pleasant orange. *Currently* rose and fell to the gentle ripples of the bay. I lay down as if to sleep, keeping my back to Maggie, as I always did when I had emotions to hide. Then, motionless and silent, I cried for Ukraine.

CHAPTER 22

Don't Feed the Gators

The contrasting beauty and ugliness we experienced in Marco Island continued to occupy our minds as we traveled, but setting world politics aside for a moment to focus on our boating experience, Smokehouse Bay was a compelling destination. The anchorage had excellent services close by. We took the dinghy to a local grocery store and loaded up with provisions for our short journey through the Everglades and to the Keys. (Yes, the grocery store had a dinghy dock!) We also stocked up on parts for the next few oil changes. We dropped off the dog, the parts, and the groceries at the boat and headed out once again to the great burgee hunt.

A dinghy full of groceries in Smokehouse Bay

We found two boats close by and bonded with both crews immediately. We met *Betty Gail* and *Indigo* for dock-tails, at a small bar attached to a marina a mere ten minutes away by dinghy. Over time, a few other loopers joined us, and that group helped us forget about the worried world for an evening.

As early morning came, we snuck out of Smokehouse Bay, only the rattling of the windlass and low thrum of the diesel announcing our departure. We continued to nibble our way around the tip of Florida. We'd spend two days in the Everglades before joining with *Indigo* and striking out once again into the Gulf on our way to the Keys.

The first leg of the trip took us to Russell Pass. We saw winds of just about fifteen miles per hour, but they came from a favorable direction, so the seas were manageable. Though we'd been told to expect complete electronic isolation, we still had pretty decent internet. That gave us confidence because we'd be able to check weather and ask for help in need.

We dropped anchor in Russell Pass, a small channel between Indian Key and Everglades City. Reminding myself "Don't feed the gators," we decided against letting Emmy off to pee. Miraculously, she peed on our swim platform, and we rinsed it off easily with our raw water washdown. We tried over and over to repeat that miracle, but she never managed that feat again.

As we'd done in other places, we put out a fish light. Over time, it would attract small fish at first, and those would grow as the bigger fish found prey. Then we'd watch the one true version of *Survivor* play out from the cockpit. Throughout the evening, we could see shadows of bigger fish zipping by at the limit of our light's distance. Though we couldn't see dolphins clearly, we knew they were there because we could hear their blow holes hissing as they took in air.

We'd been alone before, but never quite like this. We were pushing our electronics to the edge. We might be able

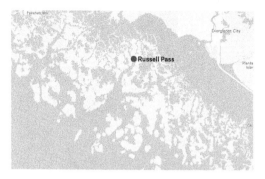

Russell Pass in the Everglades

to call for rescue should we make a critical mistake or see the weather turn sour, but perhaps not. At times, we felt not wholly fearful but definitely uncomfortable.

Evening turned to morning and the sun rose over the marsh. We made the short run from Russell Pass down to Little Shark River, the name of the place reminding us of the fleeting shadows of the night past. We saw a couple of lonely sailboats there, but we kept our distance and dropped the hook, waiting for *Indigo*.

While we waited, we gave in and loaded the dog into the dinghy and went to take Emmy and her anguish to shore to pee. Ever the coward, I let Maggie step off toward shore, and she immediately sank into mud up to her knees. That mud that looked so beautiful and black from a distance *stank*. It smelled worse than our waste tank or the fish-cleaning stations that dot the city marinas. At that moment, we learned that our love for Emmy was not boundless. I pulled Maggie back into the kayak, pushed off on the cleverly disguised sewage, and paddled frantically off the shore, though I doubt any gator would want to put anything smelling as bad as we did in its mouth.

We rinsed off the best we could, dragging our filthy limbs in the water. Emmy looked out across the water, breeze in her fur, and smiled. We poked around the man-

Little Shark anchorage in the Everglades

grove forest for an hour or so. Small paths through tunnels of trees wound their way through the everglades, a delightful maze of life and sound. Gangly seabirds on stilts fished in the shallow waters. Turtles plopped off of their perches on driftwood into the swamp, leaving concentric ripples of contrasting light and dark.

As our personal mangrove tour wound down, *Indigo* pulled up. I waved to Karen as the boat idled by, Emmy barking and Maggie laughing at the unexpected joy of the moment, the tension from our self-imposed isolation evaporating in an instant.

Still, being alone in the Everglades gave us unexpected satisfaction. The solitude let us experience the place through our own eyes, as we took our dinghy into the mangrove mazes that shoot in and out of the rivers and coastlands. We saw this tiny slice of Florida, not as we wished it to be or through the eyes of a guide. Instead, we saw the unvarnished everglades with the promise of new life. The sights and smells of decay mingled in a unified ecology. We experienced clouds of biting bugs alongside of dolphins so close we could hear them breathe. We saw the promise of

Taking the dinghy to shore

beaches dusted in white, a pretentious barrier over the foul, sticky mud.

After *Indigo* set their anchor and checked through the tasks on their arrival checklist, they invited us over for some cocktails. On their flybridge, we were above the typical swarms of no-see-ums, those barely visible biting midges. We talked about everything and nothing much. Then we climbed back aboard *Currently* to plan the next day's journey, with paradise right outside our window.

At an estimated eight miles per hour, it would take *Currently* and *Indigo* only six hours to cover forty-five miles to Bahia Honda State Park. For some strange reason, most locals pronounced the place Bah-HAY-ah HAWN-dah, slaughtering the Spanish pronunciation for *deep bay*. After we pulled up our anchors, we moved out and toward the Gulf for our next crossing. Initially, we were in protected waters with pretty flat seas.

We would occasionally see the colored dots representing the floats attached to the traps. Sneaking past the crab pots was laughably easy with *Indigo* leading the way. They could

The picture-perfect portal at Bahia Honda

drive from the top of their boat, a flybridge offering a perspective to see the connecting lines between the pots. Though they were at least twice as dense as the ones we encountered after our initial Gulf crossing, *Indigo*'s experience made quick work of them. Only a few last-minute swerves marred a nearly perfect run.

As we approached the park, the wind and waves grew, rising from one to two feet. Once we were through Seven Mile Bridge and in the Atlantic, the waves reached their peak at three to four feet. For thirty minutes, I knew with great certainty that I was more programmer than captain, but we took comfort in our buddy boat and the proximity to our destination.

We pulled into the state park and took it in. Home to manatees, turtles, and dolphins, the bay was one more remarkable testament to Florida's investment into public spaces in beautiful, shared resources. While there, we caught up with *Wildlife, Indigo*, and a handful of other loopers, including a lovely Manatee classic trawler called *Butterface*. (Yes, *Butterface*.) Score one more for the great burgee hunt. Old friends and new friends alike shared our dreams, troubles, and lives at sea.

As I watched the weather, a coming storm kept growing and shifting ever closer to the Keys until it was too close to ignore. Sometimes, conditions can lock the Keys down so tightly that nothing moves for weeks at a time. Our short-lived community would break up the way loopers do. *Indigo* would stay with friends, lucky winners of a sweet deal at a small local marina. *Butterface* would work on their boat in a self-service yard, an incongruous bargain amidst a literal ocean of tourist traps. And *Currently* would cut our plans short, using our throttle to bail us out of coming trouble. We'd run fast to make for Miami before the weather hit.

We left Bahia Honda a day early and had our most beautiful day on the full loop. Every view was a postcard with dozens of shades of blue, dusted now and again with stark-white sands. White wispy clouds set off stunningly bright blues, kissing up against the deep-green mangroves. The seas were so clear we could see the coral formations on the bottom, orange brain coral no deeper than a half dozen feet, usually less.

Back in the cabin, we communicated through the day with *Turn the Paige*. We were a few miles ahead of them and told them about the depths we were seeing through major cuts. Later, we told them to turn around, as we had less than a foot under our keel, not enough for them to make safe passage. They eventually grounded briefly, to be lifted off later with the rising tides.

Turn the Paige **in the Keys**

Eventually, we reached Gilbert Resort in Key Largo and called it a day. In a week of superlatives, the tropical drinks there were the strongest drinks we encountered on the whole loop. We stopped at a couple each and still wobbled our way back to the boat, content after marvelous company, a good meal, and the most beautiful seascapes we'd ever seen.

Though the trip only took three days or so, Florida Keys was still an important part of our journey. The trip was one of contrasts. The high waves and crab pots uncomfortably tested our skills, and the intense beauty with placid waters gave us time to reflect and recover. We took wise counsel and listened to our instincts and were rewarded.

In the days to come, the weather would roll in. Loopers were pinned between Florida Bay and the Atlantic, just as we knew they would be. Other boaters were OK with waiting, but we wanted to move on so we could visit some new friends who had a place on the Atlantic ICW. Our recognition of the weather patterns let us decide *where* we wanted to wait out the February winds and storms. About a day in front of the weather system, we pulled into the bays surrounding Miami.

CHAPTER 23

Our Party on Someone Else's Boat

In the first two months of our loop, we covered wide industrial and rural rivers, canals, bays, the ICW, and the open Gulf. The marinas had a sameness to them, recreational hubs for smallish towns. As we approached Miami, all of that changed. Though it barely cracks the fifty most populous cities in the United States, it is grand, especially from the water. We were about to experience our first urban marina experience. I pulled up the PDF with the mooring field identifying our ball while Maggie drove us in.

We rumbled up to Dinner Key, with skyscrapers all around us. Entering the mooring field, we oriented our map. This field had around two hundred floating white buoys laid out in a grid. Another field half again that large was across a channel. We did what we'd been coached to do, approach from downwind, grab the pickup line with a boat hook, and tie off to it with two separate lines. We tied off for the first time and thought everything would hold. Then we thought about the inbound gale and affirmed, yes, this would probably hold. Maybe.

Maggie at the helm near Miami

Next, we wrestled the dinghy from the roof, tied it to the back of the boat, attached the light electric motor, and looked proudly at our setup, one we'd cobbled together from West Marine, Amazon, and a few more-sketchy vendors. Then Maggie saw a dinghy flying by, spraying a high rooster tail and making quick work of the commute to the sprawling dinghy dock at the marina. We looked at the big white rib-style dinghy as it effortlessly cut through the waves. Then we looked at the shore, disconcertingly far from little *Currently*. Then we looked at our tiny dinghy, with its short side tubes and its efficient but slow little motor.

Maggie and I looked at each other, a wordless "I told you so" passing between us. We thought about the two Gulf crossings we'd already managed and thought, "We can do this." And then we looked at the dog and mentally calculated the power requirements for taking four hundred pounds to shore in the coming two-foot seas, and what it would mean to manage wet, salty clothes and grocery supplies. My smile faded a little. We can probably do this. Maybe.

In the end, we were able to throw on our quick-dry clothes, wrestle our dog onto the baby boat, slowly motor to the dinghy dock, and get everyone off. The electric 3 HP Torqeedo motor on our Saturn KaBoat were surprisingly nimble together in the surf. We walked around Coconut Grove and even found a place that would take two mostly dry people and a soggy blob of fur.

The dog in the dinghy at Dinner Key

As we melted into the city, Miami's music and culture flowed into us with a chaotic joy and international intensity. Don't get me wrong. The southeast is a lovely place with good people and world-class hospitality. Still, to this point, our loop had been immersed in a monoculture from the time we left Chattanooga to the time we arrived at Dinner Key. Boating and marinas were not exclusively white, but pretty close. The southeast has a conservative palate, and the Florida coast mostly an aging one. These cultures dominated our experiences. The colors, tastes, smells, and sounds of the city rapidly broke down our defenses. We were in love.

After an unexpectedly lovely trip into town, we motored back to *Currently* on a glassy bay, a quiet before the storm. Feeling the length of the walk, Emmy limped back on board and immediately crashed on the floor. Maggie and I slithered out the side door to the bow. We sprawled out to gape at our surroundings. After a few minutes, Maggie went back inside to warm up and make some decaf.

The fresh, salty air mingled with the distant lights of the Miami skyline and fading sunset. The emotions that tickled me were new in some ways, as I'd never seen the skyline of a large city from our own boat. Some surface emotions flashed through me. Awe. Peace, certainly. Fear of the coming gale. When all of those feelings had flashed and faded, a faintly familiar undercurrent remained. The feeling had a hint of melancholy on the surface, but something else teased fertility and depth of experience. The word describing those feelings playfully danced around the boundary between my conscious and subconscious thoughts. Eventually, the word let me get just close enough to catch it.

Solitude.

There was so much to take in. Though we shared a mooring field with two hundred other boats, we were very much alone. In a wicked irony, I recognized that we'd come onto the loop partially to flee *unhealthy* solitude. This feeling was both different and the same. To be the man I wanted to be, I would need to find ways to embrace this solitude *without* the benefits of Miami in the midst of a stunning sunset and gathering storm. I slid this memory aside to grapple with it another day.

We spent a couple of days on the mooring ball. All the while, the waves came up with the rising winds. We did meet another couple, sailors from Chicago on a forty-foot Leopard, a huge sailing catamaran with a mast just short enough to fit under the sixty-five-foot spans over the ICW. They told us we'd experience waves over three feet high in the mooring field. To make the most of Miami, we decided to bite the bullet and pay the five dollars per foot cost to move inside. There, we'd have the benefit of the breakwater surrounding the marina.

Our first day in a Dinner Key slip, we met Tony and Karen Long on another Ranger Tug, called *Long Recess*. These retired teachers are wonderful people. Tony was an excellent planner. He always took copious notes and worked hard to learn to do things the right way. When I was with him, he was almost always calm, always gentle, and liked

The calm before the storm in Miami

to listen. Karen was a woman who liked to smile and liked to serve others. Like me, she was an encourager at heart. Together, the couple put together one of the most remarkable loops we saw.

When we met them, Tony was frustrated. He was having trouble tying up his boat, and it showed in the tension in his shoulders. I walked him through the process, emphasizing the three- to four-foot tides. I showed him how to tie spring lines to keep a boat from moving forward or back. Then we controlled the stern with crisscrossed lines to cleats on the dock, and finally we made sure he looped both posts in the front. We wouldn't see the Longs again until Delaware Bay, but this relationship would be one of the most important on our whole loop. We had brief dock-tails and then went on our way.

After helping Tony wrangle his tug, I botched our tie-up. I didn't allow enough slack on the stern, but a neighbor saw the problem and loosened it for me before the problem could cause any damage more severe than a scuffed dock line. I reminded myself that I was still learning, but in Tony's bright-red tug, I could see the progress I'd made under the tutelage of boats like *No Agenda*, *Argo*, and *Indigo*. We threw our fish light overboard and turned it on. With absolutely nothing else to do, we walked up and down the docks and met people.

In a burst of inspiration, we threw a dockside party, a taste of the loop for our new dockmates. They were excited to meet the new residents, the tiny new tug with a white burgee and a home port thousands of miles away. The party grew past ten to twelve people, so it spilled out of *Currently* and onto the dock. Predictably, it began to rain. As we clamored to the safety of a Virginia boat, it dawned on us that we had just invited our party with half of the dock onto *someone else's boat*, and we were grateful for the welcome and the community.

For the first time on the loop, there were both different political perspectives and different races represented in a big circle. The common factors were that these families were retired and *rich*. The average boat size among them must have been over forty feet. They stayed in Miami in the winter and lived elsewhere for the rest of the year.

Mostly, I remember the black man, Mike, from a boat called *One Love*. I remember him clearly because he was also the *only* black man we met for more than a passing conversation on the whole loop. I was curious and sat close to him, wondering if, on the surface at least, we saw life in the same way.

The seven captains at our party were different men from different walks, but they had a few things in common. Every one of them was curious about life as pleasure boaters often are. To a person, they were easy to talk to. They were also used to being both right and in control, and it made for some humorous conversations. One man on a forty-something-foot trawler talked about the Georgia and Florida ICW. He said "Bruce, you're going to hate it." Of course, his boat had nearly two more feet of draft, six more feet of air clearance, four times the mass of *Currently*, and stabilizers. It had to stop to get under every bridge, and its keel would drag in every grain of sand that encroached on the channel. If I were in that boat, I would hate it too. I smiled and nodded, confident in my plans and in little *Currently*. We'd be going inside because we didn't *want* to skip the towns that added so much flavor to the ICW.

The conversation shifted to the high prices of diesel. We danced around the politics for a bit, but we talked more about the impact of the high prices than the cause. For big chunks of time, the circle focused on the new strangers of D Dock. They wanted to know about the loop. We told stories and shared dreams. I've never wanted to live aboard full-time, but that day, I could see the appeal. This group seemed to tolerate differences better than the dysfunctional groups at home. Maybe boating communities like this one depended more on one another. We had a few more drinks and laughed before wandering home.

I thought about the huge Trump flotillas we'd encountered in previous summers on the Tennessee River, and for the first time, I understood. The feeling of safety and community was strong in these circles, and it would be easy to associate the connectedness of this lifestyle to a political party. Maybe they longed for this feeling of togetherness rather than any particular political agenda.

That evening, the fish light was the show. A cloud of plankton gave way to little fish and then big ones. We watched the visitors slowly grow until looper midnight. Eight-thirty at night. Early in the morning, when I couldn't sleep, I got up to gaze into the green light, and I saw a massive seven-foot fish, tapered, with a predatory posture near the bottom, seven feet deep. Later, we'd learn it was a tarpon, trained to frequent the fish lights that popped up here and there along the marina.

I watched the fish show for almost an hour until I couldn't take it anymore. I woke up Maggie, and we hurried to the back of the boat, and I pointed to the corner where the monster of the deep would appear from time to time. Eventually she too saw the tarpon, took an involuntary step, and pointed, more excited than scared. Then we went back to bed, content with the evening's adventures.

Over the next couple of days, the gale-force winds came. Driven by gusts over fifty miles per hour, four-foot waves rocked our newfound friends in the mooring field hard, and they were in a forty-foot boat. We abandoned plans for dinner together, as the boat shuttle service wasn't running and no one wanted to launch a dinghy in those waves. Our little tug would have done fine out in the mooring field, but it would have made her occupants miserable. The rain stayed mostly away, save some short afternoon downpours, so common in Florida. The result was more time in Dinner Key and less on *Currently*. We spent the time with people and places, forming short, intense relationships so commonly found on the loop.

Street festival in Miami

Some adventures were no further away than a hundred yards from *Currently*'s docks. In the adjacent park, next to a water pipe, we walked onto the bridge, like dozens of others we'd seen. Following a bubbling sound, Maggie looked down and pointed, temporarily excited beyond the ability to speak. I followed her shaking finger, and I saw. A giant manatee was right beneath us, rolling side to side luxuriously beneath a pipe. Slowly, Maggie came to herself but never did get any coherent words out to express her shock and surprise at the marvelous beast. I laughed because I couldn't find any words either. I just put my arm around her as we danced excitedly and watched the gentle giant, willing the moment to go on. For a while, it did. I don't remember if we left first or the manatee did, but fully satisfied and smiling, we walked back to the dinghy in near silence.

A manatee in Miami

The winds stilled just as we exhausted our allocated money and time. With vows to return, we reluctantly cast off. We lowered our mast and antenna before making our way to the Atlantic ICW. Timing the bridge openings the best we could, we cruised up the waterway, bridge by bridge, mile by mile.

As the compass tipped from east to north, our anticipation built, but we were ultimately disappointed. Southeast Florida holds great appeal to many loopers with its grand hotels, expansive beaches, mega-yachts, and parties to match. It was a fascinating place, but ultimately not for us. As if to punctuate the point, a forty-two-foot Pursuit sped by, catching *Currently* in the turbulence of the unannounced wake. We shrugged our shoulders and rode it out. Welcome to Ft. Lauderdale.

On the plus side, we didn't have to hurry anymore. We'd cut through the main waves of loopers, leaving them behind in the Keys, western Florida, and the Bahamas. We began to slow down and change the pace of the trip. In the days to follow, we'd make our way north to meet with two new friends, David and Violet, who wanted to see how a Ranger Tug handled the ICW through Florida and beyond. They lived on the ICW and were dreaming about their own adventure someday on America's Great Loop.

CHAPTER 24

Things We Told
Our Kids to Never Do

The sliver of coastal southeast Florida that runs from Fort Lauderdale through Palm Beach is one of the nautical wonders of the world. I just haven't decided if it's the good sort or not. It is an outright assault on senses. Just outside the ICW is the spring-break capital of the world, with resort after resort looming over the coarse-sand beaches. Turquoise waters hammer some sections, with every kind of water sport on full display. Catamarans cruise through the cacophony of powerboats, ranging from tourist-filled pirate ships to bowriders to the omnipresent sport fishers that zip up and down the coast.

Through this amalgamation of fiberglass, saltwater, and flesh, commercial shipping lanes shoot out from the major inlets. The big dogs come in from across the sea with salvation for sale, anything America could possibly want.

In the ICW, pleasure boats seek refuge from the madness outside but typically find none, for in this hell there is no pleasure, only more of the same. In the ICW, wind-driven waves give way to boat-driven waves. Radio waves are filled with admonitions of the have-nots to show the haves some respect, only to be admonished from the VHF gods that "Channel 16 is for hailing and distress only." No-wake zones are respected only when police boats or the Coast Guard are present. Harbor tugs and pilots that crisscross the waterways are generally too big to care.

Ok, ok. Maybe I was a bit jaded because of the salon full of wake-driven galley shrapnel. Maybe it was the weather report that predicted ridiculous winds yet again. In any case, the helm and navigator station in *Currently*'s cabin was a tense place to be. We were trying to break through the increasingly impatient chain of boaters as the great harbor tugs sought to muscle the cargo ships in or out of the harbor. At the same time, we needed to find a place to stay. We had arrangements to stay at a friend's dock in Hillsboro, but we were a few days early.

We'd circled Fort Lauderdale on the map, and obviously it was a mistake. There was simply no room at the inn. Anchorages were tight, and marinas all cost more than the high-end hotel rooms. Many of the marinas would only take boats fifty feet or more. Costs were as high as eleven dollars a foot! Hello Spring Break. Instead of stopping, we pulled on through. Our blood pressures came down slowly as we pulled away from the heart of the busy port.

Eventually, we settled on the sleepy town of Pompano Beach, a welcome change from the intensity of Fort Lauderdale. We settled in at a marina for a few nights. For the first time in a great while, we had great options for walking Emmy that were close to the marina, and also plenty of pedestrian-friendly streets and sidewalks for the people on board.

We had a nice dinner at the Rusty Hook and made our final arrangements to meet David and Violet in the next few days. I'd met David online, and we'd Zoomed with them several different times on the loop to give them the taste of looping life on a Ranger Tug.

Dave and Violet in Hillsboro

David asked us about the dozens of little details pending loopers must nail down as plans emerge. I asked about the sea conditions where we would be and asked about things the award-winning fisherman and local Florida boater would know.

Increasingly, we found ourselves doing things we told our kids to never do, again. In a few days, we'd get in a vehicle with strangers we'd met online. Then we'd stay at their place. I would guess that, initially, David was excited about this plan. A personal charter in protected waters and a front-row seat to the loop was a chance he couldn't pass up.

He'd probably started to second-guess himself when the first few boxes started showing up. Our special Elmhurst Cashew Milk. Our engine filters. And pea protein. And Maggie's repaired laptop. I imagined David's face when the boxes just kept coming. Backup parts. Our special plant-based deli slices. I rationalized my behavior the way an addict might. After all, I told him we'd be sending them. Well, mostly. I asked if we could send a package. I didn't really have a problem. Even with a valid mailing address on file, I could stop pressing that yellow Buy button anytime I wanted. Probably.

The next day, we reprised dinner at the Rusty Hook, meeting David and Violet for the first time. I saw his smile, but was it hospitality or revenge in those eyes? Then I saw the boxes. Revenge, then. I ran my mentoring group while the rest had cocktails. I finished up and then joined them. David's questions started pouring out like boxes. How does a looper get reliable Wi-Fi, what does it cost, and how reliable can it be expected to be? What hardware is required for a long voyage on a Ranger Tug? How have supply shortages impacted part availability, and where do you get them? How much internet does Zoom or Netflix require?

The logistical conversations bled into conversations about our lives, our common experiences, and more. Dinner progressed, then luxuriously stretched on, and then wound down. Violet told us that the docks weren't for liveaboards. We could possibly stay on board if we were quiet. She thought it would be better if we slept at the condo. The dog was another story. Maggie and I were torn about what to do.

The condo canine situation was one of the stranger living situations we encountered. The community wanted to build a quiet retreat, one without the messes and noises that come from pets. The problem was, a ton of them had dogs. So they capped pet size at ten or fifteen pounds, limiting the size of potential messes or disturbances. Then they wrote in the condo rules that residents must carry their dogs off of the property.

We also noticed that the association had bolted a speed bump to the concrete, right across the front of a handicap accessible ramp and in front of the primary garage entrance. I had doubts about the wisdom of forcing someone's Gram Gram to stumble over this strip of concrete day after day. After watching a few people navigate this self-imposed obstacle course with some combination of canes, walkers, dogs, and groceries, the images became enough fuel for decades of nightmares. In any case, because we were not residents and Emmy was forty-five pounds, our pooch was a no-go.

Eventually, we decided to follow the rules. We left the dog to sleep aboard. That gave us an excuse to break away from the party, since we'd need to take her out several times a day for walks, feedings, and companionship. Quite frankly, the arrangements suited Emmy just fine. She needed more time to rest those days.

As we got to know the couple, it became clear that we were alike in some ways but vastly different in others. We shopped together, and I did maintenance on the boat, bringing David along. I dove to check out the condition of the boat's bottom and props. David introduced us to a YouTube couple, Scho and Jo, whose channel chronicles Jennifer and Elliot's Great Loop experience on their boat, *Pivot*.

We couldn't believe our luck when we were standing on the dock and saw *Pivot* cruising by, Elliot waving from the flybridge. We hailed the movie stars, generally making fools of ourselves from the dock, and called them from channel 16, all starstruck. Later, we'd meet them for real over several weeks, sending David a picture. Eventually David called, properly shocked and awed, when he spotted us on one of their videos. Fun times.

The thing I remember most about being with David and Violet was a conversation I dreaded. Eventually, our kitchen discussions drifted into dangerous territory, about Trump, masking, and Fauci. The exact points don't matter. After something particularly egregious to Maggie, she flashed her trademark smile and said, "I don't believe any of that. Tell me, why do you think so?" I remember trying to keep a perfect poker face, but I'm not sure I could have, based on what I was feeling. She'd blown up the trip.

I held my breath, willing my sweet wife to put the pin back into the grenade. David was taken aback. I mean, he literally stepped back. Violet's eyes flared, and she responded passionately. We talked about the allure of Trump, promises broken and kept, January 6, and more. The conversation even got quite animated at times. Then, to my absolute astonishment...

Nothing. Happened.

I mean, nothing. No one was convinced or converted. We kept being friends. The exchange revealed something that had been missing in our lives: forbearance. We had built enough of a relationship to survive the politics. For some reason, they saw beyond our political identities. We spent another full day together, no longer fearful of where our conversations would lead us. We asked questions of one another, genuinely curious rather than offended. Reflecting on that conversation, I've often thought back and wondered if the real tragedy of American politics is more about behavior patterns than ideologies.

Maggie's entry to the conversation worked because she cared about our hosts, and they knew it. We first established a relationship based on common ground. Then she led the conversation with curiosity. As I think back about those few nights, the beauty of the loop shines through. Common goals and experiences bind together people who would not otherwise meet. Our shared values of friendship, adventure, and hospitality overwhelm our differences.

The thing that made it possible was a single act of hospitality. David's electronic knock on our door was an opportunity to *dream* together.

We ended up staying with them longer than planned due to an arriving storm. As the hours wore on, we watched the gale come through together. For the most part, we weathered the storm on the boat so Emmy wouldn't have to be alone. We drank, laughed, and silently watched the palm trees bend. The condo made an excellent windbreak, so the storm didn't beat on the boat as hard as it otherwise would have. Once the storm broke, we had to wait just one more day for winds to taper off enough for us to go.

Walking on a South Florida beach

We said our goodbyes, and David agreed to sell off the cursed lithium batteries that proved insufficient for our dinghy. That mismatched trolling motor and battery pack was nothing but misery from the time I bought it. Hauling those batteries out of my crowded engine room was just one more kindness from the strangers on the internet. We said goodbye until we could get together again. Hopefully, the battery would fund a nice dinner somewhere, maybe in Florida, maybe Chattanooga. I'd make my favorite toast: "Here's to old friends, new friends, and the process by which new friends become old friends."

CHAPTER 25

The Grace of a Drunken Goat

After dolphins and manatees, one singular communal experience stands out to loopers everywhere. The whole Florida community comes together to share food and drink. Oh, and maybe a little vomit. Of course, I'm talking about spring break. One morning, we looked down at the map and the calendar at the same time. Big mistake. We'd be in Palm Beach right about the time spring break peaked, and we had no reservations at all.

Once we started to look for places to stay, we felt the squeeze. Marinas were hard to find, and anchorages were full to the gills, at least to people with our lack of skills. This situation was a problem because we wanted to meet our youngest daughter, Julia, for a few days. Maggie and Julia are *close*. Even in graduate school, Julia calls almost every day, and Maggie offers the companionship of a friend and the advice of a mother. I would love Julia even if she weren't my daughter. She's an amazing young woman. I cherish the times we've spent in the garage on woodworking projects, from cutting boards to dining room tables. The walnut and maple cutting board in the galley reminded me of our relationship every day. She was flying into Palm Beach, so we had to find a place that would take us.

With these concerns on our minds, we inched our way up the ICW as a minnow amongst mighty salmon. Between traffic and bridges, we had a tough time finding a rhythm. Juggling bridge schedules and lists of potential stopping points, we motored through Boca Raton, Delray Beach, and Boynton Beach on our way to Palm Beach, the monument to our forty-fifth president. What a monument it was. A lift bridge, still under construction, carried a sign announcing a security zone. The failing infrastructure stood in marked contrast to the sprawling facade of the mansion. As we were passing by, we had no inkling that the beginnings of the document scandal were starting to play out.

Eventually, we found a place, a working Safe Harbor marina that served the thriving fishing charters and research vessels so common in the area. When we arrived, particularly windy conditions blew us right at a metal-hulled research power cat, and my thrusters were powerless. Seeing the inevitable six-foot gash in *Currently*'s bow play out in my mind's eye, I watched, dumbfounded, as a tiny little rope snagged on *Currently*'s anchor, holding us off just long enough for the marina staff to leap across vessels, in a real-life game of Frogger, before we even took on a scratch. As much as we wanted to pretend experiences like these were rare, we just couldn't do it. We praised and tipped the staff, hooked up our power, and opened up a bottle of Rosé liquid therapy.

So moored, we welcomed Julia aboard. Julia is a rare perfect blend of competence and creativity. Whether she's drawing with a woodburning iron, shopping for bargains, refinishing a table, clamping a dog's artery in surgery, or skinning a rabbit, she's all professionalism and competence. She has the creativity to find options others don't even consider, the competence to figure it out, and the skill to pull it off well. She is one of the most fiercely loyal friends I've ever encountered. The downside to all of this is that she's hard on herself, and she came to us needing some mama time to recharge.

While we were in town, we took a rare trip to the beach. We ate out a time or two, giving Julia time to sample the seafood and Florida culture. We all visited our good friends Sarajane Gates and Sam Horowitz. They'd helped us put on our conference in Chattanooga, and we'd spent a good deal of time with them. They took us to the wandering bridges, decks, and patios that make up Guanabanas, a wild restaurant in Jupiter, Florida.

As we were getting reacquainted with her, another drama was playing out. We'd received the OK from the bank to rent our home. We had a whale on the hook, but one we'd not yet managed to reel in. This potential renter was an executive on a schedule. They offered us a deal slightly over market value, in exchange for a two-year lease instead of six months. They kept raising the stakes until they reached their "final offer," a staggering two times Chattanooga's typical rates. After all, construction in the area was all but halted under a lumber shortage. To us, it was an obscene amount of money, and they asked us to decide right away. We prided ourselves on weighing lifestyle consequences as we made decisions, and this offer came at a price. We'd already moved once, and if we took this deal, we'd have to add a move once we returned home. Establishing relationships is *hard*, and we had good friends there. We also needed to address the elephant in the galley—a beautiful one who still called mama every day and loved woodworking with her daddy in the garage of that Chattanooga home.

Living on a tiny boat with three is tough. Conversations are not private, and we slowly moved toward a decision to rent our home to that couple. The hardest part of that transaction was making the plans in front of Julia. We tried to assure her that we'd find a good landing spot. Heads are easy, hearts are not. Julia loved coming home but kept her composure with a grace beyond her years. Still, we could

Julia, Bruce, Maggie, Sarajane, Sam at Guanabanas

tell she was silently hurting. In the end, that customer walked and we rented our fully furnished place to another couple for six months, a perfect length of time. It didn't fully fund our loop, but it covered the unexpectedly high marina and diesel costs.

The rest of the trip with Julia was pretty representative of life on a boat. We talked, walked, watched the storms come in (even a tornado), and hit some local shops. We fed her too much plant-based food, it made her sick, and we swore we'd have more options for her next time. In the end, we lamented that our time with our daughter was not as special as it might have been in a different place or better circumstances. We said our goodbyes, Maggie's eyes leaked a bit, and Sarajane took Julia back to the airport while we motored north.

In the next week or so, we got into a good rhythm. We flew up the Atlantic coast of Florida. To save money, we planned to pick up a mooring ball for twenty bucks, less than a quarter of what a typical marina in Florida cost. The winds and waves did not cooperate. Two-foot seas and our lack of skill doomed us, so we motored to Fort Pierce. The city marina was under two bucks a foot, and it was clean. We had some middling meals, but their farmers market was incredible. The blocks and blocks of stalls had wonderful fruits and veggies. We bought one of everything and headed north.

Fort Pierce farmers market

We ticked through Titusville, across the channel from the space program. We visited the Astronaut Memorial Plaza, but neither of us wanted to brave the Covid-laced crowds with the level of virus in Florida. Reluctantly we skipped the Space Center tour, but we did see a large rocket on the launchpad in the distance as we headed onward to New Smyrna.

New Smyrna had lots of good plant-based food options, including at the Yellow Dog Café, where we had Thai-spiced nachos. Imagine Thai vegetables, corn, tomatoes, chilis, a marvelous cream-like cashew sauce, and a sweet chili sauce crisscrossed atop the mound of food. The place was quintessential Main Street, U.S.A.—cute art, great patio, and wonderful staff.

The Night Swan in New Smyrna was one of our highlights in Florida. The big attraction of the Bed and Breakfast

The Night Swan in New Smyrna

to us was the dock. After all the full marinas, it was a welcome respite to be in a slip by ourselves, with no hustle and bustle of people. Sitting in the cockpit one quiet morning watching the birds, a sea turtle surfaced close enough for Maggie to hear its breath. The lovely dock also had a deck with comfortable Adirondack chairs, where we'd lean back and watch pelicans dive for dinner. It was the best of shows.

As we prepared for the loop in December 2021, pelicans became a bit of a theme. We encountered hundreds, even thousands of huge migrating white pelicans with black wing tips on Hiawassee Island on the Tennessee River. When full squadrons of them took off or landed, the black bands rippled against the white feathers, making a formation that looked like its own creature from a distance. We'd turn the motor off and drift to see and hear formations, intermingled with thousands of Sandhill cranes.

This experience didn't at all match the stereotype of the isolated, lonely, grizzled veteran perched on a dock piling, cleverly captured in a black-and-white for a coffee-table book or gift shop photo. I might think about the comical proportions of the pouch or the famous Dixon Lanier Merritt's limerick:

A wonderful bird is the pelican.
His bill can hold more than his belican.
He can hold in his beak
Enough food for a week
But I'm damned if I see how the helican.

Around the loop, I'd play a game. Whenever anyone mentioned a pelican, I'd recite the limerick. It got old to everyone but me. Winning.

In New Smyrna, we discovered a new appreciation of the fascinating birds as honorary raptors. I was sitting next to Maggie reading, when she burst into laughter.

She cried, "They're fearless!"

I looked up to see what the fuss was about. A dozen pelicans were flying around, not in formation but scanning the surface for prey. Then they dove with reckless abandon. I'd call the maneuver a controlled crash, but there was no control to what we were seeing. One bird after another would sail along expectantly and then tuck its wings in to dive and explode into the water like a drunk frat boy on a high dive. Julia, living encyclopedia to all animal-based knowledge, informed us that they have air sacs that inflate just before impact. I imagined the air bags holding crash-test dummies in place after a simulated sixty-mile-per-hour head-on collision and immediately discarded the idea. These pelican crashes were way more violent.

We watched, and the flock grew. We watched the show transfixed. As a youth, I'd seen videos of the mighty swan divers off of the Acapulco cliffs. That image captures the momentum, but not the result. Now replace the image of the chiseled Mexican god with Flounder from *Animal House*, and you get the idea. Dive after dive, these freaks of the sky distanced themselves from the wrinkled, frizzy birds captured on the walls of rental properties across the country. Don't laugh, but in some ways these reckless minions reminded me of dolphins, and I couldn't figure out why.

A Florida pelican

Then it struck me. Joy. We spent hours at a New Smyrna bed and breakfast deck watching dozens of these birds climb up high, cruise slowly into the wind, and then come screaming down, crashing into the water with all of the grace of a drunken goat. Then they'd surface with a fish, flick their neck to flip it down their gullet, and climb up to look for more. We saw this drama play out hundreds of times, sometimes a mere forty feet from our dock and other times across the bay, between the many anchored sailboats and trawlers. I could only imagine the show they were seeing.

Then we laughed, and it felt good. I empathized with the pelican. The time before the loop felt like we were isolated on cold perches, lonely and afraid. Then we recklessly took the plunge into the waters of the loop. All of our financial commitments and professional responsibilities threatened to tear us to pieces on impact. When we started the dive, we had no relevant experience, no boat, a turbulent world, and a pandemic. We dove anyway.

Just as the pelicans had hidden air sacs to protect them from impact, we too had our own points of protection. Our planning, excellent advisors, and our love for each other insulated us from the worst of the impact. After we dive and eat the day's morsel, all that's left are the spreading concentric rippling memories of joy and love.

Part IV

Atlantic

For most people's Great Loop, the Atlantic coast has to happen pretty quickly because loopers don't want to leave Florida until it's warm out and they want to enter the Erie Canal shortly after it opens in June. We dashed right up the seaboard, spending only two days outside of the protection of the ICW, in New Jersey. For inexperienced boaters, the Atlantic ICW can be dangerous and logistically difficult because of wild tide swings and treacherous paths through the shifting sands of the ICW.

After spending most of February and March in protected waters, we felt like we had to encounter a whole new learning curve, but this time we had other boaters around to help. Like a surfer looking over their shoulder and spotting a bigger wave than they wanted, we thought, "Here we go."

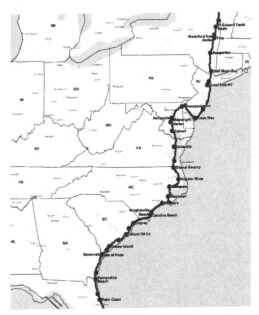

Currently's Atlantic Stops

CHAPTER 26

Lined Up Like
Lobster Tails

Diplomatically speaking, guests on the loop are challenging. Visiting well-meaning Marco Polos imagine themselves cruising through undiscovered pristine beaches and stopping at five-star restaurants for breakfast, lunch, and dinner. Since there are two captains on board, one is always available to break out the blender, throw together some mai tais, and dazzle them with stories. They see Tom Cruise in *Cocktail* weirdly crossed with Captain Jack Sparrow. That's the Hollywood version. The reality show is a bit more, shall we say, rustic.

When I thought about guests, I pictured a mountain of obstacles piled up in *Currently*'s tiny hallway, between us and potential guests. The first one was the tattered, dog-eared calendar. Would-be Gilligans wanted to book flights to their three-hour tour a month in advance, but we rarely knew where we'd be in a week. Sometimes we didn't know if we'd have a weather window to travel the *very next day*. Next in the pile was the chart book of *places*. The loop often visits off-the-grid places without airports or even Ubers. Next, throw onto the pile the Instant Pot and blender for making meals. Maggie and I both avoided foods that would kill us. Maggie is deathly allergic to soy and gluten, and I to heart attacks. So we're generally plant-based and soy- and gluten-free. Beans anyone? Throwing in these dietary restrictions to entertain guests, without good access to metropolitan grocery stores, was a good way to make Maggie abandon the loop early. Next, the growing mountain had practical things, like Dramamine seasickness pills, the weather page for the newspaper, Covid vaccines, and the huge pile of things like extra parts for oil changes we had to move out of guest quarters to accommodate crewmates. Sometimes we'd have other things in the pile, like broken generators or spare paper towels and extra vegan food, and other things as well. Add a computer, symbolizing work that had to get done to keep my business afloat. We had to deal with each and every item on that daunting pile for every guest that visited. It's a wonder that loopers take on any visitors at all.

Despite that virtual mountain and our small boat, we climbed atop that pile time after time to bring on guests throughout our whole Great Loop, from our Florida crossing to our very last day. We had more visitors than any other boat we encountered. Despite the mountain of obstacles, we craved the opportunity to break out of our 2020 quarantine to share the experience with those around us. Our loop was about people. Most of the time, we dug through the pile by setting clear expectations and establishing boundaries. We'd tell folks they could choose where or when, but not both. Sometimes we'd run with them, and sometimes we'd stay put and they'd sleep with us for a night or two. They had to arrange transportation to the boat and get back to the airport when the trips were over. Sometimes does not mean always. We found ourselves in a situation where we drifted far enough from our established boundaries that we'd need to live on a pretty rigorous schedule for a couple of weeks to accommodate the company.

We would pick up my sister, Cheryl, in St. Augustine, Florida. Then we'd run up the coast for a full day, meet the Millers, our Chattanooga neighbors, at their house in Fernandina Beach, on the Florida and Georgia state line. Then we'd run up the coast for a short day, drop off the visiting crew, and pick up our Chattanooga friend Victoria near Savannah, Georgia, to depart in Charleston, South Carolina. Finally, we'd get our daughter Kayla in Georgetown, South Carolina, to be dropped off in Wilmington, North Carolina. It was a great plan if the weather cooperated only a little.

With this pending schedule in mind, we flew up the northeast coast of Florida. We blasted through Daytona, marveling at the pounding surf. Yes, the wakes of the passing fishing charters were a sight to behold as they kicked up a spray off of *Currently*'s beam. We stopped a while at Palm Coast to give our bank account a break and, yes, wait for weather. The dock with no services was only twenty bucks a night, a small fraction of what we'd paid elsewhere in Florida. Our generator mostly held up, but eventually the impeller gave out and it wouldn't run for more than twenty minutes. That's not long enough to cook anything meaningful, but luckily the front office saved the day. They actually let Maggie plug in our Instant Pot in the lobby to cook some food for the dog on our last night. Trust me, that chicken, rice, and veggies smelled amazing. Emmy never knew she had it so good.

After Palm Coast, the next stop was St. Augustine. Here we'd picked up some additional generator parts and meet up with old friends and new. *Tailor'd for Two* was single-handing, docking in the wind with great ease. I was jealous. He introduced us to *Flying Colors*, a boat we'd see off and on throughout the rest of the loop. The next day Cheryl arrived, and we had a joyful reunion. We spent the afternoon in town, checking out the historic architecture and epic seafood.

Cheryl and Bruce in St. Augustine

The weather held up for a little while, barely. We left St. Augustine and ran through higher-than-normal winds, but the ICW protected us nicely. We watched our charts closely because sands were encroaching on the ICW. We had to go off the formal ICW channel for a little shoaling. OK, a lot of shoaling. Even other Ranger Tugs were grounding on the recommended route. Other boaters warned us away via both Nebo and VHF, and we zagged instead of zigged to stay off of the bottom. The depth alarm became practically worthless as the water became increasingly shallow. By the time we pulled into Fernandina Beach, there was no more than a couple of feet beneath our keel. Still, we got in safely to meet with Deidre and Rick Miller, our neighbors, and parents of the first mentee from our Chattanooga program for underrepresented programmers. Their son, Richard, got a job at Google; Deidre helped us put on our conference, and our friendships had deepened ever since.

As we pulled into our slip, the crew from the trawler in front of us helped with lines. They scrambled back into their ancient trawler with some incongruous repairs, materials cobbled together to keep out the sea. Later, Rick and Deidre picked us up and took us to lunch. We walked into a lunch spot and saw an artist playing for the crowd. She played through some standards for women with guitars from "Midnight Train to Georgia" to Jewel's "You Were Meant for Me." Later, she even played Patty Griffith's "Long Ride Home," a hauntingly beautiful song by an artist we'd encountered in Texas. We stayed a night at their home, taking the opportunity to sleep in a real bed. In the morning, we went back to *Currently*. While in port, Cheryl and I heard screaming and glass breaking in the distance, a reminder that people on boats have lives like everywhere else. Some are broken, and some are not.

The five of us made the brief run from Amelia Island to Jekyll Island. It was a short run but absolutely beautiful. Having Rick and Deidre on board felt like watching our kids come down to open presents on Christmas. Rick joined me in the front of the boat, picking out buoys and the dolphins that dotted the waterway. Dolphins leapt off to the side of the ICW. The guidebook said they were leaping to impress their mates, but who knows? Laughter and joy filled *Currently* as the ladies in the cockpit experienced all of this for the first time.

Cheryl, Diedre, and Maggie running through Georgia

We saw wild horses on Cumberland Island and all kinds of wildlife as we wove our way through the sea grasses so common in the Georgian marsh. Our guests had not been on many boats in the past, and it was wonderful to share that experience with them.

Early that day, we pulled into a famous Jekyll Island resort and had one of Maggie's most memorable meals on the whole loop. Massive red royal shrimp lined up like lobster tails on the plate. They were prepared simply but perfectly, and we willingly further sullied our "mostly vegan" diet with each dunk into that magical sauce: Hot Butter, a life-changing mix of Frank's Red Hot with clarified butter.

Deidre and Rick left later that afternoon, leaving us to have one last night with Cheryl. We were so full that we knew we couldn't possibly eat ever again. But we got hungry for dinner. We went back to the restaurant, and we only had a half pound of shrimp with another half pound of the sauce.

Each.

Beyond the shrimp, I wouldn't call the visit on Jekyll enormously consequential. It was just deeply comfortable, sitting around, drinking a little and eating a lot with good friends and family. We never really toured the island proper. Our meals and the giant moss-covered oak trees were separated from the dock by a couple of dozen feet. We spent a night living life in the southeast as it was meant to be rather than hustling around to see it all. There was plenty to see right where we were.

Early the next morning we sent Cheryl off, trusting one of the local wildlife guides to get her back to the Jacksonville airport. Then we picked up the pace. We ran a grueling ninety miles or so to Isle of Hope Marina, just outside of Savannah. With the growing pressure of the coming schedule, we had a fight. Maggie's capabilities were growing as a captain, but she still needed my input from time to time. Navigating that line proved difficult for us. Reversing

Jekyll Island in Georgia

our usual roles, I would nag her about the lines she chose
to take, and she would claim captain's prerogative, choosing
to ignore advice.

Maggie needed me to see her as a competent and capable captain. Indeed, with both of us working, we would
each need to spend time alone at the helm. She also needed
to recognize my experience. She needed to know about local
conditions, like shoaling and tide, and their impact on the

boat. Over time, I learned to hold back all but the most critical advice. As a result, she was more open to my advice.

Looking back, I can see that the experience was necessary. Writing about it is easy. Experiencing it wasn't. As we had these conflicts, we could choose to grow or quit. We were learning greater patience and kindness because the boat was small and we'd be in these crowded conditions for six more months.

As we talked to other loopers, a common conversation was mistakes we've all made. Brian on *YOLO* talked about screaming in Jen's ear through their "marriage saver" radio while she calmly told the dockhand to lock the line down *now*, please and thank you. Laura on *Argo* talked about making a mistake in big waves and drifting off course by six miles while Robert was sleeping. Bruce on *Sadie Bell* talked about going out into marginal weather and picking up the dishes on the floor after the fact. We all experienced hardship.

Common hardships on the loop sharpen a marriage, as do other common experiences. When we dine on our quest for the perfect fish taco, we have a basis of comparison. Whether they're the savory-spicy-sweet, folded bits of Miami manna or the stale, cold bits of concentrated apathy from St. Augustine doesn't matter. We share the tastes of the loop together and add common vocabulary, tastes, and bursts of joy in this wonderful journey called marriage.

In Savannah, we ducked out of the weather yet again. The Ranger Tug was a great boat for weather for a couple of reasons. The V-hull carved up bow waves marvelously well. The extra little speed we could muster let us take the tops off of the waves, like a stone skipping across the water. The speed was important for another reason too. We could go at looper speed, around seven miles per hour, and get great gas mileage. We could also zoom up ahead to choose where to wait out bad weather. This ability let us spend four days in Savannah instead of a Georgia anchorage.

Once again, the storm was bad. Spanning four days of high winds and occasional thunderstorms, we spent time on the boat or in the little eateries dotted around Savannah. We were starting to lose track of the gale-force winds we'd experienced. We ran only a few miles between two marinas to give us a better chance to see a broader cross-section of Savannah. Over the next few days, we'd catch up with some of the friends we'd been accumulating on the two thousand miles or so we'd encountered so far. We joyfully reunited with Mike and Beth on *Amy Marie*, the couple we'd encountered six months ago while we were harbor hosts in Chattanooga. They were also in a Ranger Tug. Theirs was a blue-and-tan diesel twenty-seven-foot version, and Mike could drive the heck out of it. We also caught *Dog House*, the boat we'd first seen off the west coast of Florida, somewhere between Fort Myers and Marco Island.

We could also see the staggering impacts of the weather, but the impact was bigger under the waterline than above. Some of the inlets were no longer navigable. The erosion and shoaling were starting to outpace the ability of the U.S. Army Corps of Engineers to maintain it. As it was, they were barely holding on. The storms would continue to shift the dredged canal, especially in places where the dozens of rivers wound around it like so much ribbon candy. We cut across channels, with names like Hell's Gate, and witnessed wildly shifting buoys with no resemblance at all to the charts drawn just months ago. Not for the last time, I wondered if there would *be* a Great Loop in twenty years, even ten. The infrastructure required to hold this route together in an age of violent storms, erosion, and shoaling was beyond my ability to comprehend.

The weather finally let up for just a morning. With two more visitors to go, we left Savannah and headed back into the ICW for a short run. We ran for just two hours, thirty miles or so, and arrived at a marina called Skull Creek. Our Chattanooga friend Victoria, a sailor originally from Chicago, joined us for a weekend. Her Savannah flight was delayed from the storms, so she had to get an Uber to Hilton Head. To keep our schedule amongst the raging storms, we had to run on fair-weather days. She got in before lunch and pointed out a lovely restaurant on the water. I destroyed some pretty good fish tacos. In the morning, we had a few hours of good weather, so we picked our way up the coast to an unlikely place called Dataw Island. It was a dock in a private golf course community. They took transients to help pay the bills.

Dataw Island in South Carolina

With Victoria and Maggie, we walked around that wealthy neighborhood. We saw numerous little ponds much like the ones we'd seen in Florida's marshlands. Some of these oversized puddles had signs that warned of *gators*. Others warned about a *gator*. On foot, those scared me more. I suspected that those ponds had a specific active occupant rather than potential occupants, but I didn't know for sure. We also saw these weird little concrete pads off of the main pathway, with ice machines. With all of the marvels we've seen on the loop, I don't know why that stands out so much, but there it was. There in the middle of a residential street stood the stoic servant, a lonely mechanical waiter perfectly placed to capture the whims of the occasional visitor. We decided, yes, we were thirsty and, yes, I'd like an extra cup of ice each to pour into a whisky and coke, please and thank you.

We came back to the boat that night. The island's great restaurant was closed, so we ate in. I can't remember what we had, but I'm sure it was good. The winds whistled, keeping the bugs away. We sat on the boat, watching the sunset together, sipping our drinks, and then melting away one by one toward our beds. The next day, we cast off toward Charleston.

We pulled up into one of the biggest marinas on the Atlantic. The locals called it MegaDock. The quarter-mile conglomeration of concrete and steel is 1,530 feet long, over a quarter of a mile of ego and testosterone. MegaDock topped Tarpon Point with the biggest pleasure boats on the whole loop. One of the boat's dinghies had a dinghy nearly as long as *Currently*.

We docked the boat, dropped off Victoria, and settled down for a few nights in Charleston. The beautiful city gave us a chance to meet up with Tracy and Stuart on *Dog House*. I loved docktails, but these little intimate dinners and lunches defined the Great Loop for Maggie and me. Stuart and Tracy had recently retired. Since Tracy was a veterinarian and Julia was training to be one, we immediately had something in common. We also had common Texas memories. The Dallas couple had connections to the Texas beaches, and we'd had coastal property there. We all had similar dietary restrictions, and similar outlooks on life. Lunch with them felt natural, like they were old friends. Afterward, as Maggie and I walked alone, I zoned out a bit.

In truth, I was a little spooked. I'd been thinking about the boat ride with Rick and Deidre, the joy on their faces. Looking back at the marinas we'd encountered so far, it wasn't surprising that they'd experienced so little boating. In fact, I could only remember one black boat-owner face on the whole loop, the gentleman in Miami. We were in a bit of a monoculture. Was that why we got along so well with *Dog House*? As I thought a little more about it, I decided the best I could do was to strive to be kind in *all* relationships and invite people unlike me into the experience, much like we'd done in Amelia. As we walked along the riverfront, Maggie and I talked about these things and reflected about the first shots of the Civil War and the fact that we were wrestling with some of the same issues a century and a half later.

Charleston was quickly becoming a place for self-discovery for us. We walked around the many courtyards, with statues of heroes, most of them from either the Civil or Revolutionary War. A couple of days later, we picked up an Uber and were talking about these issues. The driver was a black man who heard the conversation and picked up on our internal struggles. We talked with him briefly and noticed him going off our expected route.

"Trust me. It's worth it."

A few blocks off of the sanctioned route, we paused in front of a church. In front of us was Emanuel African Methodist Episcopal Church—Mother Emanuel, the oldest AME church in the South. It was the site of the murder of nine African American members in a 2015 shooting spree. I still remembered with great clarity when the families forgave the shooter. The driver sat quietly in the car, and we looked at the church silently, moved. Maggie started to take pictures out of the window for remembrance, and he encouraged her to step out of the car to get better photos.

Emanuel African Methodist Episcopal Church

The loop is a strange and wonderful thing. We'll physically cross our wake after undertaking some six thousand miles of travel and, God willing, wind up in the same place with very little change in the launch point or vessel. These waterways have physical connections that can be navigated with the right boat, circumstances, captains, and timing. That is the unvarnished truth of the loop.

Spiritually, this voyage is anything but a loop. Whenever we sojourn together, we come home to many of the same trappings, but drastically changed. Maggie was already more than she was when we left. She had more confidence.

She had a beautiful peace about her and was completely in her element in the midst of this epic adventure.

I was too. I had built new skills, challenged myself, and learned just a little more patience. We couldn't help but be changed.

Sometimes, the changes come from something as consequential as an encounter with elements much greater than we are. Other times, the changes can come from unlikely places, like an Uber driver who decides to break the rules in the best possible way.

CHAPTER 27

The Treadmill
at the Cardio Lab

The loop is a funny thing. The way we react to certain kinds of stimuli depends on our state of mind. The sound of waves breaking played gently through my Bose sleep-buds, drowning out the sounds of…um…Emmy snoring on the floor and arrhythmic waves slapping on the hull right under our chines, until I drift off to sleep. Those same sounds without earbuds, a few moments before the dawn of a treacherous crossing, will ratchet up my heart rate. Wave sounds after our crossing from a restaurant overlooking a bay provoke feelings of peace and accomplishment. It's all context.

So it is with excitement. Take the sights of the chartplotter, the depth sounder, and a shallow-water alarm. When I'm exiting a known marina from a point right between green and red, I'm feeling pretty good because such points are often on the shallow side. Those exact stimuli in the middle of the ICW and near the side of the channel, will likely make my heart rate spike a little. After a whole day of the same sounds, my heart is going to beat like I'm a guppy in the piranha tank.

I'm built for excitement in small doses, but sometimes too much happens in one day. The treadmill at the cardio lab wasn't a stress test. The loop, now that's a stress test. On the loop, we experience many different kinds of tension, and sometimes it all comes at once, as it did when we crossed the border between South and North Carolina.

While Julia is the embodiment of creative competence, Kayla is wonderfully spontaneous, energetic joy. Don't get me wrong; the spontaneity has both strength and purpose. Repeatedly, she made audacious plans and then realized them. Climbing Mount Long. Hiking five hundred miles of the Camino de Santiago. Studying abroad. Watching the solar eclipse from the top of a Wyoming mountain. Getting a college master's degree without help from her parents and now pursuing a PhD. She wants to do it all and does it.

It was a bit of a dream to share part of this voyage with her. Kayla and I would be voted the two most likely to loop by just about anyone who met us. To make it happen, we had to get her to her departing flight in Wilmington, and that meant we needed to run more than two hundred miles in six days. We were to pick her up in Charleston and drop her off in Wilmington. We just needed the weather to hold up. It didn't.

First came the flight delay. Due to storms, her flight was cancelled, putting her in Charleston a day later than we needed her to be there. We looked at a whole week of iffy travel days and decided we couldn't afford to wait. We'd leave anyway and let our world traveler take an Uber to meet us. Then came the winds and storms. They took a couple of more potential travel days off of the calendar. Eventually, we decided to make up the time by building one long travel day into our schedule.

The problems kept popping up, and we kept navigating mostly around them. We planned to pick Kayla up at McClelandville, but one last delay pushed that plan back. We put Kayla up in a hotel in Charleston and planned to

Georgetown Marina

have her drive down one more stop to Georgetown. We finally picked her up there.

The next problem was our map study. During our regular preparation, we read about two navigational hazards. The famous Rock Pile near Myrtle Beach and the Cape Fear River in North Carolina were places that caused even experienced loopers to pay close attention.

Rock Pile is a three-mile stretch of ICW so treacherous and narrow that mariners must announce their presence as they enter the hazard to prevent the arrival of commercial and private opposing traffic from coming through at the same time. Cape Fear is famous, or infamous, for unpredictable depths, shifting sands, heavy currents, and high tides. As we continued to prepare, we read about a third hazard, an inlet called Lockwood Folly. As the tides sweep in and out of the rivers and inlets that border the Intracoastal Waterway, it often carries and deposits sand at inconvenient places, in a phenomenon called shoaling. Lockwood Folly is famous for shoaling. On our big day, we would be running through three notorious Great Loop obstacles in the same day.

We cruised up the ICW to Osprey Marina, near Myrtle Beach. As we talked to boaters there about Rock Pile, we heard two dramatically different stories. Most of them seemed to believe we'd be fine if we stayed in the channel. Occasionally, we got an alternative perspective. I could almost hear music play with ominous minor tones when one particular captain talked about the rocky channel. The agitated dockmate had once strayed too far outside of the channel and took tens of thousands of dollars' worth of damage as a result. After more reading, we learned that mere inches out of the channel, barely submerged rocks waited, shallow enough to rip the bottom out of even shallow draft boats like *Currently*. Most captains suggested running through at low tide. That way, the surface would fall and the jagged rocks would be visible just above the surface. Looking at our schedule, I noticed we'd reach Rock Pile precisely at high tide. In the end, we decided to go anyway.

We also talked to boaters about Lockwood Folly and Cape Fear but decided our boat's shallow draft and beefy engine would be perfect for the conditions, so we'd approach them with little more than healthy respect. We didn't expect to find much trouble there. Our final obstacle would be weather. We expected higher winds around sundown, but we'd be safely tucked into Carolina Beach State Park a few hours before the weather arrived if all went well.

When we were in Osprey, we spotted a Ranger Tug and walked over to say hello. They saw our Great Loop flag, and we walked them through the boat. They graciously offered to take us into town to have some dinner. We enjoyed the time there, though our Uber driver got lost on the ride home. A bridge was out, and the maps had not yet caught up.

As the day started, we woke up early to eek through Rock Pile during the best weather, with the lowest winds of the day. Maggie and I cast off, leaving Kayla to sleep in for a little while. I drove while Maggie made coffee and passed out a cold breakfast of bananas and Kind bars. The radio was turned up a bit higher than usual because it would warn us about the approach of other vessels. Around

Kayla in Carolina Beach

a half hour before we began our northbound run through the hazard, we heard other northbound boats announce their entrance:

"Sécurité, sécurité, sécurité. This is southbound vessel *Sea Belle* entering the Rock Pile. Interested vessels can hail us on channel 16 or 13."

We flipped over to channel 13 to hear the same announcement. We slowed down so we wouldn't have to encounter the approaching pleasure craft in the heart of the danger zone. After they exited Rock Pile, we announced our entrance in very much the same way:

"Sécurité, sécurité, sécurité. This is northbound vessel *Currently…*"

and so on. I pulled back on the throttle, slowing to just over idle speed. I looked over at Kayla, who was smiling. She was actually enjoying this! As we got deeper into Rock Pile, we could see the dangerous rocks just beneath the surface of the water. Quite frankly, we didn't see anything particularly treacherous. We'd seen narrow channels before and shared rivers with commercial tows among the great bends of the Black Warrior. The channel did narrow from time to time, but there was always plenty of visibility. My heart rate was up a little, and a third of the day was gone.

The reality of the loop is often like that. Our Gulf crossing was absolutely trivial because we didn't have the winds or waves typically encountered by others. Our Rock Pile was easy because we followed procedures, slowed down, and didn't encounter other vessels. We also had days in not-so-dangerous places that were bad because we weren't smart. The big one was Decatur, when most loopers would not have traveled. We simply never checked the weather, and we paid the price for it. I was aware that our schedules were pushing us to take chances we might not otherwise take, like counting on the inbound weather to hold off until after sunset.

Later, after a hot lunch underway, we approached Lockwood Folly. Winds kicked up unexpectedly. Our boat handles high winds well because it's relatively flat, but this day the winds dug under one of the cushions on the bow and blew so hard that the snaps gave. For the briefest of moments, it covered our windshield and I couldn't see a thing. An instant later it had blown over the boat and into the water. I spun *Currently* around to give chase.

I thought, "What am I doing?" I was in the second major hazard of the day and chasing a hideous cushion, putting our boat and family at risk. The winds quickly blew it out of the channel, so we waved goodbye to the three hundred dollars, said our last respects, bowed our heads for a moment of silence, and left the cushion to carry on elsewhere. I spun the boat back around to act like I'd done this before. We'd entered North Carolina, and Lockwood Folly had claimed another victim, but I hated those cushions anyway. Our heart rates were still up, and two thirds of the day were gone. With a little less padding in the front and a little more storage available in the back, we headed for the third danger point, the aptly named Cape Fear.

The river was low and strong when we entered. The Atlantic ICW was full of shoaling and had a high-tide swing. Put those factors together, and it was hard to trust the buoys or our charts. We'd need to pull up a navigation aid called

Bob's Tracks, the actual line of a legendary boater who helped the Coast Guard and other cruisers by publishing his extensive knowledge in the form of tracks, guides, and other information. The whole system had to work together. Mapping, buoys, dredging, and maintenance all played a role in the success of the ICW. The storms that raged around us constantly moved all of that sand and mud, stressing infrastructure and maintenance crews alike. Interestingly, every little buoy that was missing or out of place felt like a lie and eroded our trust in the whole system. Throughout the day, doubt increasingly crept in as we encountered shallow depths where they weren't expected to be. Less trust meant more attention at the helm and more tension. That's what made the ICW from Georgia to North Carolina so difficult. Through it all, we kept going.

As expected, the beefy Volvo pushed us briskly along while the winds kept climbing and the seas ticked past one foot to just under two. Amidst the last of the three expected obstacles, we turned the corner toward our campsite. Under the protection of the riverbanks, the swells dropped off, but the wind gusts of greater than twenty miles per hour blew with increasing frequency. As we looked out, we saw our friends on the trawler *Turn the Paige*. They were grounded hard, right in the middle of the channel. We tried to make sense of the buoys but couldn't understand what to do. At low water on the Cape Fear River, sometimes this channel was hard to find and harder to navigate because of the huge tide swings and the dramatically shifting bottom. We were very close to dead low tide. We talked to *Turn the Paige* briefly, told them what we were going to do, and then tried to see if our two-and-a-half-foot draft would let us do what their four-foot draft could not.

I slowly tried to feel my way into the state park while *Turn the Paige* sat beside us on the bottom, waiting for the rising tide. It was Easter Sunday, so no one was available to guide us into the marina. I slowly poked my nose forward until we felt the slide on the bottom, backed up, and then did the same once again. After trying to feel our way around the waters, we determined two things. We couldn't help *Turn the Paige* because the winds were too high and the area was too shallow. We also couldn't get into the state park marina without help, and no staff were there that day. With the winds rising, we made sure Sea Tow was on their way so our friends were safe. Then we continued to head north to find a dock before the storm came in.

At this point, I was exhausted, the stress and length of the day taking its toll. We saw a wind-battered marina with a working fuel pump and a barely serviceable dock. I couldn't navigate the current and wind to park *Currently*. After two attempts, Maggie slipped next to me and said our code phrase. "Perhaps I could be of some assistance?" The words cut through my despair, and I passed the helm to her. Two were able to solve the problem where one had failed. I could read the winds and current. I could tell her exactly what to do with the throttle and the wheel. We had two large fenders deployed so there was no danger of holing our boat.

She angled the boat upstream and toward the dock. She let the nose slip a little downstream, going quickly toward the dock. In this way, she docked the freaking boat the very first time. I jumped to shore and muscled the boat to the fuel dock, getting a line tied on, and in the meantime popping off a cleat from the aging structure. The cleat blasted off of the dock like a cannonball but missed the boat, the body, and the fuel pumps.

Cognizant of the incoming gale and the aging dock, it was all hands on dock. We tied up every line on the boat using every cleat we could reach to spread the load on the rusting hardware and aging wood. When we were done, the dock was covered in enough trip hazards to give an OSHA inspector an instant coronary. Kayla? The sometimes climber was jumping off of *Currently*, dancing between the lines like Spiderman, tying us up to cleats perfectly, and checking everything over. We looked at the weather map,

Carolina Beach fuel dock

looked at our lines, felt the dock, and thought there was no way they were possibly going to hold, but we'd done our best. I prepared the anchor just in case we needed to drop it in the night. I hooked up power and then collapsed in a pile.

Maggie handed me a drink. After the long day, I took a sip. My word, it was good and blessedly *strong*. It needed to be. Oddly, it brought unexpected comfort and then the smell came to me. Early in our relationship, Maggie and I would eat Werthers butterscotch candies by the case when we traveled to her family's homestead in the Finger Lakes region of New York. The Jack and Coke brought me back to those calm sweets.

Then she made a dinner. Kayla excitedly talked about our shared adventure to her boyfriend (now husband). I made good progress with my stiff whiskey and coke, barely staving off a nervous breakdown. Maggie was drinking up her time with family, buzzing happily in the kitchen and reveling in her docking success when we absolutely had to have her skills. We all got what we needed.

In the end, we laughed, commiserated, and broke bread together as a family. We had a sleepless night, but the ropes held. I got up when the boat didn't move quite right. I balanced the stress on the old dock the best I could by adjusting

Shells on Wrightsville Beach

this line or that one. It was the only night of the loop that Maggie dreamed fretfully all night about capsizing. As the night wore on, the waves of the river grew more rhythmic and less frantic, a lovely counterpoint to the raindrops on the fiberglass top.

The next couple of days, we docked our weary bodies. We spent two nights at Carolina Beach and snuck up the coast for a couple of hours to Wrightsville Beach. We ate some good lunches and dinners, sampling some of the best seafood we'd encountered so far. We did what families do, and it felt good. We laughed so hard, people at other tables turned around to glare. We had one particularly poignant conversation about an unsettled past, and we cried together.

We also walked for the first time to the great Atlantic Ocean. The six-foot waves exploded onto the shore, leaving the omnipresent foam to flow upstream. We waded out ankle high into the low suds. As we did so, we felt the tensions of the previous days in our toes. Slowly, we left them to the waves to be carried out to sea by the rhythmic tides of the beautiful blue Atlantic.

CHAPTER 28

Swamp Minions Both Miserable and Lethal

Our time with Kayla was nice. The challenges of the trip fed Kayla's sense of adventure, and the conversation fed both mama and dad in ways only direct connection with our children could. Once she returned to school to continue her graduate work, our collective memories would shrink the physical distance between us. We were grateful. The end of our time together was chaotic, as a seventy-foot yacht was coming into our transient space at Wright's Marina ahead of schedule. We unceremoniously booted tearful Kayla and her gear from our blue tug as Maggie put on a brave face and made the promises moms do, and I took care of the details of getting underway.

As we left, we admonished ourselves to slow our departures down so we wouldn't forget anything important. Miraculously, even through our hasty departure, all of the lines were off, electric was unplugged, and there was no traffic beyond the yacht eyeing our spot like a hungry shark. We turned on all of our electronics, set up our electrical system to inverter mode, and made our way through the just-opening bridge. For the first time, we didn't have a schedule to keep. We worked our way up the Atlantic coast amidst the borderline weather. As we cut into the North Carolina ICW, we eyed three dangerous sounds. Like most of the larger bays on the coast, any one of them could work us over if we hit them on the wrong day. We also eyed an announcement that popped up on the forums and the waterway guides. The Coast Guard would close the ICW throughout the day to work through some exercises.

We managed to work our way to an exceedingly shallow Dudley's Marina, one that didn't charge for power and was only a buck a foot. We couldn't get anyone on the radio to walk us through the approach, but the guidebooks were just accurate enough and we made it in approaching low tide, kicking up a cloud of sand as we dragged the keel across the soft bottom. We pulled in slightly miffed, but we reminded each other that Dudley's was a buck a foot. I tried to tie off on a post, and it came off in my hand. I grunted at my new splinters, managed to work around the obstacles and rustic decking, and finished tying up, still muttering "a buck a foot." We wandered into the store and saw, annoyingly, the VHF on the counter, turned off, and the phone ringing near three employees having a casual conversation. At that point, we thought we might not be getting our money's worth. Still, the sunset was nice, so we called it a win.

The weather settled down a bit, so we picked our way up the coast. We stopped in a quiet Beaufort marina with half a dozen loopers. We stayed a day or two and then took a calm day to cut across the Neuse River Sound. The crossing was a little choppy, but not too bad. That one gave way to the massive sailing community called Oriental. The rustic Carolina towns had an authenticity we hadn't seen since Appalachicola. Marinas, restaurants, shops, and the like were distinctive instead of the formulaic sameness we'd encountered throughout the lion's share of Florida.

There, we met a Canadian and American couple on *Knot Fantasea*. We gave them props for two nautical puns in the same boat name, but *Nauti Fantasea* seemed like a missed opportunity. We met Jen and Elliot on *Pivot*, the YouTube crew we'd first encountered in Florida. We shared a dinner with them and enjoyed the time tremendously. We had seafood nachos and took a walk. We walked them through some of our decision-making, and they told us about the free docks we'd encounter throughout the North. Both exuded a humility and kindness that was rare amongst captains. Through the year to come, we would see them several other times. To make David from Hillsboro jealous, we snapped a selfie with them, sent off the picture, and posted some obnoxious message. He oohed and awed, paying the appropriate tribute.

After Oriental, we cruised up the canals, creeks, and rivers that made up the ICW in Carolina. A combination of grasslands and swampy forests, these waterways got progressively greener. We slowly puttered through the second sound on our list, Pamlico. The weather was nice, so we saw waves no higher than a foot. Then we arrived at Belhaven, an important stop for two reasons. First, I needed to teach my second class on the loop. Second, Maggie and I wanted to update our Covid boosters. We'd get our fourth shot at a tiny rural Walgreens.

We tied up on the rustic dock, and then we took in the facilities. Many loopers considered Belhaven a stop to miss, but we disagreed. The facilities were great, everything was reachable by bike, and the townspeople were as friendly as any we had encountered. We settled in for the week. I would teach the class, walking around between the docks between class segments to stay fresh. After the second day, we biked down to the Walgreens to get our booster. We met a man who seemed nice, and then we said a completely socially unacceptable word to him.

Vaccine.

Suddenly, we were buried beneath a verbal torrent of microchips, agricultural remedies, conspiracy theories regarding some of the most respected and decorated doctors in our country, and other things we've long since blocked out. Eventually, the visibly agitated man moved on. I just didn't understand. My loop was one started amidst the Covid pandemic, one that still raged around us. We could see the data about waning immunity and efficacy of boosters. As a high-risk pre-diabetic patient with a heart condition and asthma-like symptoms, the vaccines weren't just conveniences. They were lifelines. We saw the projections of a Covid-inflamed New York City and timed our boosters to arrive there with peak immunity.

Throughout the loop, Maggie and I wondered about how we got to this place as a nation and as a community. To me, the vaccine represented a fact like "the sky is blue" or "today is Tuesday." These were the basic red and green buoys we needed to drive our lives through to stay safe. Call them truth, or facts, or news like Cronkite (not news like social media). These markers weren't infallible, but I believed the people that laid them had our best interests in mind. We got our boosters, jumped on our bikes, and rode them through the idyllic streets of Belhaven, and pushed our troubles aside.

After several days of classes, a growing pod of boats docked in Belhaven, pinned once again by the weather, just in time for our ominous crossing of the feared Albemarle Sound. Boats with names like *Smile with the Rising Sun*, *Compass Rose*, *Positive Latitude*, and more dotted the docks. More were docked at another marina a mere mile away. We planned to finish our class and leave on Friday afternoon. We had some of the biggest docktails groups on the whole loop here. We got hammered by storms, mostly overnight. One afternoon, one of the marina employees walked from boat to boat, asking captains to adjust their lines and fenders in one way or another in advance of a still larger storm with sustained gale-force winds. For *Currently*, he wanted more slack on the bow line and less on the stern. He walked me through the expected winds and why he thought that tie-up to be best. In the end, he was right.

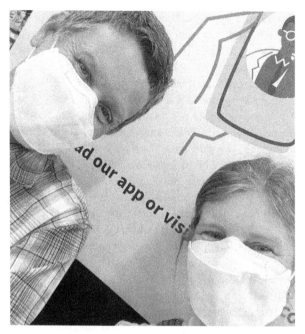

Getting shots in Belhaven, North Carolina

That night, we planned to go for docktails and dinner. We scheduled the meal early to beat the inbound gale. After the loopers lost track of time amidst all of the stories of rough weather and the ominous Rock Pile, Maggie eventually looked at her phone to see a large red storm cell rolling in. Around the table, loopers looked down at their phones, and then heads popped up like prairie dogs. Foregoing credit cards, each couple dropped a wad of cash on the restaurant table and left. We ran all the way back to beat the pending tempest. For a night, we were action heroes as lightning crashed behind us, and we made it to *Currently* mere minutes before the weather system unleashed pandemonium, just one more gale in a whole season of them.

By Friday, the weather had eased up, but just barely. We left Belhaven, and the waves reminded us that Mother

Nature was in charge. The waves were between one and two feet, and they were right on top of each other. Why, yes, we would like a generous portion of tolerable misery, please and thank you. We dialed in the speed and direction until we were at least moderately comfortable. All of that changed as we rounded the corner to the Alligator River. The seas were a solid two feet and growing as the heavens opened. We encountered a lonely sailboat and called them to arrange for a slow pass. They laughed and said wakes wouldn't make a bit of a difference out there. Eventually, Alligator Marina came into view, and we threaded through the shallow, narrow entrance, and the rain stopped as if all the drops in the world were finally depleted.

We docked, fueled up, and stared at each other. The rain had relented but the winds were still howling. An unspoken conversation passed between us once again. Maggie hated moving the boat in bad weather once we were docked. Her eyes said "Please, let's just stay on the fuel dock this evening." Mine said "Relax. I can do this." For the first time on the loop, I won a staring contest on the fuel dock. But let's be honest; no one really wins such a contest of wills. I turned around and got in the boat and started the engines. She reluctantly climbed aboard, and we moved the boat. It was rough and awkward, but we made it into the slip in one piece, so we'd have heat and power amidst the coming cold, wet evening. Maggie hugged me with relief. By morning, the weather would hopefully be better.

It was not. We made the poor decision to go into the Carolina sounds in borderline travel conditions. We expected no more than two-foot waves in the dreaded Albemarle Sound, a place that beats nearly everyone up. We got waves from three to five feet, hitting us right on the nose. Maggie was driving, and she absolutely hated it. The dog was shaking on the floor. Something metal was rattling hard, and cabinets were flying open. I tapped Maggie on the shoulder to utter our safe phrase: "Perhaps I could be of some assistance." She gratefully passed over the helm. I marveled at how far she'd come in the past two months, but this was too much for her, and we both knew it.

She taped the cabinets and drawers shut and then climbed down on the floor to hug the dog. I'd glance down from time to time, and she'd smile back up at me. I couldn't tell if she was on the edge of tears, or just content to steel her own courage by helping the dog brave the waves. Sometimes on the loop, every boat makes the choice to take weather that's uncomfortable but good enough. Albemarle was our day. We broke through to the canal on the other side into blessed protection. The winds slowed down and the waves lay down to nothing. *This* was the calm weather we expected, just two hours too late. From this experience, we learned not to go out in weather conditions that were barely good enough.

After leaving the sound, we had a choice to make. Along the ICW, boats can choose to take the Dismal Swamp route through Elizabeth City to Norfolk or the eastern route that goes through Coinjock, North Carolina. Instead of taking the eastern route through Coinjock, we elected the western route with the name only Tim Burton could love. The very name of the Dismal Swamp suggests unsavory images twice. As a husband of an extrovert, the word *dismal* screams lonely isolation. As a son of an artist, I saw dismal as melancholy masses of sepia tones and indistinct edges. True enough, the swamp did have plenty of isolation and shades of brown. When we saw some fleeing geese, the typical white froth stirred up from their dragging feet wasn't white but the stout brown of espresso coffee or dark chocolate.

As if Dismal is not enough of a burden for a single name, the Swamp steps forward with promises of things miserable or lethal. Misery comes in the form of gallons of oily mud and air thick enough to pour into a muffin tin. If it's in a swamp and doesn't ooze misery, it's probably lethal, like a gator, venomous snake, or black bear. Sometimes, swamp minions like ubiquitous mosquitos and disease-ridden water are both miserable and lethal.

Geese in Dismal Swamp

Put the name on a piece of paper, and it's little wonder that few loopers would ever put the place on a potential list of favorites before their trip. After visiting the swamp, we can both say our journey through it was a loop highlight.

Dismal, as it turns out, is a name Europeans used to refer to swamps or other areas of stagnant water. The Great Dismal Swamp covers an area of over a million acres and spans parts of coastal Virginia and North Carolina. Historically, the landmark was visited by George Washington in 1763 and became a refuge for thousands of slaves throughout the years. Construction on the canal started in 1793 and finished in 1805, in very much the same form we see from the water. The Dismal Swamp cut covers over twenty miles and goes through two locks. One goes up and the other goes down. Both change only eight feet of elevation.

As we approached the North Carolina/Virginia state line, we hailed the lock operator and asked to lock through. We pulled into the lock, which had historical placards, and passed the operator one bow line and one stern line. He looped the rope around a fixed bollard, a metal pipe that served as a pulley of sorts for our line. Each line passed from a cleat on our boat, around the bollard, and then back to a passenger on *Currently*. Then the lock closed and began to fill with water. We took up slack until the boat had come

Reflections in the Dismal Swamp

up eight feet. The lock opened, we took our lines back on board, and departed. The lock operator left the lock, drove a few feet to a bridge, and opened it for us. This one-man show has operated in roughly the same way for years.

We passed through the lock and went back in time. Our boat sliced through the mirror-calm water. We could see the diffuse emerald-green light from the trees reflected back to us with slight rippling distortions across the surface of the water. Both Maggie and I spent a little time on the bow to take in the full grandeur of the experience, silent moments of inspiring beauty and peace.

After five short miles over about an hour, we pulled up at the North Carolina welcome center. Incongruously, this rest stop served both as a visitor center for the park and for the North Carolina highway. We'd never encountered a truck stop marina before. This one was only a mile from the Virginia state line. We spent an hour or so with the two other vessels tied up there and then went to sleep.

The next day, we cruised seventeen more miles through the park to the second lock. We experienced more of the same, and then some. We saw eagles almost close enough to touch, flirting geese, and more. Though we saw plenty of logs on the river, we didn't so much as brush a single one of them. We emerged from the experience rested and optimistic.

Great Dismal Swamp, we now love your name. We will carry with us the beautiful memories that can only come when low expectations meet surprise and delight.

CHAPTER 29

From Dock to Dock and Bar to Bar

Once we hit the Virginia state line at the Dismal Swamp, we closed out one chapter of the loop and moved on to the next. We'd already completed the southern rivers, the Gulf Coast, Florida, and the southern half of the Atlantic. We'd gone from several months behind to surfing the leading edge of loopers, putting ourselves in a great position to do a couple of side trips we'd tentatively circled. Our next stop opened the next chapter, Chesapeake Bay. After the great bay, we'd have only another couple of weeks on saltwater. These were massive accomplishments.

Still, we had a couple of moments of what I would call modest concern. Most sane people would call our mental state full-on, hysterical freak out. True, we'd caught the wave of loopers. At least three-quarters of them were in Norfolk for the ALGCA Spring Rendezvous. This year, at least three hundred travelers would attend the convention of boaters. The problem was that we also caught the wave of Covid, which was heating up in Virginia and was expected to be in full bloom about the time we reached New York City.

As a spouse and a high-risk heart patient, our imaginations got away from us, and our fears were in full bloom. By the time we got to Norfolk, we "reasoned" that the loop was mostly old people in boats with a healthy portion of anti-vaxer mixed in. Then we imagined seeding that group with a super-spreader event. Then we'd race from dock to dock and bar to bar. By the time we worked ourselves fully up, we wondered how there were any of us left at all!

Looking back, we could see another perspective. Loopers are not typical boaters. Most of us *did* get vaccinated. People made informed decisions based on their risk profiles, and we generally did a good job of protecting one another when we got sick. There were good reasons to attend the event since we'd be encountering a few serious obstacles, including the treacherous Chesapeake and Delaware bays.

Still, in our mental state, we weren't going to get anywhere close to the rendezvous, and looking back, that was the right decision for our circumstances. Instead, we'd catch up with a few people who were there early enough and could make some time for us. In that spirit, we visited with *Pivot* and were delighted to be on board when Jen took a turn at the helm for the first time in a while, with a great warship in the distance and a ferry operating right in front of her. She handled it like she'd been driving every day on the loop.

We talked with them about their hair-raising trip to the North Carolina Outer Banks. They had both a failed bilge pump and alarm, and perhaps scupper problems as well. I was terrified for them, and pretty much made an ass out of myself admonishing them to check these systems with a greater regularity. Elliot took it all in stride, and I mumbled an apology that maybe he even heard. That awkward start led to a great day together. We enjoyed their company as people who viewed travel as a way to understand more about the world and each other. We cruised across the river to the rendezvous marina and filmed a short segment with

Jen pilots *Pivot* in Virginia

them on Dismal Swamp vs. Coinjock and then picked our way across the docks, waving at other boats we recognized.

Instead of hanging out while the rendezvous went on, we would use this great meeting as an opportunity to put some distance between us and the fleet, making more resources available to us, like space on free walls or in marinas. We'd work our way up the bay and then decide where to teach our classes, maintaining some distance from the massive wave until we reached New York. Then we could take a lesser traveled route through Lake Champlain and Montreal.

Pulling into Norfolk, we saw the greatest naval base in the world sprawled out before us. The river was intense because it was so wide and the current so powerful, but it was otherwise easy. We gassed up and moved into Tidewater Marina in Portsmouth, Maryland, across the river from the mass of fiberglass, coffee, and good cheer at Waterside. We walked mostly in Portsmouth, seeing the lightship and eating crab cakes, stretching our vegan plus seafood diet in ways our doctor at home would not approve. The closer we got to Maryland, the better the crab cakes got.

We also got a chance to invite Mikey, my brother's oldest son, aboard. He got to take pictures of the boats, step aboard, see how the electronics worked, and spend a bit of time doing the things families do. He told us about his job on the naval base and the *Iowa*, the ship where Mike Sr. served. In response, we told him about the loop and the places we'd visited. Then we said goodbye.

Bruce's nephew Mikey in Virginia Beach

After a day of rest, we got out onto the bay with pretty decent weather. Our first obstacle was a cruise ship. We waited a bit for it to pull out, but their captain waved us through, saying it would take a while for them to depart. We moved up the river toward the Chesapeake alongside one warship after another. We could hear announcements of boats as they made their way out to sea, but we didn't have enough knowledge of the area to understand the radio chatter, so we just kept pushing up the river.

Eventually, our luck ran out. We pulled out just ahead of a destroyer. We could see the 95 on the bow, and Maggie looked up the ship. She was the destroyer named *James E. Williams*. We expected some unpleasant radio chatter, but it never materialized. As the *Williams* picked up speed, the voice of a woman broke out on our handheld radio, the one we had tuned to commercial and military traffic on VHF 13. She announced that the *James Williams* would be picking up speed, and that we were on the edge of their safe range.

We thanked her and opened *Currently*'s throttle as wide as we could, shooting off into the bay at forty-five degrees from the massive vessel. We could see a boat just in front of us doing the same. They snapped a shot of tiny *Currently* running from the destroyer. We were probably a quarter of a mile away when the picture was snapped, but it looked much closer when we saw it.

The *James Williams* in Chesapeake Bay

Over the next few weeks, none of the days were great for travel, but some were good enough. We ran about half of the days. Each day, we'd run far and fast. We went through Deltaville, the first of many sailing communities we'd find on the bay. The change from fuel to wind-powered vessels was welcome. The sailing boats threw off tiny wakes and were generally good citizens. In Deltaville, we'd planned to teach a class, but we wound up slipping the schedule a week.

Next, we visited Solomons, home of a great World War II naval base. Calvert was a founding family of Maryland, the namesake of the naval base and our marina. We hung out there for a couple of days, waiting through the unrelenting wind and visiting the museums there. A recurring theme was the discovery of plenty, settlement, industrialization, and the depletion of resources. The loop was continuing to shift my perspective.

In the past, I'd been pretty ambivalent about global warming. On an Alaskan cruise, I'd witnessed receding glaciers and changed my mind about climate change, and this trip intensified my opinions. We saw the carnage from the escalating power of hurricanes arriving with greater frequency. We saw record low temperatures in Tennessee and Mississippi, winds twenty miles per hour above norms on the Atlantic, and we'd continue to encounter extreme weather throughout the loop. Zooming out on our storm charts, we saw storm after storm working its way across the Atlantic coast, and it frightened us.

Despite the weather challenges, we enjoyed this section of the loop tremendously. From North Carolina on up, we'd continue to encounter looper boats at each marina we visited. We got a chance to slow down, in part because of the weather. We sampled local foods, but more importantly, we came to understand more about the people in each geography we visited. In this section, we were able to take on occasional visitors instead of the steady stream of them we'd seen from north Florida through North Carolina. This pace helped reduce the stress and opened up more options for making safer decisions due to weather.

In Solomons, we also had the opportunity to visit the Drum Point Lighthouse. We learned that the lighthouses that dotted the Chesapeake Bay are often shorter because they don't have to project any more than five miles or so for the most part. Others on the Atlantic or the Great Lakes are much taller. We visited the three-story structure and ate it up. Like green and red buoys, for us lighthouses became metaphors for truth and guidance. When we saw them, we thought of important people in our lives, our mentoring program, and more. I was ever more cognizant of those who worked hard to mark the way for Maggie and me on the trip. We took pictures of hundreds of them throughout our loop. Over the years, many of those massive structures have given way to automated buoys or other structures, but their story is an important one. I casually wondered if a lighthouse tattoo was in my future. Maggie considered the same.

Drum Point Lighthouse Museum

We had planned to zip across the bay to visit St. Michaels, Smith Island, Tangier Island, and other destinations on the eastern shore, but one by one, we struck them off of our list, another casualty to the demands of our work schedule and the weather. With higher winds coming in and precious few travel days, we looked for a safe place to land for two classes. The weather in 2022 was strange. In truth, the 2022 hurricane season wasn't bad, save a particularly bad one on September twenty-fourth in Fort Myers. Still, we found weather extremes throughout our entire run. I had a theory but couldn't verify it one way or another. The Great Loop builds its travel seasons around a particular weather pattern, based on the wisdom of the crowd. When the weather changes, the pattern shifts a little. If so, a small change in our schedules or in weather patterns could lead to drastic changes on the loop. Just a difference of four miles an hour to wind speed in the wrong direction can mean the difference between one-foot and three-foot seas on that bay. We saw a travel advisory with four-foot waves in the south bay with sustained winds of only twelve miles per hour!

To handle our class, we settled on Shipwright Harbor in Deale, Maryland. It was a small family-owned marina recently acquired by the larger conglomerate. We ran through the bay with pretty hefty one- to three-foot waves angling across our bow, but once we sped up, the Ranger Tug took them marvelously well. We skipped from wave top to wave top traveling in the morning when the waves were lower. On the way, we negotiated a great two-week rate in Deale, Maryland. We pulled in after a half day of running fast and hard and immediately felt ourselves relax. The place was full of smaller slips for the many sailboats that dotted the bay. Our little tug slipped into place easily, perfectly at home with our ten-foot beam. We were happy to be tucked in tight because the big winds would roll in and wouldn't stop for a good long while.

We had an unexpectedly pleasant time in Deale. I don't mean to say that the facilities or staff were poor; the opposite was true. Still, the weather was going to be miserably drizzly, and many of the services in the resort town were still closed for the spring. Amidst the wind-driven vessels of the Washington, D.C. weekend warriors, we found a pleasant community of liveaboards. They were sailors, a new community to us. They were a jovial, competent lot. Most had encyclopedic knowledge about the places we'd been and those we wanted to go.

Modern boats use cheap sacrificial metals called anodes on their propellors, hulls, engines, and rudders to prevent corrosion. The type of metal must change depending on the type of water where the boat operates. We had to replace some zinc anodes with aluminum ones for our pending switch from seawater to fresh, so we bought aluminum ones and had them installed. They pulled out the boat, switched the zincs, washed the bottom, and touched up the fiberglass in places we couldn't reach from a dock. The technician seemed to do a little of everything at the marina, and he made quick work of the transom plate that I thought might be a permanent fixture due to corrosion. These anodes looked horrific, but I knew that they attracted tarnish and corrosion to protect the other metals on the boat.

Changing the transom anode in Deale

To save a little money, I would have to change two engine zincs myself. The two little bolts containing them were difficult to access in their tight corners. After the staff once again proved their worth wrangling us back into our space in high winds, I set out to replace my two engine anodes, a five-minute job that extended to two hours and three bloody knuckles before I finally gave up. Even the on-call mechanic couldn't break it loose.

Ryan, a local liveaboard, agreed to help me out by breaking it loose, and wrestled with it for a good long while, laying on his stomach with his hands high before climbing all of the way down into the cramped engine room. We pulled and pulled on that little bolt and put several gallons of thread penetrating oil on it. Finally, it gave way. Ryan wouldn't take a penny for the work, so we gave him one of our aluminum Currently Crew mugs, and the guy was absolutely beaming with pleasure. He carried that cup everywhere. We caught two hours of low winds, so we took *Currently* to the fuel dock to pump out waste. We looked across the little inlet and saw Ryan waving with his Currently Crew mug up high in the air. When we went to a little outdoor pool-opening party, we spied him before he knew we were there. He waved the mug, full of exquisite Pappy whisky, back and forth, pantomiming the story of the frozen engine zinc. A little connection goes a long way, and we were hungry for it after years of quarantine.

One of the great pleasures of the loop was to meet up with good friends. Over the past couple of years, coworker and acquaintance Frank Hunleth became increasingly important to us. When I was ready to leave a particular professional programming community, I had a job circled and was just about to take it. Frank's kindness convinced me to stay. He spent time with me, guided me through some fun projects, was a listening ear, and was basically a terrific human being.

Later, his daughter started to attend our mentoring program, which tightened our relationship a little more. It goes without saying that we buried the Hunleths in a pile of Amazon boxes because they were our only close contacts in the area.

Frank and his daughter Alexa joined us for the weekend. We planned to use a projected break in the weather on Saturday to visit Annapolis. We had a nice dinner together, Maggie deftly navigating the food allergies among us like a dinghy through MegaDock. Alexa and Frank built a gift—a printed circuit board that showed a map of the Great Loop. Alexa wrote an Elixir program to show our progress on the trip. It was a stunning accomplishment for a programmer in high school and is to this day one of the best gifts I have ever received.

Alex presents her gift as Frank looks on

The next day, we planned for a day trip to Annapolis, but the weather wasn't cooperating. The wind and waves were low, but a thick fog hung over the bay. Most loopers don't have the experience and confidence to run in the fog. We certainly didn't have much experience doing so, but we did have the equipment and knowledge to make such a run. After looking at the weather, we decided to let the fog begin to lift before departure. We waited for a little while and then decided to go when we could see the first buoy outside of the marina. We decided to get the whole crew into the routine of safely navigating. We turned on our nav lights, powered up our radar, and cast off.

When we got out into the bay, we found a thicker fog than either our instruments or senses had led us to expect. Still, by watching our radar, going slowly, and sounding regular horns, we could safely make way. We let Alexa set two-minute timers, and we hit the horn to warn boats in the area. As we rounded the first corner outside of the marina, the radar picked up a slight return, so we changed course ever so slightly. Incredulously, we saw a lone kayaker emerge like a ghost. The slight contrast of white on white was barely visible, and his dark red jacket was only marginally better. A local sailor and a fisherman looked at us with annoyance. To us, the fog was remarkable, but locals had a special name for days like this. Saturday.

Fog in Deale delays our departure

We worked our way north through the stubborn fog, the distance taking us three times as long to cover as we expected. Alexa said, "Time"; I hit the horn; repeat. There were no buoys to site because there was nothing to hit out in the middle of the bay, so Frank and Maggie were free to just enjoy the experience. As we got close to Annapolis, I saw a huge cargo ship, right in our path. I slowed down *Currently* to idle speed and looked out. The whole bay was full of container ships. I was ready to turn around and flee, but Maggie smiled and said, "The fog is lifting." Of course. They had been there the whole time, and the vessels lay down before us like skyscrapers, much further away than I thought.

As we got to Annapolis, the fog cleared the rest of the way, and we could see a regatta in full swing as well as several tall ships in the harbor. We nibbled our way around the edges of it and snuck into town. We docked the boat on a mooring ball downtown and got a water taxi to pick us up. Frank was the consummate host, because he'd been there many times, and walked us through the area. We visited the schooners on the docks of the harbor. We had lunch together. I had two crab cakes and swear that one of them was as big as a grapefruit. No, my doctor would not be pleased.

We ran fast and smoothly on the way back to Deale, Frank and Alexa talking to one another about the day. Frank had a map out, and they were speculating on some weird formations they saw on Google Earth. Alexa got to take the wheel briefly when there was no other traffic around, and Frank asked about how things worked on board. They had an obvious affection for one another. Frank was so gentle and Alexa so bright. Being with them was one of the highlights of my trip.

After staying two weeks, we left Deale and headed up the bay. We went quickly to keep working ahead of the wave of loopers from the rendezvous. Many of them had been pinned for weather, as the southern bay was choppy enough to rattle a battleship. We had some healthy chop of our own, but we were used to it. The last few miles we were running from a storm that looked closer than the weather radar on our iPhone showed it was. We were also fighting nightfall, but we docked in Chesapeake City at a place called the C&D Canal.

In the end, Chesapeake Bay was not all that we wanted it to be. We missed the whole east coast of the bay. We fought winds and waves at sea and endless cold with healthy rains in port. As always, the loop provided plenty of highlights, though. Our times with *Pivot* were priceless, and the connections with the Hunleths were profoundly meaningful. Experiencing Alexa's growth firsthand through an amazing gift gave us a look at the promise of the next generation. Rather than places, our highlights of this place were the people we encountered there, and that was OK with us.

With the bay behind us, we'd approach the biggest nautical challenges the loop had to offer, Delaware Bay, the Jersey coast, and New York City. Then we'd head north toward Lake Champlain and Canada. The loop called, and we were eager to answer.

CHAPTER 30

A Boat Sank There

The mysterious looping folklore blows some areas of the loop way out of proportion. We'd been through the Gulf crossing and the Rock Pile formations and did not understand all of the consternation about either place. Other places get barely a mention at all and *are* big deals. The Jersey coast is perhaps the most significant of these places.

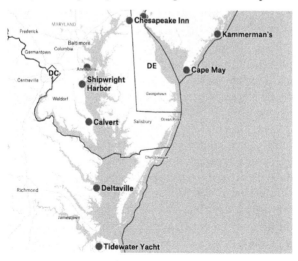

The ever-treacherous Delaware Bay

The trip begins with the Chesapeake and Delaware Canal that has a four-mile-per-hour difference between peak ebbing and flooding tides. Flood tides are rising, and ebb tides are falling. When the distance between two bodies of water is particularly great, currents can get quite strong.

While the run isn't technically difficult, the canal does complicate logistics significantly by forcing travel at certain times and focusing boats to one of two major marinas. The canal dumps into Delaware Bay, where marriages go to die. Perfect days on the bay can and do take miserable turns without warning. Building currents against the wind combined with significant commercial traffic can build enormous waves rapidly, and there's no place to stop. After these obstacles, the looper must navigate the treacherous ICW, barely deep enough to accommodate the shallowest of drafts on the loop. Alternatively, captains can choose to venture outside where the Atlantic waves can blast unimpeded onto unwary beams. Then loopers must navigate New York Harbor and all of its traffic, before heading up the Hudson River.

With these thoughts, we tried to pull into the free wall in Chesapeake City, but it was full. Instead, we pulled into Chesapeake Inn Marina after barely avoiding running aground, an inauspicious start to our journey. We backed into a narrow, shallow spot that was perfectly located. The dockhands in this area could mostly tie up a boat by whipping the rope up and down at waist level, flicking a ripple in the line around the cleats in a move I never began to master. They could also manage boats in close quarters. Boat hooks, experienced staff, and good instructions were the order of the day, and they made docking a pleasure.

The inbound storm veered north instead of hitting us, so we did our normal arrival dance, using burgees to find the dozen or so loopers scattered along the three or four short docks that made up the marina. We got a credible group together, each of them tired from a wavy, rainy day of running. Strangely, Maggie and I found ourselves among the more experienced loopers. We had a short time together and realized that no one knew the looper toast. We told Eddy's story, and then gave the toast with several of the loopers recording it.

Then the blonde-haired captain on *No Agenda* broke out into a toast of her own. I should set the scene a little bit. The most popular boat make on the loop is called a Mainship. Normally, the big trawlers are old, white, reliable, and slow. Go to any big marina in a small town in the deep south and you can find dozens of them. They're the stereotypical old lake cruisers. When I saw *No Agenda*, I had to look twice. This Mainship had a bright, bright-red hull, polished like a New Year's champagne flute at the Ritz. The ship fit its occupants perfectly, a party-sized package for two. She was bright and bubbly, and her well-rehearsed toast had wonderful comedic timing and exaggerated gestures. I can't recall the exact words, but it went something like this:

> Growing old's a bitch,
> He can't see, I can't poo.
> Growing old's a bitch,
> I can't see, he can't screw.

It was very funny, with a shockingly abrupt transition. None of us knew quite what to make of it. After a long pause, the group exploded into laughter and applause. By this point, this group of loopers understood the challenges the next few days would hold. The two toasts were exactly what we needed, one to build community and another to break the tension.

In the morning, we cast off for a brief one-hour run through a tide with a huge four-mile-per-hour current in our favor. The weather let us through to Delaware City the next day. We pulled into a weathered commercial fuel dock to take on diesel fuel. The approach and landing were easy enough because of our river experience, but it still got the heart pumping after we docked the boat, when we had to lean out over the dock and the four-mile-per-hour currents to pump the diesel. Any mistakes there would be costly.

Delaware City fuel dock

That night we took in the famous briefing in Delaware City. The intense gathering walked us through all of the various things that might kill, sink, or otherwise incapacitate unwary loopers. Tim Konkus, the marina owner, started with a detailed weather report, including the intensity of the winds and tides at any given point in time. Because we didn't want opposing winds and tides, he pointed out the schedules a typical fast boat or slow boat might keep. He showed us important checkpoints and the few places we could duck out if the conditions turned bad.

He showed us a place near the shore where another tug had sunk in a ferry's prop wash. At some point, when some of our attention span faded, he asked for the hands of captains on sailboats. All of us looked up, confused because everyone was under power. All of the masts were down in anticipation of the inland bridges. He deadpanned "You sailors will be fine. You'll pop back up if you flip over." Then, with all of us in rapt attention, he pointed out the various shoals next to shipping channels. These were very dangerous when they magnified the already huge wakes of the massive cargo ships. He told us never to get caught between Ship John Shoals and a cargo ship, and I've never forgotten.

Most of us tentatively determined that the conditions should be good, so we'd need to aim for a five in the morning departure to time the tides. The run didn't happen. Tim knocked on our windows and said, "No go." I had come to the opposite conclusion, but I'd missed the spiking winds on one of the weather buoys. A few boats went anyway and had a safe but rocky run, but the point remains. Those kinds of days *could* turn bad. After the briefing, it was a chance most of us were unwilling to take. So we stayed in port and connected with Tony and Karen Long on *Long Recess* to plan for our run the next day.

Bruce and Tony plan our Jersey coast run

We'd not seen *Long Recess* since Miami, and we didn't know them well, but we enjoyed their company. Their newer Ranger Tug 27 transmitted AIS, meaning they'd project one of those nice triangles onto our electronic display. Because the system also showed speed information, *Currently* would fall in behind them and match their speed. After a morning predawn departure, we were deep into the bay with all aboard *Long Recess* and *Currently* going through our list, pointing out the important buoys, shoals, and bail points on VHF as we went by.

The waves were mostly tame until we were six miles from the entrance of Cape May. There, they rose up to just under two feet. They were steep and uncomfortable but workable. After the intensity of the briefings, it seemed like we were all holding our breath for the entire eighty miles or so. When we arrived, our depth sounders seemed to always be firing because of the shoaling in the ICW. Almost perpetual dredging was happening to hold the sand and sea at bay—a losing battle.

We pulled into Cape May and took stock of the deteriorating weather. Both boats joined our friend Loren on *Das Boot* for a walk and dinner. Loren was single-handing his tug with his old black lab, and we talked often. After dinner, we parted to check the weather and ask the locals about the ICW. Most loopers ran outside along the Jersey coast, navigating up to four inlets, one small stop at a time, and eventually crossing into New York waters after crossing a landmark called Sandy Hook. Our little Rangers gave us options. Because we had a shallow draft, we could run inside. Because we could run fast, we could cover greater distances. We decided to nibble our way down the ICW until we were in range of a single, long run into New York.

We decided to pass on the first segment of the ICW in favor of a short weather window, running from Cape May to Atlantic City in projected two-foot waves. We knew that meant we'd likely see occasional waves up to four feet. The Atlantic surf didn't disappoint. Shaken but not stirred, we pulled into Atlantic City, ducking in among the big commercial fishing ships to avoid higher waves in the afternoon.

We pulled into Kammerman's Marina, a small family-owned business that could handle our smaller boats. We knew we were close enough for a long one-day run into New York if we could get outside and open up the throttle, but it all depended on the weather, and the winds didn't appear to be ready to cooperate. The weather apps said we might have one more day to run, but winds would speed up after that. We'd be locked down hard, unable to move and paying high New Jersey rates for one to two weeks, until the next weather window opened up. None of us wanted that.

The options were just maddening. We had the shallow drafts that would allow us to traverse the ICW, but most loopers said that path was madness because the buoys were just not reliable due to shifting sands and bad shoaling throughout. We thought of buoys as truth. We needed the buoys to tell us where the bottom was. If they were wrong, we would be at a huge disadvantage. In the inlets, shoaling was especially bad, so we had limited options. That meant some sections of the ICW would open to us only on a high tide.

Along the Jersey coast, four inlets were adequately marked and opened to navigation. First was Atlantic City, the inlet we'd use to exit to the Atlantic if we went the outside route. Next was Barnegat Inlet, the surliest of this bunch. Shoaling and partially submerged jetties made it a famous place to get into trouble. Next, was Manasquan, a wide and beautiful inlet that's especially well marked and

New York and the Jersey Shore

well used. Finally, the Sandy Hook inlet is wide enough to hold a few city blocks. We'd use it to reach the Hudson.

Marginal days outside often meant big waves in inlets. As we planned the travel, it looked like the morning winds would be too high for us to run outside, but they would settle down in the afternoon. Conversely, the ICW would get too shallow to run inside, so near New York we'd eventually need to move outside. A plan started to crystalize. To travel the one hundred plus miles to New York, we'd need to start inside, exit the questionable Barnegat Inlet, hoping to reach it at slack tide. Then we'd run outside to New York. By choosing the surly inlet, we'd be able to miss the worst of the big water and reach the open Atlantic in time to make it to New York by sunset.

Harbors, marinas, and major bodies of water like Barnegat Bay in New Jersey have strong banks to keep the hot, rolling anger of the oceans out and let in the water, wildlife, and boats that form the lifeblood of the towns along the bay. In the best of times, engineers must bolster inlets to keep the sand and shore where they should be and able to hold up to the inevitable time and tide with minimal intervention. Jetties in New Jersey are usually raw piles of stone that form walls to hold up to the relentless pounding surf. These piles slowly move. Barnegat Inlet has two such jetties that bracket the inlet like a vertical equals sign. Sometimes they were visible, but most of the time, they were partially covered with water. Hitting them would quickly destroy a boat. It had happened with alarming frequency, and a boat sank there a month after we passed through. We needed the temperamental Barnegat Inlet to make a hundred-and-twenty-mile day possible. With a plan in our pocket, we took an evening walk on the famous Atlantic City Boardwalk.

Atlantic City Boardwalk with *Long Recess*

We left at nine, a time we picked that offered four advantages. First, we'd run the whole inside ICW on a rising tide. If we grounded, the tide would hopefully lift us off. Second, we'd be able to spend some time running slow, conserving the precious eight-dollar diesel. Third, we'd time our exit to let bad weather pass outside, hopefully leading to a kinder, gentler Atlantic. Finally, we'd hit the beast at dead slack tide, when water would be near a standstill. This one was important because Barnegat had a reputation for six-foot waves and greater on a calm day.

The first part of our plan worked brilliantly. To give Tony a break, I led throughout the day. Along the way, we picked up a hitchhiker, a buddy boat called *Superior Passage*, who filled in behind *Long Recess*. The three of us started at low tide and worked our way northeast along the Jersey Shore. The shorelines were mostly rural and had a mixture of grasslands but a slightly different ecological mix than what we'd seen down south. We couldn't pay much attention because our depths were regularly seven or eight feet, so we'd often spread out and find the deepest water. *Superior Passage* had a real knack for it.

When the channel got more and more shallow, we'd spread out from left to right and call out our depths over the VHF. Then we'd find the deepest water and work our way toward that part of the canal. At one point, we passed a Sea Tow vessel. Tony called to him, and he gave us the local intel. The tow captain told us there was one more shallow spot and to hug green buoys through a particular section. From there, we'd be in well-marked waters. We followed his directions and saw depths no worse than five feet the rest of the way.

Just before slack tide, we started our approach to Barnegat Inlet. Maggie was driving, but I'd be the one to head through the big waves of the inlet. By this time in the loop, I should have been seasoned enough to show as much grace under pressure as Sean Connery in *Hunt for Red October*. My wife looked over to find her stoic salty dog, but in his place was me, hyperventilating, with a face as white as a sheet. I wondered if she even noticed, and then she said, "Are you ok?" I was not.

I had watched too many videos and seen one too many Google maps. I knew the north sea wall, to our left today, would be slightly submerged. I could picture the prominent red and green markers on the sea walls of the inlet. I played our future run and saw *Long Recess* or *Superior Passage* slide too close to the wall and hit the piles of rock or the submerged north jetty. Logically, I knew that the boats behind me knew exactly what I did, because I had told them, over and over. Emotionally, I had gone full mama duck and was leading my flock right to Barnegat blender. I could still see the Google map in my head, with all of the shoaling and the barely visible meat grinder that was the north jetty.

The underwater Barnegat Inlet shoals from above

I pulled out into the surf anyway. I passed the numbered green markers at the south jetty. As expected, the north wall was underwater. I picked up the less conspicuous green cans toward the middle of the channel and called back on the radio to make sure *Long Recess* and *Superior Passage* saw them too. Next, we throttled up and aimed right for the five-foot haystack-shaped wave in the channel. It crashed straight into our bow, submerging it slightly. We held course to avoid the slightly covered north jetty. We turned around in our seats and saw our baby ducks tracking sweetly and safely behind us. I wanted to say, "Stuff it, blender!" What came out instead was "We'll head north at the big red marker."

In the Atlantic, the seas were from two to three feet with a few outliers higher. These were among the biggest seas we saw on our loop. *Superior Passage* decided we were running too fast for her, so she eased off of the throttle. Later, she planned to duck back into the ICW through the Manesquan Inlet and stay the night. They didn't have the speed to make it all the way to New York. With that, the two tugs headed out into the Atlantic alone.

I called *Long Recess* to ask Karen, "How's it going back there?" After a pause, Tony answered in a low and steady voice, "Just fine." I chuckled and asked him to put Karen on. After a slightly longer pause, she said, "We're fine." Maggie and I chuckled. Then I told them seas would settle a little bit in an hour, and a little more after that, and they did just that. Two hours later, we were looking at seas one foot high, with an eight second period, simply lovely conditions for the open Atlantic. The tense undertones melted out of the conversation, and we settled into pleasant banter about the day's run. They eventually opened up their throttle to give the folks at Great Kills Yacht Club a chance to process our boats one at a time. Later that night, as the sun was setting over the Jersey Shore, we sailed around Sandy Hook, across two shipping lanes, and into New York.

We said goodbye to the Atlantic Ocean. We'd leave behind the saltwater that slowly dissolves boats one flake of rust at a time. We thought about the difficulties of the day and considered that it was a fine example of the seamanship we'd learned throughout the loop. We'd had to balance weather, fuel consumption, ocean conditions, and ICW shoaling all in a 120-mile day. We used local resources, including a local inlet most loopers didn't consider. Then we navigated the busy shipping channel without incident.

When all was said and done, this would be the day we'd point to that best demonstrated our cruising skills. We pulled into Great Kills Yacht Club in New York, tired but content. We'd crossed the last open saltwater on the loop, and it felt good.

CHAPTER 31

Some Days, You Are the Show

As we pulled into Great Kills Yacht Club, we knew we'd hit a significant landmark. We'd cut across both of the main bodies of saltwater on our voyage—the Gulf of Mexico and the Atlantic Ocean. Though we'd be dealing with tides for another week or two, we'd effectively made the transition from seas to rivers.

That night, we shared docktails with our buddy boats and Kim on *The Perch*. The director of the America's Great Loop Cruisers Association mostly listened as the surrounding boaters discussed the previous day's run and our pending entry to New York Harbor. Maggie and I talked about feeling inexperienced. She smiled and said everyone has days like that. "Some days you watch the show, and some days you *are* the show." We also talked about the coming challenges of Fleet Week.

Every May around Memorial Day, ships representing the United States Armed Forces enter New York Harbor. This year, the six participants represented the Coast Guard, the U.S. Navy, and the U.S. Marine Corps. Each year, the proud parade enters the Hudson River, squeezing all other traffic aside so they can maintain a security barrier around each ship. Usually, Fleet Week vessels arrive late in the morning, when the adoring public can celebrate the vessels.

This year, the Fleet arrived just before *Currently* and *Long Recess*. Today we were following *Long Recess* in their familiar twenty-seven-foot tug. Remarkably, fire boats were saluting the fleet by blasting huge geysers of seawater into the air. The massive ships passed right by Lady Liberty, an iconic scene of power and majesty.

As we arrived, the Hudson River was squeezed down to about a quarter of its usual width, leaving scant space for the many container ships, ferries, police boats, and the barrier around the fleet. Inevitably, our two tiny tugs were squeezed between the arriving parade of warships and New York's everyday fleet of ferries, cargo ships, working craft, and private vessels. Something had to give.

As we swam our way upstream, like so many minnows among mighty migrating salmon, we were squeezed closer and closer to the places we were not supposed to be. Eventually, we got intolerably close to the fleet. As a rule follower, I watched horrified as the escorting military police boat peeled off of the fleet and politely but firmly pulled up to *Long Recess* and then *Currently* and asked us to leave, pointing vaguely toward the turbulent wall of chaos occupying the constricted Hudson. As we struggled to nudge our way back among the big fish, a smallish container ship emerged into the harbor. Now, a harbor police boat skittered alongside, first *Long Recess* and then *Currently*, to point vaguely back behind us toward the fleet to tell us to wait until the fleet had passed.

I was completely freaked out. Meanwhile, Tony had slipped out of our temporary time-out, unnoticed by the harbor police. He pointed at the Statue of Liberty, wanting to get some photos. Tony said on the radio that we'd worked hard to get there, and we'd get our pictures. I looked out at the chaos and at my electronics and couldn't tell what was going on. Around this time, Karen got a text, a picture of the military police approaching our boats from some harbor cam. It was from Kim, asking if we were the tugs in the picture. It was the last straw. My dyslexic brain had too much input to process it all.

"Perhaps I could be of some assistance."

Maggie's hand was gently on my shoulder. At some point in all of the chaos, Maggie noticed that I was overloaded with too many rights and lefts among the buoys and ships and escorts. She gently gave me a camera and pointed me to the back of our boat. I said I could do it, but she firmly placed the camera in my hand and pointed firmly to the cockpit. I'd been promoted! Head photographer it is, then!

The lie was preferable to the undeniable truth. That day, just forty-eight hours removed from my crowning marine achievement, I'd been banished from the helm. Maggie calmly put *Currently* through her paces as we posed for a shot in front of the Statue of Liberty, and *Long Recess* did the same—with the fire boats, Coast Guard, and ferries dancing around us, all plotting our demise.

Later that night we were tucked in at Liberty Landing, a wonderful marina a stone's throw from the Statue of Liberty. We showered off, walked off our stiffness, and began to work through some of the wonderful pictures of the day. I even took some of them. There were Karen and Tony in their cockpit right beneath the Statue of Liberty. There was the fireboat blasting water into the sky, welcoming us to New York. And then, there was the tiny, low-resolution picture of a police boat right beside two insignificant tugs, captured by New York's harbor webcam. I smiled. On the loop, some days you're the show.

All in all, we spent just two nights in New York. One was at Great Kills. From there, we walked to a family Italian market and bought one of just about everything in the store. From Liberty Landing, we took a ferry into New York. Because of the scorching Covid rates, we decided to do outdoor walking tours instead of indoor activities.

The public parks and spaces in New York were some of the best in the world. We walked the High Line, a converted train track several stories above street level with plants, shops, sculptures, and interesting walkways. We meandered through the Hudson River Park, staring dumbly in surprise at a handful of outdoor classes, with teachers in headsets singing to babies—a personalized mini Disney. Maggie liked New York much more than she thought she would.

As we left New York, we had several ferries to contend with, but the traffic thinned significantly as we went further north. We wound our way up the Hudson, noticing the striking resemblance to our own Tennessee River. Eventually, we settled in to Half Moon Bay, just as Henry Hudson did in 1609, pausing for a week to get a good rate and catch our breath. We spent our time hiking along the river and hanging out with the dozen or so loopers docked there.

One of the great memories of our loop was visiting West Point on Memorial Day. Kip and Insel on *Fourth Dimension* invited us to go, and we gladly took them up on it. The tour had three different stops, including the cathedral, the drill field overlooking the Hudson, and the cemetery. I remember clearly looking at the candle in the chapel, marking a seat for those who could not join, the empty chair haunting and moving. My brother had been on the *Iowa* when the turret exploded but survived uninjured. Maggie's uncle had been shot down and killed in Vietnam. Our daughter was engaged to a man who had a four-year commitment to serve. We knew the significance of empty chairs and memorials to the fallen.

We also saw an interesting placard in the chapel on a wall of heroes, of a sort. The tiny slab felt wrong. It was partially behind a column, had a name crossed out, and had no death date. It didn't seem like a way to treat a hero. Then it became clear. The tiny memorial was to Benedict Arnold. The navy hero blocked the British incursion on Lake Champlain and then turned on his country to join the British. We would later look down on the Hudson from the Plain, the parade field at West Point. We could see the distinctive S-turn that made the fort so effective as a bulwark on the river.

A candle memorializes the fallen at West Point

Back at Half Moon Bay, we said goodbye to the Longs and ate our fill of the best Greek food on the loop. We finally cast off and headed up the river. We passed beneath the cannons of West Point and headed up to Saugerties Marina near Kingston for three days. Though we'd see tiny current changes due to tides until Federal Lock 1 and the Eerie Canal, at that point, we'd left the worst of the tidal currents behind.

We visited our friends Sophie and Steven from a podcast we hosted together. Sophie had us over for a great party, and Steven's family stayed with us on *Currently*. Marven, their son, even got to go out in *Currently* and "drive" from my lap while Steven and his wife, Yeli, were in the back with our dog, grinning ear to ear. We saw the Saugerties lighthouse, puttered around for an hour, and then headed back in.

The next day, we packed up *Currently*, headed through Albany and into Troy, and looked at the map. We were less

Historic Half Moon Bay on the Hudson

than a mile from Federal 1, the first lock on the Erie Canal. We stayed a couple of days, and I kicked off my final class before traveling up into Lake Champlain. We prepared to take on Kayla and her fiancé, Alex, and we again made a planning mistake. We committed to a pretty aggressive schedule so they could travel all of the way to Montreal with us. If the weather cooperated each and every day, we'd have a pretty good chance of making it, but the weather *never* cooperated.

In retrospect, I should have recognized that teaching, traveling, and hosting over that great a distance was a mistake. Traveling by boat is stressful enough with just two. Passengers, work, and schedules each add their own stress to the system. Throw in the expectations of family members without the time to communicate, and something will always go wrong.

Our problems started with *Currently*'s temperature gauge. It ran just a little hot at high speed. I could troubleshoot the problem, but it would take time. Then the winds started kicking up. We calculated that we'd lose three days to weather over the next week, too many to absorb if we wanted to reach Montreal. All the while, I was trying to juggle teaching through the bulk of the day and an off-season canal schedule with closed locks after six o'clock, so we'd have a tough time getting to where we needed to be.

In the end, we decided to slowly work our way up the lock system between classes. The Champlain Canal locks didn't work like the others we'd seen. They would hang slimy ropes from the sides. We'd pick them up, kill the engine, and keep the ropes tight as the boat moved up or down. Sometimes, the ropes had cyanobacteria. They can produce a toxin called microcystin that harms livers. Winds could easily blow the boat off the wall, but we knew we could pass the rope around a cleat for leverage. I don't mean to say that locks are miserable places. They aren't. They just have a different set of challenges and conditions to consider.

Kayla works one of many locks

After locking through to Waterford, we picked up Kayla and Alex. I was able to steal enough prep time, and the family left the boat long enough for me to focus on the class. I had great chemistry with the students, and we were able to get through all of the material we needed to. Next, we nibbled up two more locks to Mechanicville before the class started. I taught day number two, and then Alex and I fixed the temperature problem. Then the shower bilge broke. That would take at least a half hour to fix.

I crammed myself into the narrow compartment, scooping out the nasty stagnant water. Then, after cutting and burning my fingers as I spliced the wires together and heated the connection up, it blessedly ran. Two and a half hours after starting the job, I was done. I snuck into the cockpit, had what was left of the dinner, and went to bed, hungry and frustrated.

The loop can magnify family dynamics, both for better and worse. When I get frustrated and tired, I get more abrasive and lay down the law. Kayla likes to sleep in and be taken care of and is independent enough to not respond well to authority of any kind. Maggie likes guests to feel comfortable, no matter the cost. Over the next day or two, these dynamics swirled around the boat like a toxic oil slick on an eddy. Eventually, I blew up and Maggie was the target. I'd thought that Alex and Kayla weren't on the boat, but they'd heard the whole shouting match. I felt terrible. It wasn't our only fight on the loop, but it was one of only a few bad ones.

The next day, I taught the final half day. The students were in high spirits and were able to work through the final complex project. It was an important course, and we'd done well. Still, we decided to remain in one place for each of our remaining classes. We were equipped to handle classes on the move, but it put too much stress on the crew.

Along the way, we started running with Sherri and Mark on *Positive Latitude*, and it was nice to lock through with buddies. We had a number of nice dinners with the easygoing couple, and we enjoyed the company. Even with all of the people around me, for the first time on the loop I felt lonely. I'd been waking up early to get us ready to move. I taught through the day and maintained the engines after each class. I took the time that was left to prepare for class. Then, exhausted with the work of the day, I would go to bed early, and alone. Compounding the problem, I'd also been hungry, my strange dietary requirements and the hectic schedules contrasting with my ability to get enough to eat.

So we picked our way up the Champlain Canal, stopping at Ft. Edward where I brooded, once again hungry and lonely. I was also ashamed of my outburst and didn't know how to bridge the gap with my family and crew. Maggie and Kayla desperately wanted to make it to Montreal, so I put my energies into working hard enough to make it happen. This extra pressure compounded my loneliness and stress.

Right after the second to last lock of the system, our engine threw a low-coolant alarm. We asked the lockmaster for permission, pulled off, and tied to his lower wall for a while. We waited for things to cool down enough for us to add coolant. Alex and I took off the coolant lid, filled the tank, and then checked the various valves. Miraculously, I noticed that one of them was out of place. When Ryan had helped me break loose the engine anode back in Deale, his knee had switched off the return valve from our bus heater. I opened it up, we added coolant, and then headed up the river through our last lock at Whitehall. *Currently* was still running a tad high.

We pulled up to the Whitehall wall, and I went diving. I threw on a mask and fins, grabbed a rope, and dove over the side into the dirty water to remove the wad of grass from the engine intake, one last task in a day full of them. The wad of grass blocking the intake was huge. When the engine wasn't working hard, the natural spring of the branches in the vegetation pushed out, allowing enough water in to cool the engine. If we had opened up the throttle, the engine would have thrown an alarm and eventually overheated. Luckily, the gauges warned me about little problems before they turned into big ones.

Weeds from our water intake

While *Currently*'s engine was reliable, the water intake was pretty congested. Whenever the gauges told me something was off, I had to address the problem. I thought about the engine and our need to address the pressure before something blew. I could relate. I pulled Kayla aside and told her I loved her, and that I loved her mother, and that I was sorry. Then the very next morning, we headed up to Lake Champlain with light hearts and a fresh start.

Part V

Canada

Our Great Loop route took us through Canada. Because the country was closed to marine pleasure craft in 2020 and 2021, we had lots of company. Currently entered Canada on Lake Champlain, went up to Montreal via Chambly, then headed west to Ottawa and the Rideau Canal to Kingston. From there, we cruised the Trent-Severn, Georgian Bay, and the North Channel.

Most of our best days on the loop and a few of our worst were in Canada. The cruising was technically demanding, our circumstances were emotionally challenging, and we were in some of the most beautiful places on earth.

Currently's East Canadian Stops

Currently's West Canadian Stops

CHAPTER 32

We Wondered
Who Was Pranking Us

With Kayla and Alex still on board, we tiptoed through the morning routine of casting off. We'd need to get through one more lock and then more than seventy miles to make it to Montreal for their flight back to Texas. We started working on a backup plan in case the fickle Champlain springtime weather derailed us. If we couldn't make it all the way to Montreal, we'd let the visitors off in Chambly, a small town to the southeast of Montreal. The quaint tourist destination was about an hour away by car, or seven by boat if we hurried.

We went through the last of the locks, with one other boat in the chamber. Then we picked our way over the shallow river and made our way north. As the river opened up, we realized we were in Lake Champlain. I should say a few things about the management of the lake that impacted our trip. Champlain is a breathtaking glacial lake, which cuts through the hills between Vermont and New York. It's a sensitive ecological area that the park rangers vigorously protect. Due to algae blooms and invasive species, they are particularly concerned about waste tanks, hitchhiking mussels, and plants. Managing the hitchhikers was relatively easy. One of the locks in the Champlain canal went up and down several times quickly to rinse the bottom of vessels inside it. The waste tanks took more work.

To prepare our black water tank for the traversal, we were supposed to completely disable the waste discharge from the tank by completely removing a section of piping. On *Currently*, we didn't have enough access to do so. Unable to find a way to remove the last length of tubing, we decided to disconnect the discharge pump electrically and block it mechanically. I looked around for a suitable stopper and found nothing. No dowels, clamps, or fixtures anywhere on the boat seemed to fit. I don't think I could have ever imagined writing this next sentence, but here goes.

We blocked our poop tank with a champagne cork, the same one from the bottle that christened the boat. I cinched it down with every available hose clamp on *Currently*. We were quite sure we didn't want to pop that cork unexpectedly. To us, the law wasn't absolutely clear, so we didn't know if we satisfied the letter of the law. But let's be honest—if you were a ranger and you saw a champagne cork so employed, would you be able to stop laughing long enough to write that ticket? To my dying day, I will tell the story about the Champlain champagne cork.

Over the course of the next few days, we found ourselves in the pages of our history book. Benedict Arnold lost his fleet but provided the time the rebellion needed at Valcour Island. The colonials won their first victory with the capture of Fort Ticonderoga. Ethan Allen's homestead was north of Burlington. We saw these places and more, but this great glacial lake didn't need these historical markers to hold our attention.

On the loop, we mostly felt an artificial safety due to shallow depths. In many places, we'd be able to stand on top of the boat and breathe if it sank in calm weather. Other places, like the Florida Keys, we could stand *next to* our boat and keep our head over water. Not so in Champlain!

We saw depths around four hundred feet and shivered at the thought. The lake reminded me of an American version of the storied Loch Ness.

After a long day of cruising, we stopped for provisions and rest at Burlington. The town was absolutely delightful. For such a small city, it had an impressive waterfront. Also, the place reflected our own value system, with excellent shared public spaces and the preservation of small, quirky businesses. Our family came from Austin, and we all valued the Keep Austin Weird vibe. We experienced things we would not find elsewhere. Maggie and Kayla had Maple Creamies, soft-served ice cream cones with maple and a little salt. We had fire-roasted bagels. These nontraditional morsels of delight were a brilliant surprise in a town full of them.

When we were there, I reconnected with an old friend, Brian Goetz. Years ago, we'd been on a speaking tour together, and he helped to kindle in me my love of programming languages. Over a nice dinner, nearly twenty years dissolved away through the magic of the place and the people around the table. We were delighted to stay one more day to wait out the weather, but with Montreal beckoning, we needed to head on to keep our aggressive travel schedule.

As we packed up our boat early the next morning, we prepared ourselves to leave the United States for a while. We didn't know how long we'd be gone, maybe a month and maybe three. What's more, we really didn't care. I was ready to enjoy a few more days with our daughter and then rest for a bit. The three historic canal systems we'd visit would give us a place to do exactly that. When we cast off, I was feeling a little less isolated, but the tension between Kayla and me was still high. She wanted to sleep in. Of course she did. This *was* her vacation. Still, I felt an enormous amount of pressure to get folks to Montreal safely, and we butted heads a bit. I suspected she was still angry at me for the fight she'd overheard.

Brian Goetz, architect for Java, in Burlington

We headed to the top of the 120-mile lake, and then crossed the border. There was no line, no sign, and no fanfare. We saw only the thick black line on the GPS. We crossed the border and then headed up the lake a bit until we reached a tiny dock that was little more than a shed on a couple of barges and a floating dock big enough for three or four modest-sized pleasure craft. One other boat was there, but they hung out just long enough to help us tie up in a stiff breeze, and probably more so for us to help them cast off. They were a couple with a tiny craft, and the wife had only one arm. They were having a bit of trouble with the wind and getting off of the dock cleanly, so we helped. We pushed them off hard, tossed their bow line on board, and they were off.

We'd heard story after story of boats being waved through the border. We weren't so lucky. Maggie was terrified that they'd stop us and find fresh fruit or vegetables with seeds. Our few raspberries, or our meager amount of wine, or something else we hadn't considered would condemn us to whatever punishment they use for such offenses. We'd squeezed our lemons and cooked our sweet potatoes, so there wasn't anything else for them to find. They took a little while to do their inspection. Family and dog waited patiently outside while the Canadian border guards satisfied themselves that we were either who we said we were or far too smart to get caught, and then we headed off into the wind and the great white north.

A few hours up the river, we ran into a lovely system of ten locks, called the Chambly Canal. It connects Lake Champlain and the Richelieu River to the St. Lawrence Seaway near Montreal. Honestly, it was so absurdly nice that I wondered who was pranking us. We approached the first lock, and the lockmaster acted like someone who had studied history and hospitality (she had). She walked us through how to tie up in her lock and told us that we'd keep the formation with the same boats for each of the rest of the locks in the system.

At every single lock, we were asked if our plans had changed and if our visit was going smoothly. In some of the previous locks, we'd secure *Currently* using fixed lines coated with copious slime, silently suggesting gloves and a preventative course of antibiotics. On the Chambly, every lock had staff to lower each line. There was no sign of mold or slime because each line was dry, new, and sparkling white. It was all so very clean that we didn't quite know what to do.

Alex holding clean white Canadian lines

The people were also impossibly…Canadian. While we were there, we saw hundreds of people riding bikes, eating, drinking, and doing everything to watch the boat show. Since it was early in the season, there were only a handful of boats in the show, so we got questions. The French Canadians were friendly and had a hunger for all things Great Loop that we couldn't possibly satisfy. As the boats slowly lowered in the locks, we drifted down and had beautiful conversations with the locals as they took in the show.

We spent the night on a wonderful wall in the Chambly Basin. We took in the town and had a little dinner out, our first Canadian meal. Remarkably, even this small place had good vegan and gluten-free options. We'd have a pretty short day the next day, so we got to sleep in. The historic district had nine total locks, followed by an open stretch of river and an independent lock called St. Ours. The locals affectionately called it "Lock 10," and our goal was to get through the lock to park on the lower wall.

A café with "Lock 10" in French

The tension between Kayla and me remained, and it was frustrating to me. Mostly we butted heads in areas of control. When should we leave for dinner? Where would we go? Was it OK to fire up the microwave to cook a lunch when we were approaching a lock? How close to the lock would we have to be to actually care? It all sounds ridiculous, and it was. I knew I needed to relax control. Once I did so, I knew she'd relax around the important stuff. I knew this instinctively, because in many ways we are the same.

Once things slowed down and we got into the lock system, I kicked up my feet and just watched her. Alex would tell an outrageous joke and her blue eyes would sparkle as she laughed. She'd pantomime a punch, and he'd drop to the floor. From a certain angle, she looked so much like Maggie that I could barely tell the difference. After hours of relaxing into the rhythm of the locks, the bikes whizzing by, and the beauty of the countryside with the different flora and fauna, I finally let go. I pulled Kayla aside once again and told her I loved her, as she was, with no preconditions or exceptions. I couldn't tell whether she'd forgiven me for the fight she overheard, but it didn't matter. I'd let the matter go and made amends the best I could. The rest was up to her.

We departed St. Ours and headed up toward Montreal. Things got increasingly commercial, and the current grew stronger. Once we made the turn to the St. Lawrence River, we were in a constant state of shock and awe. Gone were the quaint recreational vessels of Chambly. Instead, we saw massive container ships lined up like storm troopers at Comicon, one after another. Some were moving and some were at anchor. The current was mighty, four to five miles per hour and getting stronger. Once we reached Montreal, I saw a cable ferry underway, barreling right for us. We'd need to exit right, and there was a pretty stout dock there, leaving no room to maneuver. I felt the hand on my shoulder, heard the catch phrase, "Perhaps I could be of some assistance," and I let Maggie take the wheel. She passed the ferry without issue.

Our Volvo was running at 3,000 rpm, nearly full speed, but *Currently* was creeping along at seven miles per hour. We saw our turn, and I slid back into the driver seat to handle the aggressive eddies of the harbor. This was my domain. We wheeled around sharply to break through the jet of water forming the harbor opening. Abruptly, the current slowed, and we pulled into Port D'Escale, or Old Port. This quay is a massive, recessed cutout that used to house wharfs that fed the old city, but now it houses a full modern marina and many tourist boats as well.

Docks of metal and plastic spread out around us. Everything was a portable structure on a floating dock.

Dozens of boats dotted the ribbons of docks around the edges of the quay, and even more occupied the comb-like structures that spread out across the back half of the harbor. On the other side, long ferries lined up to take diners for a dinner cruise or passengers for a waterside tour.

In Montreal, little *Currently* was not the show. We were happy to be absorbed into the greater show. Adjacent to us, the impressive circus tents of the Cirque du Soleil show were permanent fixtures. In this city, we had our best meals of the loop. We indulged in seafood, like a mussel stew, a salmon tartar, wonderful breads, and nice wines. We encountered uniquely French architecture that fit the people and the place. At long last, I had plenty of time to explore and rest.

Mussels in Montreal, my best loop meal

While Kayla was with us, she visited one of Alex's friends. Alex and his friend both taught English as a second language in Spain, and both fled the country as the United States shut down their borders due to Covid. From time to time, we joined the trio, inviting them to dine with us. The next day, Kayla and Alex departed on their flight. Conflicts aside, I was grateful that we were able to share that time in Montreal with them. It was a beautiful time, and I will remember seeing how effortlessly she glided through that place.

Mostly, we took in the Montreal way. Local shops displayed a radically different value system than we were used to. The grocery stores featured produce instead of processed foods. There were flower markets and three regular farmers markets. The public parks were among the best we encountered on the loop. There were shops for lounging and taking a sip of coffee or a cool bite of ice cream. Sidewalk bistros encroached on ample sidewalks and even the roads, and meals took hours instead of minutes.

I did practice as much French as my meager two weeks of Duolingo would allow. We'd been concerned that we wouldn't feel welcome in Quebec. We needn't have worried. The locals *did* want to see visitors invest in their ways. What we offered was enough. The French Canadians were happy to smile patiently as we tried, enjoying visitors eager to embrace their culture.

Our two days stretched out to three, then four, and even five. We settled into a long luxurious stop with great food, excellent access to the provisions that had been so hard to secure, and blessed sleep. We slept late just about every day, and our bodies adjusted to the pleasant new schedule. But while we were resting and touring, life interrupted. We were broken out of our reverie four days into our stay by a call from my sister. Mike's son had called, unable to reach his father. A few hours later, we got the call confirming what we already knew. Mike had suffered a heart attack in his sleep. He was gone.

I don't mean to minimize this moment, but the truth was that Mike had distanced himself from his family. We were sad, as we should be. We also knew that Mike had been very sick for a long time. He had come back to Chattanooga to live, five years before, on death's door. He was

Mike passed as we crossed Canada

a heart patient who had a six-way bypass. He wasn't taking his medications, and he looked like it. He healed well enough to travel to Thailand and Ukraine. Then, when Covid happened and his health slipped again, he moved back to Chattanooga. For all of these reasons, we'd known his passing while we were on the loop was a real possibility.

We felt for the two adult sons he'd left behind. Both were on the autism spectrum. We tried our best to support them over that time and to step into some of the void he'd left. Both sons, and their father as well, had visited us on the loop. We talked to them about doing a special memorial when we returned home. My sister told us not to come home; there was no reason to do so. His sons both wanted to do a memorial on the boat and were happy to wait for us to return home to do so. Other than the few family members, there just wasn't anyone else to invite.

So my sister, Maggie, and I took on the responsibility of planning a brief memorial over Zoom. We spent time with each of the boys and walked them through how their lives would change. Since each of the boys had his own job and apartment, they'd both continue to live as they had done, but with a Mike-shaped hole in their lives.

Make no mistake, some of the challenge of the loop comes from the logistics and trials from extremely diverse environments. Some of the challenges are more mundane. We are humans, and we each have our own life to live. We have imperfect relationships and lives that present challenges having nothing to do with the sea. Our loved ones live their lives somewhere far away, and sometimes they die. Mike, I'm sorry we weren't closer, but I'm glad we got to experience a bit of the loop together. Without you, Tampa Bay would have been miserable. With you and your smile, it was magical. Thank you, and I love you.

CHAPTER **33**

We Chuckled Condescendingly

When we left Montreal, Mike's death was on our minds. We were worried about his sons and a bit angry at him for not planning for this moment a little better. We felt despair because we wouldn't be home to help my sister, Cheryl. We thought about Mike's last lonely years, a self-imposed isolation.

Maggie and I struggled once again about whether or not we should go home. In the end, we decided to continue. The critical question for us was, "What could we change by going home?" In truth, we weren't going to have a funeral. Most of the details of his death would be managed from a distance. The boys needed ongoing conversations, and we could have those anywhere.

And yes, we were looking forward to the next part of the Great Loop adventure. Canada would be a great place to reflect on *his* death and *our* lives together. We trusted my sister to manage the arrangements and details surrounding Mike's death. And we all agreed that we were only a phone call away if there was a need. We continued on and looked ahead to the next phase of our voyage. Two routes were open to us, but we'd already decided where to go next.

On the loop, recommendations reign supreme. Invariably, loopers would give one of a few answers: Georgian Bay, the Trent-Severn Waterway, or maybe Florida. Kip and Insel had a different answer. We spent a few hours together touring West Point with the veterans on *Fourth Dimension*, and we asked them about their favorite places on the journey. They liked the Rideau Canal the best.

The historic waterway connects the Ottawa River to Kingston in a route roughly parallel to the St. Lawrence Seaway. Even after we had tentatively planned to go to Montreal, we'd not planned on going through that waterway, because it would take ten days to traverse, but we kept the waterway in mind in case things changed.

Weeks came and went. We wound up racing weather and schedules through the Hudson and Champlain Canal. We kept up the pace through the Chambly system, had good luck, and timed every lock perfectly. Finally, we didn't have a reason to hurry anymore. The long side trips to the Florida Keys, Lake Champlain, and Montreal were all behind us. The Trent-Severn was backed up because of flooding. We found ourselves a week or two *ahead* of schedule, so the Rideau came back into focus. We decided to take that route.

After we pulled out of Montreal, the eight knots of current that had been in our face were behind us. We were cruising at twelve miles an hour and had a fuel economy more like a sedan on a highway than our trawler. As we approached the commercial St. Lambert Lock on the St. Lawrence Seaway, we jumped onto the VHF to announce our arrival. We were immediately, gently chided for using our radio on commercial channels, as it was against Canadian protocols.

We hadn't carefully read our instructions, but we did have an appointment to lock through with other pleasure craft. We came to the lock at our regularly scheduled appointment and tied off on a little wall, hiked up a tall set of stairs, picked up a phone that would be at home in the 1970s between East and West Germany, and announced our arrival. We heard nothing else. When the lockmaster told us on the loudspeaker to cast off, we slowly approached the red signals marking our limit-of-approach. The bright red lights flickered off one at a time every few seconds, allowing us to creep forward a few dozen feet at a time. Those lights showed us precisely where to be at any given moment. Then we pulled into the lock, looked up, received a rope, and hung on as the waters rose. In true Canadian fashion, the ropes were dry, and the staff let them down only far enough to reach us, not to splash into the water. Shielded from the wind at that point, locking through was easy. So, intermingled with the big container ships, we headed down the canals of the St. Lawrence Seaway.

A ship on the St. Lawrence Seaway

With a little confidence under our belt, we approached Côte Sainte Catherine, a taller lock in a trickier crosswind. The crew in front of us had no control of their boat. Maggie and I smiled at each other, remembering the time when we were beginning boaters too. We chuckled condescendingly and waited for our turn. We didn't see karma loitering around the corner.

Maggie pulled up to the lock and promptly got blown sideways in the lock, just like the previous boat. She struggled and struggled until she felt the gentle hand on her shoulder. "Perhaps I could be of some assistance."

Then I took the helm and brought the boat in hard, only to have the line hands, several dozen feet higher, struggle to get the line down accurately to our bow. By the time Maggie had control of the boat, it had started to drift away from the wall, and our thrusters were worthless in the high crosswinds. Then the line hand dropped a line to me at the cockpit which tangled ever so slightly at the end, tantalizingly close to my extended hand. OK, karma. We deserved that.

I crept up the cockpit stairs with a fully extended boat hook. Then I reached out a little more on the rocking boat and barely snagged the line. I looped it once around the cleat and we were in business. Though we thought the boat was far from under control, the doors closed and the turbulent waters began to rise. Maggie slowly wrangled the boat closer to the wall, and we survived the lock-through in the howling winds. With our egos bruised, we exited the lock and made our way through the waves toward the mouth of the Ottawa River and headed upstream.

A short way up the river, we arrived at St. Annes, a bustling tourist town packed to the gills with pleasure craft. We pulled in to dock, barely missing a brand-new runabout on the wall. Tourists strolled in and out of the little restaurants. The lock staff told us we could go through right away if we loaded right then. With a longing glance back at the diners, Maggie reluctantly pulled out into the current, and we were on our way.

A few miles up, we stopped at Carillon Lock, after they'd closed for the day. We'd need to spend the night there, so we docked on the blue wall to signal our intent to take the next available lockage. A lovely cruiser called *Via Mer* was there for the evening. French, then. Before we could say a word, they came up, pointed to our burgee, and started a nonstop barrage of questions. They knew just enough English to befriend us and ask us about our adventure. In return for conversation and expertise, the *Via Mer* crew cooked a lovely appetizer for us to share, a salmon tartar much like the one we'd experienced in Montreal. Marc was an engineer who understood English but didn't use it every day. Josée knew just enough English to strike up a conversation. My French was still awful, and Maggie's was worse. They were new boaters and wanted to buddy boat with us up the river and into the canal. We were happy to oblige.

This lock on the Ottawa was different from the others we'd seen. The staff in the lock tied us to a floating dock, and the whole thing floated up with the water level, making traversal a breeze. Then we cast off and were on our way. We'd need to enter the upper Rideau right outside of Ottawa.

That night we anchored right outside of the Rideau system, at the waterfall with the same name. In French, Rideau means curtain, and we docked close to the water that was sheeting over stone like floating silk. We heard the roaring water in the distance, shining white in the fading hours of sunset. We launched our dinghy and took our dog ashore, followed by Josée and her dog from *Via Mer*.

The next day was the best on our entire loop. We woke up and piloted our boats into the canal, one after the next. Eight locks majestically rose into the heart of the capital city, disappearing into a scene right out of *Excalibur*. The flight of those eight locks flowed from one into the next so that they worked as one connected aquatic staircase. Each of them was operated strictly manually by uniformed staff. We waited for the signal. Rather than a horn or a loudspeaker, a staff member came down to the base and beckoned us closer. He explained the rules of the lock system and told

Our route through the Rideau waterway

us we'd go through all eight locks with *Via Mer*. They would be on the starboard side and *Currently* would be on the port. They also had some advice about how high to set each fender in each lock.

We pulled in, and lock by lock, we slowly ascended as the water poured into the chamber. This luxuriously slow voyage was our introduction to the most beautiful part of the capital complex. The cascade of waterfalls was pretty in its own right, but the Gothic and Romantic architecture slowly enveloped us as we rose up into the city. We could see the Canadian Parliament on one side and the classic picturesque castle of a modern hotel on the other. Tourists from around the world excitedly chattered to one another as our two boats rose slowly through the flight. After just over two hours, we exited the last lock and tied up to the walls for a few days in Ottawa.

Rising into Ottawa on the Rideau

We spent our first three days on the Rideau on the wall in the heart of the Ottawa capital district. The routines of the day were different in the lock chambers below and the government offices above. Our first morning there, instead of the hard work of governance, we saw the lock staff joyfully chasing a gosling from the chamber and back to mama. Another evening, we saw a red fox, the copper trickster staying just on the edge of the gardens. *Via Mer* headed down on day two. On day three, *Stray Cat* and *Currently* followed.

We made our way slowly toward Kingston, taking eight days to wander through the historic waterway. We stayed on lock walls, hanging out with boaters we knew on one wall and making new friends on another. We'd do around five locks a day. Stops like Black Rapids, Merickville, and

Smiths Falls scooted by. Then the canals broke through to marshy lakes, with huge swans flashing white, and black loons singing their mournful songs. After one lock, our engine intakes sucked in some sea grass, setting off the telltale alarm. We dropped anchor in the marsh, letting out a scant ten feet of chain. I cleared the clump of grass, and we headed on down.

As we poked down through stops at Chaffeys and Brewers, the topography changed. We traversed most of this way with *Stray Cat*. Shane and Beth are gregarious and generous and made excellent company. They were hard-working business owners from Mansfield, Texas, and the four of us had visited many of the same places. Unlike us, they were most at home at parties, especially those thrown by the hardened tow operators. We howled with laughter at the story of their experiences with the families and crew at Bobby's Fish Camp.

Stray Cat stayed behind to sample some of the rocky lakes, and *Via Mer* caught up. We called this fluid happenstance "loop frogging," the fluidity of our community as people came and went. No one became hurt or frustrated. We just moved on when we were ready and headed down the canal toward Kingston. The swampy shallows gave way to rocky splendor, with narrow channels among boulders and cliff faces. The depth gauge plunged down past one hundred feet, and we knew we were in glacial waters. Rather than individual locks, the lower Rideau had several flights of locks with tremendous dramatic backdrops. Because the chambers tended to be a little bigger, the locks and dams in this area were among the most beautiful in the whole system.

Via Mer **on the Rideau**

The navigation got more and more precise, but we found the buoys and charts were excellent. The Canadians' continuous investment in their infrastructure paid off. Whenever an official buoy broke off or an unmarked rock surfaced, the locals were more than happy to mark these obstructions with milk jugs, impromptu markers that we learned to respect. In these rocky lakes, anything less would make navigation vastly more difficult.

We cut through several dramatic gorges, and the topography became clear. From 1826–1832, the excellent Canadian engineers flooded these hills to provide an alternative supply route, should those pesky Americans rise up again and take the St. Lawrence Seaway. We could see the hilltops. Our chartplotter showed crescents of blue—tiny individual lakes between the major canals of the system.

Along the way, we'd see more cable ferries. They kept an aggressive schedule, offloading cars and taking on more in mere minutes. Timing runs between them was sometimes frustrating, especially in the many no-wake zones that limited our speed to five or six miles per hour.

Among those manual wooden locks and the dozens of mountain cottages that dotted the shores, we were transported far away from the other places and people we'd encountered. It was tempting to think of Canada as Little U.S.A. or Little Great Britain or Little France. It wasn't. The people had their own ways, the reverence for public parks was transforming, and the embrace of summer and leisure was eye opening. It was glorious to share with the people we met on the way.

When we entered Jones Lock, we found ourselves waiting alone, with no other boats in sight. We didn't mind. The area was deep green and beautiful, with a series of four locks and their associated dams, separated only by a short turn of the river. Unlike the utilitarian feel of the Champlain canals, these were all aesthetically magnificent. I struck up a conversation with the lockmaster, who was standing next to an open gate. He told me they were raising the level of the chamber for a boat with a deeper draft to go through. Boats with deeper drafts had to sign a waiver, but the lockmasters would do their best to get them through. At this moment, the valves were wide open. Valves were nothing more than paddles extending down into the water. The staff would use hand cranks to block a pipe with the paddles to stop water or open the paddles with those same cranks to let water through. By opening the valves at both ends of the lock, they could let water through to the river between the locks, and it would rise.

As we were talking, the young man told me about the locks and pointed out several of the massive blocks making up the chamber. He told me the blocks were numbered. Whenever they needed to change out a block, they took the lock apart one block at a time. Then they shaped the replacement and put it into place, restacking the wall in the reverse order, using the numbers as a guide. He told me about the rafts we'd seen from time to time along the shore. These were made up of timbers that fit together and were used to block off side channels or let more water through, depending on the needs of the waterway. Rather than diesel cranes, they'd use hand tools to move these timbers too. These solid rafts were much heavier than the docks we encountered elsewhere. They felt like concrete slabs.

In mid-conversation, the lockmaster turned the valve off. I looked at him incredulously. He had no radio and wasn't looking at any gauge. He smiled and then let me in on his secret. He'd been watching a rock on the shore. When it was covered, the chamber was full enough. Mid-conversation, he'd stolen a glance at the rock and shut the valve. For his conversation and his service as a lockmaster, we gave him a Currently Crew mug, just one more gift to someone who helped us on our journey.

A Currently Crew mug for a lockmaster

As we pulled into the lock wall at the end of our day, we tied up. As we'd seen often at other locks, families with kids were swimming off of the docks. Fishermen in kayaks were in the water. Then we saw a big cloud of smoke and an old forty-foot cruiser coming way too fast toward the kayaks and kids on the lock wall. He got the boat under control before a younger man, maybe thirty years old, leaned outside and apologized, mumbling something about a broken transmission. That night, those on the docks noticed that he was stoned out of his mind. The next morning, there was another close call with a kayak, and we could hear him screaming at the lock staff. He was obviously not right. We went through the rest of the flight with him and then took our time pulling away. We hoped the lock staff at the final lock would send him through alone.

Eventually, we got word that the man had racked up $10,000 of bills at a marina and was trying to make it to Lake Ontario before his transgressions were discovered. He made it out of the Rideau but was caught in Kingston. We didn't hear what happened to him after that, but that interaction was the only unpleasant one we had during more than a week on the Rideau.

Up ahead, a flight of Kingston locks tied four more locks together. The renegade cruiser was nowhere in sight, and we waited our lockage with three other boats. Eventually, we pulled in one after another, with *Currently* going through last, as the smallest vessel of the group. Maggie and I were silent through this last flight of locks. The Rideau had been an unexpected pleasure, and we would miss it.

We caught a bit of wind and rain, but *Currently* had no problems in those protected waters. Each of us alone with our thoughts, we pulled into our marina and tied up. We stayed briefly on the outskirts of town before moving downtown. We pulled into the marina, which had great lighthouses and castles on the bank of the first of our Great Lakes.

The Rideau is merely a side trip on the loop, but it was the best part of our trip. The culture, stunning beauty, and kindness of the locals we encountered made for an experience we will always remember. It was much more than just another day on our adventure. Though we didn't know it at the time, Canada had much more to offer. Looking out across historic Kingston, we couldn't wait to experience it.

CHAPTER 34

She Was Gone

Canada felt like Oz. Endless days of beautiful weather and slow speeds led us to a voyage in an alien and wonderful place. A short week in Kingston provided more of the same. Once we moved to the public park downtown, the incongruous mix of an old locomotive with stunning sunsets, towers rising up from the sea, and the vast Lake Ontario made for a heady mix.

Magical Kingston was once the capital city

Kingston was the third major Canadian city we visited. The old capital of Canada had all of the trappings a showcase city should: a central location, dramatic architecture, and varied culture. We spent those few luxurious days taking in the fusion of foods from French, British, and American cultures. We walked, had docktails with the dozens of loopers coming through, and prepared for the coming bash on Canada Day on the first of July.

Of all of the dishes we sampled, we loved the potato-based fish cakes the best. The mix of smoked fish dip and hash browns with nice sauces was delicious, and about as healthy as a bowlful of gravy. We rationalized that moderation would be key. We split an order the day we arrived. Then we reprised the meal to be sure we liked them, and even went back for dinner, with each of us getting our own full portions. If we went back for them a fourth time in three days, I won't admit it in writing. If my cardiologist is reading this, I'm sorry I lied to you.

At last it was Canada Day, and the holiday was everything we hoped it would be, and more. The Canadians came out in their red and white gear, just daring the tourists not to participate. Most of us found flags and T-shirts in the local stores and donned them joyously. The boaters in the marina put out flags and banners, forming a sea of red and white, backed by towers rising like fat lighthouses out of the lake. Bands playing in the park played music, both skillfully and not, in styles from around the world. We heard rock, folk, and even an expertly executed Brazilian samba. Through it all, the flags fluttered happily in the wind, and the boats in the marina swelled with more and more people in anticipation of the fireworks.

The sun settled slowly with an explosion of color, gentle winds blew, and the temperature was absolutely blissful, leaving us just slightly chilly in shorts. On either side of *Currently*, our neighbors invited more and more guests aboard, bringing back food from the nearby festival and sitting in the cockpits to wait for the fireworks show. A

The flags come out for Canada Day

South African immigrant shared a local beer with us, and we told him stories about our loop. As we sat in the cockpit awaiting the fireworks, we were curious to see how Emmy would do with them. Mostly, she was tolerant of fireworks but never really enjoyed them.

The show started with a boom and a flash. Emmy barked curiously, then joyfully as her paws popped up on the swim platform door, ears up and tail wagging as if to say, "I get it! Why didn't you say so?" She watched and barked, and we did nothing to silence her. Rather than being put out, the Canadians laughed with us, basking in her joy. The little girl in the boat next door was pointing at her and laughing. The fireworks settled down, and we got down to the floor to pet Emmy. She smiled, we smiled, and everything was good.

The next day, we cast off, content with our brief stay in Kingston. We headed off to the one highlight Great Loopers mentioned more than any other. Like the Rideau, the Trent-Severn is a waterway that stitches together a system of rivers, lakes, canals, mechanical locks, and engineering masterpieces into a beautiful and memorable experience. The 240-mile route was first imagined as a military site, like the Rideau, but by the time it opened in 1922, it was a commercial system to move timber between Georgian Bay and Lake Ontario. Today the area is almost entirely recreational. It runs from the Trent River at the top of Lake Ontario to Port Severn on Georgian Bay in the southeast corner of Lake Huron.

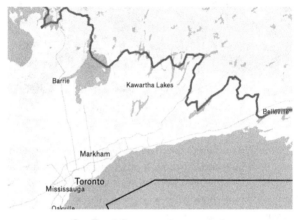

Our Trent-Severn waterway route

After Mike's passing, the challenges of his two sons facing life with their autism and without their dad slowly came into focus. One was a victim of fraud, and the other was having difficulties making ends meet in an increasingly expensive economy. Each needed his own guidance from family, but we were half a continent away. We were burdened also with a few other tensions. Because the Canada border had been closed for two years because of Covid, there were more loopers than usual. In a typical year, there would be 150 to 200 boats. This year, over 500 were making their way around the loop, and most of them took the Canadian route. Also due to Covid, Parks Canada had fewer staff to deal with the mighty hoard making their way across the country.

In Trenton, we started to encounter the crowds that we'd read about throughout the loop but had seldom encountered. During the beginning of the summer season, flooding on the Trent River shut down several of the locks, and there were other problems as well.

The Trent-Severn Twitter feed said the waterway had a backup of a couple of dozen boats at the Big Chute, a tiny overland marine railway that loaded boats onto a cable-powered railway car, went on rails over a sixty-foot hill, and unloaded the boats back down into the water. Staffing turnover and labor shortages caused a growing backlog of boats. The new staff didn't know how to safely load the plethora of boat designs without damaging them. Pod drives, stabilizers, prop shafts, and even rudders were features on boats that could bend or snag in a sling, and they varied wildly from boat to boat.

I imagined myself as a summer student from the local college taking a job at the Big Chute. I didn't know much, if anything, about boats. Then, amidst flooding conditions and backlogs, I thought about the experienced staff leaving one by one. Maybe the senior lockmaster retired, and the lockmaster in training quit, only to have the only other experienced staffer catch a bad case of Covid. I wondered what standing on that rail car would be like if a million-dollar yacht pulled up with the captain yelling at me to be careful, dang it. Then I imagined the scene playing out over and over as an unexpected backlog cleared. Would the perks of the job, like a park pass and the beautiful jobsite, be enough to lure me in, or would the angry boaters caught in a backlog, leading to stressful conditions, chase me off? That's essentially what happened to them. The staff needed to place the sling correctly, and the people who knew how to do so were in short supply. Through the backlogs, they had to keep short staff hours for retention, leading to more backlogs, and so on.

Problems at the Chute led to backups

We were reading about all of these problems, and we didn't know what would happen to the crowds once we entered the system and closed in on the Big Chute. No one did. The number of boats, Covid, and the weather made a cocktail that made the system sick, and the only thing that would make it better was time. In these circumstances, we made our way across the upper reaches of Lake Ontario. We started our journey in the Z-shaped Bay of Quinte, marvelous wetlands with a variety of birds we'd not encountered elsewhere. The only winds that could give us problems were west winds. We had west winds.

We expected waves mostly a foot or so, with some creeping up to two feet as the day wore on. That's exactly what we got. Like most lake waves, these were shorter and steeper than ocean waves, making our trip a bit uncomfortable but not dangerously so. Based on our experience over the first four thousand miles of looping, we strapped down everything that could move and hunkered down in the front seats. Emmy slept and groaned her way through it, salty dog that she was. As we approached the head of our canal system in Trenton, we broke out Nebo to see what boats were nearby. We counted more than ten boats there, and there would likely be at least that many more locals plus loopers not on Nebo. The constant stream of boats would surely add to the stress of the system.

Trent Port Marina was a huge marina, positioned at the head of the Trent River. It existed to serve the wild variety of boats visiting the waterway. We got provisions for a week and then planned our departure. We knew the locks opened at nine in the morning, so we talked with several other boats we knew about our plans to leave early in the morning. Our friends told us about their plans to either go later in the day or possibly wait a day to avoid the crowds. Based on that advice, we woke up at seven o'clock to leave at eight. As we stepped outside, our friends were leaving, waving to us. It felt a bit like cloak and dagger, and it put us behind a lock's worth of four boats.

The locks in the park system in Canada were mostly the same. There was no signal system, and they didn't respond to the VHF. Instead, parts of the wall were painted blue. Boaters on the blue line were announcing their intention to lock through. The rest of the lock wall was available for overnight stays. Some had power and others didn't, but they were mostly the same otherwise. We pulled onto the blue line, announcing our intention to lock through, and waited. As expected, our other friends were in the lock. Another boat pulled up behind us—Al and Arlene in a Kadey Krogen called *Arion*. They became our companion boat for the next three weeks of our journey. We immediately hit it off. Both had been sailors until they bought their powerboat a few years ago. Al had led a construction company, and Arlene had worked with travel agencies to plan trips. They were fabulous travel companions. That first day, we went through six locks together.

That first night, at Frankford Lock, the other boats who'd left early told us there was room for one more boat in a site with power, but we declined. We decided to travel with *Arion* for a while. We had dinner together in the Kadey Krogen—salmon from the grill and a marvelous salad. They traveled with higher-end dinnerware, with napkins and a nice tablecloth. Such luxuries were for bigger boats, not tugs like *Currently*. We talked for hours about our loops, our lives, and our families.

The rhythm of the canal system turned out to be much like the ones we'd experienced before. We got used to full locks, entering and exiting the locks quickly, as directed by the lock staff. After the Rideau, we'd learned to handle the cable systems well. In the Trent-Severn, the tie up systems were a bit different.

These locks had several different tight cables running from the bottom to the top of the lock. Boats would loop fixed lines from their own boat around the lock cables. Then the crew could hold their boat against the lock wall by pulling the free end tight. In the Trent-Severn and Rideau, we'd wrap one such cable on our bow and the other on the back of the boat.

With one boat in the lock, the other boats would come in one by one, per the lockmaster's instructions. Sometimes we'd tie to the boats already in the locks, a system called rafting. Since we were familiar with *Arion* and we trusted each other, most of the time we were loaded in the same way for an entire day. With the boats tied side to side, either Maggie or I would talk to Arlene in the cockpit, and we got closer still. After seven locks and twenty-five miles, we pulled up for the second night on the Cambellford town wall.

There's a certain comforting sameness of life on the locks, and it's comforting and restful. We'd left the bad weather behind, and the six-mile-per-hour pace was comfortable and nice. We'd let *Arion* pull into a lock and let them collect the lines from the lockmasters to pull their forty-one-foot trawler to the side of the lock. Then we'd pull in beside and tie our boat to *Arion*. The routine was the same each time, and the boats we traveled with were also mostly the same since passing boats was rare.

On the third day, that sameness was shattered. Emmy had a seizure in one of the locks. She was standing at one moment, and then she froze up hard and keeled over hard, like a sack of cement. She then lost control of her bladder. I was manning the lock line, so the best I could do at the time was to wrap the rope around a cleat, hold on with one hand, and comfort her with the other as the rope slid up the cable. It was heartbreaking. She was laying in her own excrement, and this loyal dog *hated* to make a mess. She didn't understand what was happening to her, so we cleaned her up, carried her inside, put her on a towel, and as we moved up the river, we loved on her when she was awake. It was all we could do.

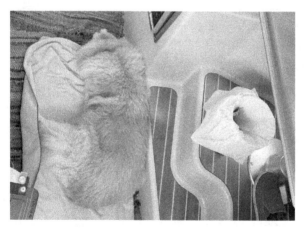

Emmy hurting after her seizure

We rose up within the lock, and the wonderful staff told us where to find a vet. Throughout the rest of the day, it became clear that Emmy's time was near. Our home vet, our daughter in vet school, the vet on *Dog House*, and local vets all confirmed what we already knew. Emmy was in pain, and she would not get better. We would have to find a place to put her down. As we continued down the river,

I held my own emotions in for Maggie so she could have time to cry, and plan, and spend her last day with Emmy.

Loopers loved Emmy, and news travels quickly, so it was no surprise that when we docked at Hastings, there was a space for us prepared on the busy wall and boaters to help us tie up. Everyone there offered to help, but what could anyone really do? Ken on *Knot Fantasea* offered to buy us dinner, while other boaters knelt with Emmy and made her comfortable. This was community, brought together by our humanity, and it touched us.

Maggie made arrangements to take a local taxi to the closest vet in Peterborough, about an hour's drive away. Emmy was in pain, so it was worth it to find an after-hours clinic to put her down instead of saving a couple of bucks and make her wait through the night. In that foggy reality that encroaches in stressful situations, we silently held hands over Maggie's shoulder in the taxi. I was in the back of the three-row van with Emmy and Maggie in the middle. I couldn't see her tears, but I knew they were there. I heard the raspy voice of the driver telling stories that didn't really register, a light cough of maybe uncomfortable grief through a mouth blessedly covered by a mask. Emmy's shallow breathing and low moans told us everything we needed to know. She was dying and hurting.

We pulled up at the vet. Due to Covid protocols, or maybe safety, we had to wait outside while the vet was preparing to see us. There were a few chairs, and a cooler labeled "Drinks. Please help yourself" offering little comforts. Sadly, it was empty, but then we were too.

We spent a bit of time with her at the vet, and the staff were lovely. The doctor saw her quickly, agreed with the diagnosis, and gave us some time with her. Then she put in the IV, looked at us for the silent signal, and I nodded. The IV opened, Emmy's breathing slowed, then relaxed, and she was gone. Our tears came and didn't stop for a good long while. We opted not to have an urn filled with

The empty cooler at the vet

ashes. No piece of mere pottery could fill the void or give us the comfort she did, so we didn't even try.

Not many people will understand this, but Emmy's death hit me harder than my brother's did. Maybe saying all of this makes me a bad person, but I don't think so. Emmy and I had daily interactions. I had not had a close relationship with my brother for over thirty years. He had moved away from our family, and we wouldn't hear from him for years at a time. He came home at death's door, and there was a distance that we were never able to close because we were slowly saying goodbye. Any one of three or four serious conditions could kill him, and Mike wasn't willing to take the medications to give him a chance. I don't think he had a death wish. He just didn't like to listen to his doctors, and we all knew it would eventually kill him. It's hard to build a relationship in those circumstances.

We drove back to Hastings heavy with grief. We weren't hungry and we were emotionally and physically exhausted, so we readied for bed. We shuffled our feet to avoid a dog that wasn't there, and we saw her food bowl, or leash, or bed. Having slept restlessly, we woke up the next day and continued on. We drove through beautiful Rice Lake. At thirty miles, the lake wasn't particularly long. It also wasn't deep. It was nice, though. With space to just be and grieve, we followed *Arion* at a slow, steady pace.

The Trent-Severn was nice, but it never quite measured up to the Rideau. Whether the crowds, the circumstances, or our expectations, we never found the same level of connection with people and places as we found on the Rideau. I don't mean to say the experience was a negative one. The towns and landscapes were beautiful, the people friendly, the staff wonderful.

Maybe it's because we did the Trent-Severn after the Rideau. Thinking back, of course that would be true. We saw many times the traffic, which made resources like access to power and water more difficult. Emmy had just died. We had the circulating anxiety about the Big Chute and constant rumors about its opening and closing, sometimes several times in a day. Whatever the reason, the voyage was nice but not to the level of some of our other experiences in Canada.

We pulled into Peterborough in a fog of sadness and stayed for a couple of nights. Our many friends came by to give condolences. We were sad, but we spent our days walking with Al and Arlene anyway. There, we also met up with two long-awaited Instagram friends on *Tortue de Mer*, Mike and Bobbi. We all walked to the famous Lift Lock 21, two detached elevators full of water that moved boats up or down sixty-five feet in mere minutes. Water, the only power in the whole system, operates the gates for boats and the valves that let water in and out of the chambers to move the seven-foot hydraulic rams. Like locks elsewhere, water and gravity provided the real lifting and lowering power.

The Peterborough Lift Lock

I'd been in elevators, and I understood how they work, but the scale of this lock was incredible. Walking up to see this lift on foot was absolutely the right way to experience this engineering marvel. We were able to walk around and see it from every angle. We could see the huge hydraulic rams that tapped deep into the earth and powered the beast.

After a couple of days, we were ready to leave Peterborough. Still distracted and lacking a disciplined checklist, we began to drive off with power attached. Our dockmates screamed out a warning, and we pulled back in before we did any damage to the power tower or our boat's electronics. Then we cast off properly.

We tied up at Lock 20 immediately downstream of the Lock 21 lifts about an hour before it opened. Then we got out to walk around while the lock staff arrived. As we climbed the stairs to the lock chamber, a strange site spread out in front of us. The whole section of river between the lift and Lock 20 was almost empty, only the barest trickle running through. I did a double take. How could a river just evaporate? The always informative staff told us we'd have to wait four hours or more for the canal to fill up again. The station was beautiful and we had nice positions on the wall, so we didn't mind.

The whole river was drained dry

As we waited, we talked to the lockmasters and listened from a distance. Once they'd opened the upstream valves, they could only wait too. We heard several different stories about what had happened. One of the staff thought someone had come in under the cover of darkness and opened the downstream lock valve, perhaps a prankster or a disgruntled employee. Another thought perhaps the staff was overworked and made a mistake. In any case, there was nothing to do but wait.

As we talked to the staff, we heard what we suspected. The number of boats and the delays were taking their toll on the staff. They wouldn't tell us so directly, but we overheard the truth. To us, this staff was tremendously supportive in difficult circumstances. Boaters are generally good people, but throw enough money at some folks and entitlement can creep in. We don't always treat people as well as we should.

We walked back to the boat to get some lunch and then wait. Still distracted, as I cooked some salmon on the boat's grill a brief grease fire started, but we quickly put it out with some quick thinking and the help of a pan lid from Bobbi on *Tortue*'s bow behind us. I was sure the good citizens of Peterborough would be happy to be rid of me, the distracted walking disaster cursed with dying pets, empty locks, and fires. Through the next six hours, the staff waited as the river between the locks slowly filled. Eventually, they locked us through. We went through the lift locks and marveled at the silent speed of our rise in the lift. The surreal experience broke me out of my fog, and we laughed for the first time in a while as the ground fell away beneath us and we rose to the upstream side.

Currently **pulls into the lift**

As we worked our way through the waterway, the locks got progressively taller and the scenery more dramatic. Over the next few days, we got our groove back. The locks were invariably lovely. Often, the locks would occupy splits in the river, with the lock on one side and picturesque waterfalls on the other. Unlike in the United States, the lock machinery was left for the evening with no more than a padlock to protect a few miles of river from being drained dry by a prankster or, worse, by someone doing more than opening a lock gate. We passed locks at Lakefield, then Buckthorn, with bald granite rocks, churches, and quaint villages.

Next was Bobcaygeon, the busiest of the walls on the Trent canal system. As we approached, *Arion* called with the interesting news. He'd spotted a unicorn, two free spots on this wall with power. We decided this was an omen too good to pass up. We pulled in, though many of the restaurants were closed for the day.

We hung out enjoying the rocky river bubbling nearby and the people show of looping trawlers and locals in pontoons or speedboats. The speedboats we saw were much smaller than the ones we encountered in the United States, because of the shallow drafts and rocks throughout the system. We did a round of docktails, and I started feeling bad. I silently feared what must be true after the hour cab ride in Peterborough with that nice man with a scratchy cough. I took a Covid test, and it was positive.

Susan and Theresa on *Masquerade* asked if there was anything they could do, but nothing could help us but time. Maggie talked to Al and Arlene and told the older couple they didn't have to worry about us, but they didn't leave us. They knew Maggie was concerned and that I was a high-risk case, so they stayed close. We kept our isolation on our own boat and slept in different compartments, but we kept running with *Arion*, our friends and security blanket.

This first positive test was a big deal for us. The more data we saw when Covid broke out, the more I was convinced it would eventually kill me. The kinds of people who were getting badly sick had the same comorbidities I did: heart disease, high blood sugar, and pulmonary disease.

I was modestly overweight. I wasn't old or black, but I had almost all of the other issues on the CDC list of high-risk people. Our great hope was that our vaccines would provide some protection and that our isolation in 2020 and 2021 had bought us time for medicine to evolve and remedies to be developed. At least, we hoped so.

We thought a bit about what we would have to do if my case turned ugly. We had trappings of civilization with towns, boats, and crowds of people but none of the infrastructure that could help us, like major hospitals or grocery delivery services. A massive crowd of boats was working the way down the waterway, making the competition for resources tough. No power meant no air conditioning. None among that wave of loopers had anything on board that could help us if my case turned south. There was a backlog of boats at the Chute, between us and the kind of hospitals that could help us.

In the end, we reasoned that our fears were mostly based on a little line on a testing strip. We had data on our side because we'd stayed on top of our vaccinations. To date, vaccines had kept Covid patients out of the hospitals and morgues. We called our doctor at home to keep him posted on my status. We decided to keep moving down the canal slowly, picking our way toward the large city of Midland at a relaxed pace. We'd quarantine on the move, allowing plenty of time to rest. We'd suck it up and try to tamp down our fear.

CHAPTER 35

Shake Me Off
This Board Game

After I tested positive for Covid, Maggie moved into our tiny midberth cabin, and we picked our way slowly down the river. The space was small, but dark and comfortable for sleeping. Maggie did most of the driving as we continued our journey. This first bout with Covid left me with an unrelenting middling fever around 101 or so.

We opened up every window on the boat. We'd read that aside from vaccines, ventilation and masks were the key to keeping a case isolated, so that's what we did. Between locks and on the walls through the day, I slept. I must have slept sixteen hours that first day, every minute that I wasn't eating, docking, or locking. We moved twenty miles or so up three locks over four hours to a lovely station called Rosedale.

After the first few days, my symptoms began to fade. More and more, I would sit across the boat from Maggie with both of us double-masked and all of the windows and hatches open. As we worked through the lock system, we read about a cruise ship called the *Kawartha Voyageur*. The ship alone was interesting enough in its own right. It had a bow that folded up and was shaped to have exactly the right dimensions to make it through the locks in the system, including the massive lift locks in Peterborough behind us and Kirkfield in front of us. We would have another reason to care as well.

Where Peterborough lifted us up, Kirkfield lowered us down. Once we were through, the topography became more rugged at the west end of the system, cutting the canals that crisscrossed through the alpine lakes. That led to waterways that were both narrower and more jagged, thus more demanding and less forgiving. After we saw the various cuts near Severn, we laughed at our earlier concerns about Rock Pile in South Carolina.

Boats weaving through the Cut

We went through the Kirkfield lift locks, every bit as impressed with the down-bound lift, which was just a few feet shy of the Peterborough locks. Ken on *Knot Fantasea* told us to be careful at a particular cut, especially if the River Cruise *Kawartha Voyageur* was nearby. In fact it *was* nearby. The Kirkfield staff told us that the Talbot Lock would keep us in the downstream chamber for an hour or two so the cruise ship could pass us all at one time, just downstream of the lock.

We descended in the lock and were told to tie off and make ourselves comfortable. We ate lunch and chatted between boats, marveling at the coolness of eating in the lock chamber and the excellence of the waterway management. We ate outside with me on the bow to keep my distance from the healthy folk. The lock chamber doors were open, so we could enjoy the breeze and the view while we ate. At the appropriate time, the lock staff told us it was time to go. They told us exactly where the canal was wide enough to safely pass the *Voyageur*. So a lock's worth of boats lined up like baby geese behind mama *Arion* and picked our way down. The spot looked nice and wide when we saw it on the map, but when we got there, it was choked with weeds. Al on *Arion* seemed to pick the perfect place, but I discovered a nice little patch particularly snarled with weeds and exposed to wind. I sat brooding while every weed on the river slid toward my prop, wrapping it tighter and tighter. Any weed scraps that were left immediately made a beeline to my engine intakes.

After I had successfully collected the weeds from the river, the majestic *Kawartha Voyageur* cruised on by, breaking radio silence by thanking us for cooperating. We were stunned with the uniquely Canadian experience. We'd never had such a pleasant encounter with a commercial craft. We could see the whole cruise ship up close, with the bow that folded up and the two levels of windows around the boat. Visitors came from around the world to travel on this waterway, and the cruise ship was a great way to absorb the magic but give the tedious details away to someone else. It was probably more like a country bed and breakfast than a ship. I waved and smiled but also gritted my teeth, knowing I would be cutting the vines free from my prop with my body's internal temperature regulation fighting against the chill of the river, one last bit of misery extracted from my bout with Covid.

We make room for the *Kawartha Voyager*

Less than two months later, the forty-five-passenger cruise ship would be headed up the Kirkfield lift lock, on its way to Peterborough. At that time, the lock gate would malfunction, releasing water when and where it wasn't supposed to. The *Voyager* would be brought back down in the chamber, and water would pour over the top of the upper pool onto the rocking *Voyager* below, and from there to the downstream canal. No one would be hurt, but Parks Canada would evacuate the ship and close down the waterway through Kirkfield for a while. We didn't have any hint that anything would be wrong with the lock or the *Voyageur* as we slipped down the waterway.

With the floating country inn safely behind us, Al announced our traversal of the narrow canal on VHF, hopefully to warn any approaching vessels of our presence. The cut was gorgeous but exceedingly narrow. We could see the sharp, jagged edges of the canal beneath the surface, no more than ten feet to either side. I could feel the wobble of the prop announcing our herbaceous stowaways around the prop shaft, but it wasn't so bad that we'd need to stop. We locked through Portage Lock, number 39, and then at Thorah, where we stopped to spend the night.

We tied up, and then I dove into the cold water. My fever must have been completely broken at that point, because the water temperature didn't mess with my internal temperature at all. We had docktails that evening, keeping a good eight feet downwind from our friends on *Arion*. We agreed to stay one night and then continue to nibble our way down the river.

As we moved through the waterway, we learned more about the backlog of boats at the Big Chute in front of us. As we progressed from lock to lock, the Canadian Parks staff revealed information slowly, encouraging boaters to slow down earlier in the system to avoid adding to the congestion ahead. They were trying to conceal the overall situation so they didn't cause panic, but the staffing and skill problem was worthy of concern. Most of the locks in the system worked the same from one boat to the next. The locks didn't care whether a boat was a fifty-four-foot power catamaran or a twenty-five-foot tug. If the boat could fit through the doors of the lock, they'd tie themselves to the wall and go through. The lockmaster had to know only how many boats could fit into the chamber.

The Big Chute was different. It was a rail car, positioned at an angle. Vessels would pull onto the car, the front of the boat would rest on the front of the car, and a sling would hold the back of the vessel. This rear sling was the problem. When I first started boating, I had no idea about the complexity of modern boats beneath the water line. Propellers had shafts that could be many feet long. Stabilizers looked like wings that jutted out beneath a boat.

Pod drives were increasingly popular, and every new year bought new features and, with them, more cost and complexity. This type of propulsion mounted a gearbox and drive beneath the boat, much like the gears on a bike. Pod drives were much more flexible than alternatives, allowing boats to be controlled completely by a joystick. The downside was that river bottoms or systems like marine lifts or the Big Chute could easily damage them. That meant that the marine railway's operator had to know about what was happening below the waterline. The year 2022 brought staff turnover through retirement, floods, Covid-19, and record numbers of boats, so the needed expertise to load the railway was in short supply.

The staff didn't want to talk about how bad the backlogs were, but we got better and better at asking the right questions. The Big Chute was Lock 44, and the backlog of boats at its peak had covered all locks all the way back to Lake Simcoe between locks 41 and 42. Marinas were full, and facilities were stretched to their breaking points. Some boats waited weeks. The staff was on the verge of working through the backlog on weekdays, but on weekends the short staff would all go home to get much needed rest, and the backlogs would begin anew. We also learned that simple boats with short lengths or skinny beams could go through. With this information in hand, we decided to inch down the waterway. With my Covid, we didn't want to move fast anyway.

I woke the next day feeling good. I still couldn't focus for long, but with major Covid symptoms mostly behind us, we were two days away from the Big Chute. We had about forty miles and three locks to travel to wrap up the waterway. We'd see what was ahead of us at the Chute, but rumors were more and more promising as we got closer. We also gave Maggie daily tests, and I tried to keep as isolated as I could. We kept all the windows open, and I would wear a mask whenever I wasn't in the cabin. Before too long, we were following *Arion* through the narrow Lake Simcoe inlet.

We ran three hours through Lake Simcoe and off the main channel. The entrance to the lake from the canal had a slightly hysterical sign about potentially hazardous conditions. I guess it made sense, but considering that the lake was between Lake Ontario and the frightening Lake Huron, it seemed like a bit much. It was also stone-cold beautiful, the way Alaska is beautiful. The deep blues and greens were foreshadowing what we expected to see in Georgian Bay. We saw our first deeper waters in a while as well.

Lake Simcoe is sometimes violent, but wasn't for us

We cut across from the east end of the lake to a bay on the north end, called Ojibway, and pulled into a marina of the same name. I was in this weird quarantine state, having mostly bounced back from Covid and being outside of the U.S. standards for finishing my quarantine but still inside of the full ten-day Canadian parameters. To respect their laws, I continued to shower on the boat, stayed away from others, and socially distanced with others outside when possible.

I spent the time walking a bit, working up my endurance, and sleeping. Oh, and more sleeping. Sometimes, I would sleep up to sixteen hours in a day. Those days, Maggie did the lion's share of the driving, and I would come out to help with locks, wearing a mask for any interactions with the lock staff.

Through all of this, *Arion* continued to stay with us, and we'll be forever grateful. We would continue to do docktails with them, and Maggie would walk with them when we stopped in towns or on hiking paths at the walls. Other loopers, too, offered to help any way they could. Through Emmy's death, Mike's death, and the bout with Covid, we had all the help we could ask for and more. We didn't start the trip with lifelong friends, but we sure did accumulate some along the way.

In the morning, the last day of running through the Trent-Severn stretched out before us. Covid was gone save the lasting remnants, a periodic dry cough and a bit of lethargy. Our last day would have just over thirty miles and three locks, around six luxurious hours. We expected some of the prettiest cruising country in the world, and we were not disappointed. Lake Simcoe melted into the bay and jagged coastline with a canal cut, marked with the land-based triangles and squares that the Canadians used to highlight common canal openings and such.

From there, we went through a picturesque canal, with cottages along the deep-green banks, each one with sprawling decks and omnipresent red Adirondack chairs. The interplay of those dominant colors was like bright-red berries on holly. It felt like hospitality. We locked through at Couchiching, the last lock built on the system. It was a big lock, and a fast one. Then the canal opened up into Sparrow Lake, an exceedingly beautiful and rocky place with narrow channels, lots of shallow-bottom boats, and lots of homes dotting the channels. The uneven lakeshore sprawled all over the maps, unlike the valleys below. This was flooded high country, one of those few manmade creations that must have rivaled the original country.

As we thought about the lake around us, we imagined rocks and channels like these but open to the elements. That's what we were expecting in Georgian Bay. This place was rural, but Georgian Bay was downright remote. We hoped against hope that Maggie wouldn't contract Covid, and after about five days it seemed possible.

After we went through Sparrow Lake, we all extolled the virtues of life in beautiful country at ten kilometers per hour. The big trawlers were increasingly replaced by pontoons, jet skis, and tiny speedboats. Many of the speedboats were the jet-boat types that had less beneath the waterline to break off on a rock or root. They seemed built for this place. We went through giant Swift Rapids Lock, the only one we saw with floating bollards. We fit into the lock with at least a dozen tiny craft. It's perhaps the only time on the loop that *Currently* felt *big*. We dropped nearly fifty feet, let the traffic clear, and headed on our way.

From there, we nibbled our way among rocky, uneven channels, deep greens broken by cottages, businesses, side passages, and house-sized boulders. Eventually, all of this opened into a small body of water leading to a couple of long docks. We saw two sets of railroad tracks, which just disappeared into the water. These were the Little and Big Chutes. The little one was no longer in operation, so we shifted our gaze to the big one. We didn't see at all what we expected. We tied off at a long, shallow dock. I masked up and then we all stepped out onto the dock to take stock of the situation.

***Currently* on the Chute railcar**

We'd arrived on a Saturday. They must have done a great job of communications and dealing with the backlog, because we could see only two other boats here. At the lockmaster's booth, no one was home. That made sense; they were short-staffed and wanted to focus on getting boats through. We walked back outside, and I saw the marine railway car come over the hill. I was glad my mask was on, because I just stared, dumbfounded.

The Chute was a mix of Japanese anime, steam punk, and old west tech. It was not the technological marvel I'd been led to expect. It looked like a flatbed car with an engine, mounted about ten feet high, that spooled a cable. Underneath were a series of arms and levers to keep the boats roughly level as the cart wobbled over the hill. On closer inspection, I could see a track within a track, making it possible for the device to index the level of one set of wheels against the other.

To be honest, the device freaked me out the way that Fleet Week did. I could see why you'd want someone experienced to load it, and how it would be progressively harder to fabricate parts for this thing as it aged. We talked to the…lockmaster? Load master? Rail master? Engineer? Conductor? She told us that the big boats had to stay, but the little ones could go. We decided that it would help with the backlog if *Currently* went through. I'd pull on my big-boy pants, load *Currently* on the train, and then we'd stay overnight on the docks below.

I'd like to say I wasn't scared, but that would be a lie. We were sitting on the bow of our rattling boat with just enough angle to make me wonder if the device would shake me off of this board game like one of those 1960s plastic linemen on a vibrating electric football field. Maybe they hadn't tested this particular mix of pants and fiberglass, and maybe I was destined to be the first man ever to survive Covid and Fleet Week only to be run over by his own boat on a marine railcar. To fool my crew, I laughed, recorded video, and did all of those things a sane person would do in this moment. When we reached the water and started to float, I didn't even shout "Thank You Jesus!" Instead, I looked at Maggie, and said, "Shall we?"

The staff held our lines until we were in position to leave. Maggie centered the wheel, I gathered the lines, and we were off to park at the docks a few hundred feet down-stream. We switched roles because the parking job was particularly tight, not because there were too many boats but because two jet skis were docked at precisely the right intervals to keep everyone else off of the dock. Someone was even on one of the jet skis reading, without offering to help in any way. I resolutely slid the boat between them and turned the boat off. Then I nudged the jet ski with the swim platform as I slid it back into position on the cleats. The passenger looked up, mumbling "sorry" and then sliding the jet ski a couple more inches down the dock. It was a weird interaction, and we giggled about it for a long while afterward.

We had ice cream with *Arion* and another boat and then headed off to go through the last lock. Port Severn marked the end of the Canadian canal system. The whole Canadian public parks system was amazing to behold. Their kindness and respectful attitudes were stereotypically Canadian, and that's one of the greatest compliments I can offer. They treated us (and every other boater) as royalty, engaging with us with one thoughtful conversation after another. We contemplated the place, the people, and our own situations back home. We wondered out loud about how to bring this Canadian hospitality into our home.

We picked through the last of the canals and approached the open waters of Midland Bay on Lake Huron. These little channels were tricky, but nothing like what we had navigated through the shallow waters of the canals. The channels looked like they'd been laid down by drunken sailors, but the truth was simpler. The channels were just confusing, but the clear charts and buoys made them easy to handle, even with visible rocks all around us. Before we knew it, we were pulling into the dock in Midland. As if on cue, Maggie's head began to hurt and she sneezed. We didn't need a test. Maggie had Covid.

CHAPTER 36

Here We Go Then

Certain places on the Great Loop compel healthy respect, if not outright fear. Georgian Bay was near the top of that list for us. The bay was so remote that our tow insurance would be worthless, and we'd need to go for days at a time without seeing a port of call. The channels were sometimes exposed and difficult to navigate. The narrow and winding small-ship channel we'd favor had a rock bottom rather than the sand or mud we'd seen most other places. It was also a Great Lake, meaning the waters would often be exposed to wind and waves that had been absent so far in Canada.

I remember as a kid, I would swim in the warm waters of the Gulf of Mexico. A few days before we left, I saw the movie *Jaws*, over the protests of my parents and siblings. When I was in the water with my dad, I looked around at the surf as a four-and-a-half-foot boy in three feet of water, jumping up on my toes as the waves rolled in. I asked how I could *see* a shark if one were there in the turbulent, murky waters. My dad said, "I guess you couldn't." About that time, something brushed against my leg. I threw both arms in the air like I'd been shot, throwing a sprig of seaweed high into the air, to the delight of everyone around me. Maggie had a similar fear of the Great Lakes. They were big and untamed, putting her on edge. We needed a good boat buddy, and *Arion* was a perfect companion.

As a small boat, *Currently* was not bound by the same restrictions that delayed bigger boats. We were able to clear the lock on the weekend, but *Arion* couldn't get through until Monday morning, when they cruised through the last of the canal to meet us in Midland. Our buddies would be with us when we hit the remote, open waters.

In many ways, Midland was Bobcaygeon in reverse. Maggie had Covid, and I was clean. I did the shopping, and when I could talk her into it, the cooking. I bought local fish and local produce. I still remember some yellow plums that Arlene found. They were perfectly ripe and on sale, so we bought scores of them. They seemed to have a separation of tart and sweet that blended together in each bite.

Back on board, Maggie had a moderate fever and felt terrible for a day or two. She had a constant headache and pain in her back and shoulders. Her ears hurt. We pondered the prospects of jumping into the great isolation of Georgian Bay and the risks of Maggie's virus getting worse. Still, Maggie didn't have the same comorbidities I did, and she never developed more serious symptoms. All of our consternation was unnecessary. As with my case, her vaccines did the hard work of keeping the worst of the virus away. As quick as the symptoms came, they faded away.

Near the end of our time in Midland, Maggie decided that she was on the mend. Arlene too had a headache but never developed a positive test or severe Covid symptoms. *Arion*'s crew, too, was fully vaccinated. After a day or so, the two boats got together and talked from each end of a long picnic table. We paid close attention to the weather reports, which predicted poor traveling conditions for the first time in weeks. Of course they did. We noticed a pretty serious blow coming in and predictions of relatively high waves out in the open bay after that. Wind direction would not be in our favor until we reached the top of the bay. We'd

Trent-Severn through Midland Bay

have to carefully pick our way through, staying in the lee of the many islands.

As a longtime sailor who had done similar trips many times before, Al was a tremendous asset in route planning. We would take the small-ship channel in short segments. The route was the most popular one through the great bay, but there were thousands of variations to consider. We'd leave soon to take advantage of a short weather window for crossing Midland Bay. One of his skills was identifying good anchorages with the right kind of protection. If a storm was blowing out of the west, we wanted cliffs or trees on the west side to tame the winds, and rocks or islands on that side to block the waves.

We did the last of our preparations, and soon enough, we glided slowly into a packed Frying Pan Bay. The skillet-shaped formation was a great place to wait out a storm because it was protected from the wind in nearly every direction.

We wait out the storm in Frying Pan Bay

Currently was lucky enough to get one of the free docks in the park system. Protected almost 360 degrees by the frying-pan-shaped bay, the anchorage made an excellent place to wait out the expected high winds. Through it all, Maggie would sometimes slip back into the midberth to sleep through the ubiquitous fatigue.

The next day, we cast off and *Arion* pulled up their hook. We nibbled our way up Georgian Bay, the land of thirty thousand islands. We followed the small-ship channel, a route built for ships of seventy feet long or less. Truthfully, I didn't know how such long boats could navigate these skinny channels, which had dramatic turns between them.

The buoys were plentiful and sometimes confusing, but here's the thing. They were *true*. We knew exactly where to be and where not to be. Each buoy was right where the charts said it should be. It struck me that though we were dealing with shallow channels full of granite and many sharp turns, these channels were easier to navigate than the shifting channels of the ICW.

Then we thought about our Covid experience, and the questionable buoys based on policies that may or may not be based on science. Did masks protect us or not? Was hydroxychloroquine an effective remedy or not? Did vaccines work or not? Institutions like the CDC and the evening news once kept us off the rocks of polio and smallpox. Those were the red and green buoys of our lives.

Maybe this thinking is out of place or hyperbolic, but I don't think so. I just knew it wouldn't be possible to navigate Georgian Bay without trusting these buoys and the people that laid them. I also know that the world would be a worse place without the vaccines that have eradicated scores of serious diseases. In the end, truth matters. No electronic chart could be a hundred percent reliable. I needed the buoys to tell me where it was safe to be.

We spent two nights in Wani Bay. We puttered around the little anchorage in our dinghy, our electric motor silent against the drone of Al's outboard. There wasn't really anywhere to hike, but there was also nowhere to go. We hung out on our boats during the day, met for our socially distanced docktails in the evening, and had one last planning session. Then we went back to *Currently*, ate dinner, and watched the sunset.

Remoteness and bare stones of Georgian Bay

Sadly, it was time for us to part ways with *Arion* too. We had two meetings ahead of us. We also had a planned stay with our friends of twenty-five years, Rich and Carol Keith in Mackinaw City, and we had a service appointment in Holland, Michigan. As we were planning the next day on the water, Al brought out a stack of charts. It looked like he already knew every inch of them. He pulled out one in particular and told me about it.

"Do you see this chart, Bruce? Look at this turn here. It's a turn of 270 degrees. And look at this area here. It's almost too skinny for my boat. The sailing captain I know wadded his chart up and threw it in the trash. He told me he'd never run this section."

Then he pointed out Hangdog, the name on the channel on the chart. I told myself that Hangdog looked pretty miserable for *Currently* as well, especially with the expected waves over the next few days. We looked at other charts like that one and poured over options for anchoring or mooring. Eventually, Maggie and I decided on Wrights Marina in Britt. Arlene and Al said to look for them in case something changed, circling a couple of options for *Arion*'s next stop on the map. We said goodbye, so grateful for our time with them, and mournfully motored the dinghy back to *Currently* through growing waves.

The next day, we picked up our anchor and fell in behind *Arion*. A couple of hours later, we passed Henry's, a fried-fish restaurant on most loopers' lists. We passed Al and Arlene. They set their autopilots and waved to us out of their side door. We smiled through the lumps in our throats. Or maybe it was Covid.

We opened up the throttle and immediately threw a high temperature warning. We told *Arion* we'd see them later, backed off on the throttle, and looked for a place to remove the wad of grass we knew was seated beneath *Currently*'s hull. We went back to Henry's and saw a twenty-nine-foot, blue-and-tan Ranger Tug, just like ours. They were *Magnetic North*, and they had a bright-white burgee on front. They helped us tie up, and within the first two minutes, I dove over the side to pull out the grass before Henry's asked us to leave. I plucked out the wad of grass, and as we pulled out, we noticed *Magnetic North* falling in behind us.

Leaving Wani Bay

We cruised north up the meat of Georgian Bay. As the two tugs headed across Perry Sound, we established communication on a secondary VHF channel, and the weather picked up. We found ourselves looking at a variety of inlets with seas up to just under two feet, and higher outside of the thin, rocky islands that provided an extra helping of churn without shielding us from the higher winds out on the bay. We agreed that we needed to cut inside, so we picked an inlet on the map.

Hangdog Inlet, our most intense Canadian day

The initial buoys were easy to see. White froth rimmed the characteristic orange rock famous in the bay, lightened a few shades by the glare on the water. Some bigger buoys and markers were visible far away and were easy to follow at first, but they rapidly got closer together in a jumble of concentrated evil. That grouping of buoys marked a hairpin turn. We spun around it almost 270 degrees, an inverted Nike swoosh terminated with a foamy tail of waves washing up on a slanted rock. At that point, I saw the name flash by on the chartplotter: Hangdog Channel. I let out a "Shit." I tapped the glass, and rather than tightening up, Maggie smiled and said, "Here we go then."

We held enough speed to smooth out our ride, and Maggie kept calling out the buoys. When channels get exceedingly crooked and narrow, it's not always clear which two buoys go together, but Maggie and I were in a zone. She called out the buoys, and we paired them up with what I was seeing on the chart. If buoys were side by side, we went as close to the middle as we could. When they clustered around a turn, we sanity-checked our view with our chartplotter. We got closer and closer to the inlet, but the waves stayed tall. Eventually, we crossed some magical barrier. I didn't know exactly why, but the waves lay down and stayed that way for the rest of the day.

Hangdog Channel

Throughout this run, we could hear several dramas playing out on VHF. A boat had hit the bottom hard near Hangdog Channel and was under tow. Another boat had hit the bottom and was slowly sinking in the Bustard Islands, about a half a day from us. We saw another boat up on the rocks about twenty miles north of our position. Conditions were rough enough to bring people in from the open waters and calm enough to entice them out for a run. The bay was unforgiving.

Our weather reports announced unfavorable winds for a good long while, locking us down for longer than we wanted. Once we hit protected waters, we continued to move northward until we arrived at Wrights Marina, near Britt. We circled up for docktails with the other six or seven loopers there. The loopers were happy to have recovering Maggie in the circle, but we kept her separated and downwind, and she took in the conversations. We told the story of "The Six-Foot Waves" on the Tennessee River. It was particularly funny, and particularly soothing, to be back in community.

At one point, I looked out and didn't see *Magnetic North* there, so I went and got them. They had impostor syndrome and didn't feel they belonged at docktails. We explained that the only requirement to that circle was to be willing to tell a story or listen to one. From that point, they sat in the chairs Maggie and I brought over for them, and we listened contentedly as they told the stories about the many kind and violent acts of Georgian Bay that day.

When we left the next day, Mike and Laura on *Magnetic North* were gone. They'd planned to visit one of Mike's boyhood campgrounds. We looked at our weather app and noticed that the winds were higher than we liked, but we'd be mostly in protected waters. The numbers of loopers were finally making reservations difficult for us, and we needed a landing spot in Killarney, Ontario, at the end of the bay. We'd need to take on provisions. Our friends on *Tortue de Mer* came to the rescue, securing a spot on the wall at Herbert Fisheries. We made plans to watch the dicey weather and hear from boats that were out in the bay. Based on their experiences, we'd either make a stop in Collins Inlet or push through. Either way, we planned to take our time and slowly meander through the French River Provincial Park

Currently **through North Georgian Bay**

and Collins Inlet. These two places were among the most beautiful places on the whole loop.

We left our marina at first light. We passed a spot where we'd seen a cruiser high on the rocks and cut across a sketchy channel. We went slowly, barely above idle speed, but the shortcut shaved ten miles off of our route. Then we poked out into seas every bit as miserable as we expected. We had one- to two-foot seas off the beam. The saving grace was that the waves weren't overly steep and plenty were further apart, so our ride was more gentle than it might have otherwise been. We ran quickly for an hour or so to race across the open bay and back into protected waters.

As we entered the French River park, we were transported to a vastly different scene. A tangle of channels, pools, creeks, and boulders stretched out before us, the blue of the water contrasting with the green of the vegetation and the burnt orange of the rock formations. We slowed down to take it all in. The meticulously marked channels told us exactly where to go, and we saw a new set of signs marking famous canoe routes. We passed several groups of paddlers along the way. A good while later, we heard a *ding* from Nebo announcing the ominous message, "Turn on your thrusters."

I can't say how strange this message was. We were in a tiny boat by looping standards, and we were highly maneuverable *without* thrusters. Still, we did so, and then a tangle of red and green buoys came into view. They all

Islands of the French River Provincial Park

had us hugging the starboard side with the exception of the Obstacle Island obstruction, which spanned about two-thirds of the channel. It was a frightening maze, but we were going idle speed, there was no wind, and yes, we used our thrusters.

We poked around the island, pulsing the engine to keep us under idle speed. We could see rocks about two feet beneath the surface, each sharp enough to carve out a jagged hole in *Currently*'s fiberglass. If we hit the bottom, we'd do so slowly. All the while, we nudged the boat through the strange maneuver, and we each let out a shout when we were through. We could only imagine Emmy's excited bark at the sudden disturbance of the silence.

CHAPTER 37

I Want to Survive It

After Obstacle Rock and Parting Channel, we twice more broke into open waters, with waves big enough to scare early versions of ourselves but too small to keep present-day *Currently* out of open waters. We cut through one of the most beautiful sections of our entire loop, a narrow gorge called Collins Inlet.

Collins Inlet was a looper favorite

To us, this marvelous geographical feature marked the beginning of the end of Georgian Bay. It was beautiful in the extreme, with a dramatically thin passage through a fjord punctuated by high walls. We could have lingered for a day or two, but we were tired and could see the finish line of this remote lake. We opened up the throttle and came into Killarney and Herbert Fisheries, securing the spot, thanks to our friends Bobbi and Mike on *Tortue*. This town was wild and historic Canada at its best, with big log lodges and bustling marinas marking the entrance to the North Channel. We were through the great wild bay and ready to take on our next challenge.

With the completion of Georgian Bay, we added another accomplishment to our nautical resume. The bay with thirty thousand islands was nothing like conditions on the Tennessee River at home. Rather than the shallow, muddy bottoms, we saw rocky beds that plunged down five hundred feet. Instead of the murky, swift waters, Georgian Bay had crystal clear waters. Where the Tennessee waters were mostly protected, Lake Huron was subject to savage winds across scores of miles. Reaching the end felt significant, the same way that reaching the end of the ICW did.

Tortue and *Currently* were the only two boats paying for dockage here. Mike is Canadian and had family ties that secured us both spots. Herbert Fisheries was a commercial operation, with a fishing vessel and a restaurant. Locals, including native Canadians and loopers, would pull up to the docks throughout the day, eat the fried whitefish, and then head home. Before we struck out into the elements again, we had to wait. The winds were whipping in these protected waters, but on the lake, they were up to twenty knots. They'd lay down in two to three days.

Maggie and Bobbi at Herbert's Fisheries

We settled down to watch the boat show and the people show. River otters lived year-round in the crisscrossed timbers that formed the supports beneath us. We'd catch an occasional glimpse every now and then, and when the fishing boat came in each afternoon, they would feed one brave critter scraps, his surprisingly human-like hands manipulating the carcass with ease. The fishing crew told the same sad tale we'd heard all the way around the loop. Fish were not as plentiful as they once had been. Overfishing and climate here too were a problem.

Vegan fare was pretty much out, so we ate the fish that came from that vessel. We wanted to buy provisions from them for our trip, but we never quite got the timing right. One of the days, Maggie thought she had hit the jackpot. She was looking at a freezer full of fish and couldn't decide exactly what to get. She worked her way to the front of the line and still couldn't decide. As a graceful gesture, she let the busybody behind her go first. The woman promptly opened up her own cooler and bought every scrap of fish left in the fridge. The restaurants and locals depended on this place. As a consolation prize, we did pick up a bag of tortured sadness, labeled smoked fish, whatever that was. It looked terrible.

It turns out that smoked fish is the ambrosia of the gods. We made a fish dip with it and ate pounds of the stuff. Then we bought more, thankful that the locals were distracted from the good stuff with meager fresh fish. Then we walked up two hundred yards with Mike, Bobbi, and Mike's dad, Barney, from *Tortue*. For an eighty-year-old, Barney could *eat*. Most days, we wandered over to the restaurant and had fried fish, fried hush puppies, fried fries, and a cup of fried beer to wash it down. I kid, I kid, but my cardiologist would definitely not approve. Our healthy vegan diet had transformed to a healthy plant-based diet with broiled or grilled fish to a plant-based junk-food diet plus fried fish. I rationalized that it was only temporary and that I'd have some work to do once I had better options available.

Eventually, the winds lay down enough for us to leave. The North Channel ran east to west, and it was much more restricted than the wide-open waters of Lake Huron. Still, when winds blew in the wrong directions, they'd kick up a wicked cauldron of pain and misery. The nice things about our initial destination at Baie Fine were that it was close and it was a fjord protected from almost any winds, save those blowing right into the opening. We were feeling more comfortable in moderate seas from one to two feet high, and we had to be. That's just about all we saw. On bad days, sometimes we'd poke a nose out of our harbor to lay eyes on the conditions in open waters, but for the most part, our research of multiple weather sites was sound.

Baie Fine was the most beautiful anchorage on the loop. We passed up several dense anchorages or those requiring a more sophisticated tie up to the cliff walls. We settled into a tiny cutout next to our friends on *Flying Colors*. After so many days of tough weather, Emmy's death, Mike's death, and two cases of Covid, we were feeling a bit beat down. A couple of things helped raise our spirits.

First, we took our dinghy out. The bright-white quartz cliffs along the fjord were dramatic, and the clear waters were stunning in their clarity and beauty. Throughout the day, the waves kicked up. While we were out for one last dinghy cruise, we got too close to the shallows and knocked one fin off of our propeller. To this day, we wouldn't do anything different. A ninety-dollar propeller was a small price for the moments we shared along those cliff sides.

Before breaking the prop in Baie Fine

The second thing that happened was a visit from Ron and Nancy from *Flying Colors*. They came over in their dinghy for docktails when they learned that ours was out of commission. The visit was exactly what we needed.

Maggie was wrestling with going home. Our renter was causing some trouble for our neighbors, so Maggie was afraid we'd go home to some complicated relationships. She wanted to slip in under the cover of darkness. In her eyes, one day the neighbors would wake up and there would be a little tug tucked into the marina behind the trees and a couple more residents that no one would notice. Ron heard this and paused, looking pensive. He said "Maggie,

Nancy and I are not going to do that. We're planning our arrival so those important to us can feel like they are participating in our journey."

It was exactly the right thing to say. Rather than shaping our arrival as a self-absorbed exercise, we made it about hospitality and connection. Those are two ideals Maggie and I value the most. We would find a way to experience valuable connection with those friends waiting for us at home. The other thing Ron said was a bit of a pep talk. He said, "Bruce, do you realize what we've done? Have you thought about all of the skills we've had to master to make this trip happen?"

He then spelled out the types of water we'd encountered, from gulf crossings to the wicked unforgiving rocks around Georgian Bay. We had to run everything from the shallow Jersey Shore with a mere foot beneath us to great and glacial lakes hundreds of feet deep. Then he walked through the skills we had to master, from diesel mechanic to weatherman. He reminded us of the shifting bottoms in the inland rivers and through the Carolinas, the strong crosscurrents off of Georgia, and the wildly varied tides there.

The list was daunting, and if I'd known about the list in 2020, we never would have done the loop. Like me, Ron is a natural encourager, and though we seldom saw him, I have an enormous affection for him. In the morning, we woke up late and *Flying Colors* was gone. We were feeling excited again. We had a few hours of good weather before the winds picked up in the afternoon. We took advantage of them to run fast to the Port of Little Current.

After passing next to Killarney, the small-ship channel we were following squeezed between the mainland to the north and Manitoulin Islands to the south. We could either follow a route through several little villages on the northern shore or through bigger towns on the south shore. The north route would put us in several smaller, remote anchorages. Instead, we planned to go down the southern route, based

Little Current Marina

on the coming prevailing winds out of the southeast. We took advantage of them to run fast to the Port of Little Current.

We spent three days at the quaint town, which had a party going on. The summer tourist season was peaking. They had a local festival going on as well as an art show, with sculptures from HGTV's *Carver Kings*, a chainsaw carving show. *Magnetic North* joined us, and we took our Covid-weakened bodies on a two-mile hike to see a swing bridge open from up close. The waiting boats were getting absolutely pounded in the surf, and we were glad we weren't out there. I wondered how many people had watched *Currently* earlier in our voyage, from the safety of some riverbank, thinking we were the crazy ones?

The next day, *Magnetic North* went out in the surf to visit the Benjamin Islands, so we met up with *Flying Colors* for a walk. As a fellow serial entrepreneur, Ron loved to see inventions. We walked to a pizza vending machine where we filmed the whole experience. It was a festive celebration of innovation. I looked at the vending machine and was impressed. Then I decided the pizza that came out would definitely not tempt me to break my diet.

We looked at the weather. The good news was that we had less than a hundred miles to go. The bad news was that we had one day to cover that distance to Drummond Island, two if we pushed our luck. We thought about our plans to meet the Keith family in Mackinaw City and developed a backup plan to meet them at nearby Drummond Island in a pinch.

We left Little Current early on a borderline running day and saw pretty good waves, but we thought they offered enough margin for safety. Most of the time, we'd have protection from winds blowing out of the southwest. We ran twenty or thirty miles, with plans to go further, but when seas built to three to four feet, we bailed. We headed for Gore Bay, a very nice port but one with a huge Covid outbreak. *Magnetic North* was there waiting for us. We decided to brave Covid at an outdoor restaurant. Our doctor told us that our earlier case would likely protect us if we'd gotten the strain most people in Canada did.

Magnetic North, Currently's clone

The next day was our last day of good weather in the North Channel for a while, but conditions were supposed to be great for travel, and they were. We ran all the way to Drummond Island Yacht Haven, our port of entry to return to the United States. *Magnetic North* came a day later. The next day, we ran to Mackinaw City with *Magnetic North*. Looking at them was like looking in a mirror. They had the same boat, same year, same color, and even a bright-red dinghy. We took a detour to look at the island up close, and then drove by the iconic bridge.

Once we'd settled in, we thought about how far we'd come and where we were going. As we watched our Garmin in our runs from place to place, I saw the many shipwrecks dotting the bottom of the lake. It turns out Maggie saw them too. She had a running texting conversation with Bobbi on *Tortue de Mer* as the Canadian crew watched our progress. Bobbi asked Maggie what she most wanted to experience on Lake Michigan. Maggie's answer was surprising, and not.

"I have a low bar. I just want to survive it."

Part VI

Lake Michigan and the Rivers

The final leg of the Great Loop is the same for almost all routes, with only minor differences. We traversed the eastern shore of windy Lake Michigan and entered the Illinois after near-flood conditions in Chicago. We ran a few days on a low Mississippi River, two days on the Ohio, and then cruised back home on the Tennessee.

Through it all, we felt a bittersweet tension between missing home and wanting to savor the last few beautiful miles. We needed time and space to consider how the Great Loop would mark the rest of our lives.

Lake Michigan

Currently's Home Stretch

CHAPTER 38

Unsalted and Shark Free

Back in the familiar United States, we had bittersweet feelings as we waited for our oldest family friends. We knew Carol and Rich Keith, as our dogs and later our babies played together. After we left Austin for Chattanooga, the friendship continued, and now they were sharing the loop with us. We made it a policy not to share *Currently* with guests for longer than two nights unless they were family, but Rich and Carol qualified.

In Mackinac Island with the Keiths

We visited Mackinac Island, riding bikes next to the pristine white-sand beaches. Mackinaw City, opposite the island to the south, was packed with tourist activities, from a frontier-days festival to reenacts of questionable sensitivity with "pioneers" shooting at howling "indians" from across the street. The town must have been the Amsterdam of T-shirt vendors, with everything from a barechested Trump riding a T-Rex with twin M16s to drugs to booze to our favorite Michigan shirt, "Unsalted and Shark Free."

We had nice fish—the walleye and whitefish that were so common in the Great Lake areas. We visited historic sites, like the fort on the island and the Mackinaw icebreaker, in the great flood of humanity. We hoped once again our recent bouts with Covid less than a month ago would protect us. We were wrong. As Rich and Carol departed, Maggie gave a slight sniff. I said, "No way in Hell" as Maggie broke out our test kit.

We both stared in shock as the little test strip confirmed that Maggie was in fact coming down with Round Two, the universe bringing the hammer down one more time on our trip. Remarkably, neither Rich nor Carol ever developed symptoms. Maggie had some postnasal drip, swollen lymph nodes, a low-grade fever, and a few aches. In short, it was like a bad cold. Though her second bout of Covid was nowhere near as serious as the first, I can't understate its impact on our loop. At the time, the gold standard from the CDC was ten days of isolation, which we followed. We couldn't explore Michigan together the way we wanted to.

I don't mean to whine. Our loop was a lifetime experience, but among all of these beautiful places, we did imagine the things we might have done together. The trip in this intense and glorious place became a bit of a slog. At the top of the lake, the winds were too high for traveling a good bit of the time. At least one of us was quarantining until we were more than halfway down the state. Faced with a choice between feeling sorry for ourselves and moving ahead, we carried on the best we could.

We canceled plans to see a friend in Beaver Island and decided to nibble our way down the coast in tiny increments. We puttered our way down to Petoskey while

Maggie was still feeling well enough to travel, me piloting *Currently* through a miserable one- to two-foot sloppy chop. As *Currently* slammed into wave after wave, my head started hurting, and we both hoped for a miracle but knew the truth. We got to Petoskey, docked, and sat silently. I took a test, confirmed the inevitable, and melted down into my seat at the table.

Then my fever came on with alarming speed, building from 99 to 103.7 in just a couple of hours. I can't begin to express how terrifying this experience was to both of us. This was the case we knew was possible in Canada. We'd read the stories of cases like this in people like me, and we knew how they ended. Unlike my previous case, a cough came on hard and fast. I felt like a gale was building within me, one that we were powerless to stop.

Only, we *weren't* powerless to stop it. Our hard isolation through 2020 and 2021 had bought time for science to catch up. We called our doctor, and he called in a prophylactic antiviral called Paxlovid. Unwilling to give a driver Covid, like the taxi driver had done to us in Peterborough, Maggie masked up and bravely walked a mile to a local pharmacy. She looked at the pharmacist dumbfounded when he said it wasn't yet in and wouldn't be for an hour or two.

Rather than take a chance at infecting others at the pharmacy, she walked a mile back to the boat. She took my temperature and marked a rising fever of over 104, walked *back* to the pharmacy, picked up the medicine, and then walked back. Exhausted, she handed over the goods after walking four miles with her own Covid case. If I had any doubts of her love for me, these valiant walks would dispel them. I took my first pill and went to bed shaking violently with the chills and a rib-rattling cough. By the next evening, I was feeling much better.

We stayed another day in Petoskey, and my symptoms started to clear just a little. The next morning, we broke out into open waters with a steadily pounding chop to match my headache, and the compass continued to spin from west to south toward the lower Lake Michigan towns and eventually Chicago. Maggie drove most of the way, but I was in the navigator's seat. We ran just three hours to Charlevoix. Earlier in the day, there had been a bomb threat against the bridge over the only entrance to the harbor, but by the time we made it, the bridge leading to the harbor city was cleared for marine and land traffic. It was one of the more beautiful stops on the lake, but we were unable to take full advantage of it.

Sunset from Charlevoix on Lake Michigan

The next few days ground us down with one day bleeding into the next. Sometimes the conditions were pretty good, but other times the lake beat us up. One particular day, a handful of boats traveled toward Traverse Bay. A ranger tug rendezvous was happening down in Traverse Bay. *Magnetic North* was attending, but there was no extra room for any more boats. We were cutting across the bay when some unexpected winds blew up along the length of the long bay. Waves of one- to two-foot seas blew up to two to four feet. It happened quickly, and the period between them was alarmingly short, so they were steep.

The waves continued, unrelenting, as we crossed the bay. We couldn't find a rhyme or reason for them, and a boat we didn't know fell in behind us. We couldn't raise them on VHF. If anything, the waves picked up. Drawers popped open, so Maggie crawled back to tape them shut. In my Covid-fatigued state, I could only latch onto the helm and do the best I could. Bottles secured in our shelves and racks started to fall, so she collected them and dumped them into the sink. We kept a good eye on our scuppers, those tiny drains that kept the seawater from pooling in the cockpit and outside our helm door. They were keeping up with the constant pounding of the surf.

Because big waves were my domain, I drove us through the worst of the weather. Sometimes it's hard to appreciate the wisdom of other boaters, but we could see the difference between a four-foot wave *here* and one on the Atlantic. There were just a couple of seconds between these, so they were steep and uncomfortable. I started to feather the throttle, speeding up as we climbed and backing off as the bow dove into the next wave. As the waves got more uniform, I was able to pick up speed so that the bow carved through the waves just as the hull was designed to do.

As waves hammered at us, we looked at all of our weather maps that said it should not be happening. We debated about whether to continue across the bay and around to Leland or to duck into the bay and shelter in the nearest anchorage on the coast. We decided we could get across the mouth of the bay and expected the waves to settle on the other side. Eventually the waves ticked down from over four feet, to three, to a relatively comfortable two. As things settled down a bit, I passed the helm back to Maggie, exhausted but content. I said, "You have the helm." Maybe she replied, and maybe she didn't. I wasn't listening as I stumbled down to the bed, collapsed, and was out cold.

A while later, I noticed that the heavy rocking had given way to a gentle roll. I rolled out of bed and took the helm. We docked the boat in the small, lovely town called Leland.

We picked up some provisions, and then we both crashed early. The next day, we had fair winds and calm seas. We took advantage to run sixty-six miles in just over four hours to Manistee and followed that with another pretty day at sea and twenty-six short miles to Ludington. In this last segment, we ran with our friends on *Betty Gail* and were happy to be reacquainted with them. We'd met them in Marco Island and were just catching up with them again. Of course, I was still in isolation, so we could only do docktails from a distance.

Many of the Michigan towns on the lake were shaped like keyholes. They had an inlet with two seawalls, lighthouses on one or both sides, a narrow channel, and a harbor pool, sometimes on a river and sometimes not. Ludington was memorable because of its ferry the SS *Badger*. This 650-ton vessel was sixty feet wide, one hundred feet high, and more than four hundred feet long. At regular intervals, they left to take passengers across Lake Michigan to the Wisconsin side. We would see them cruise up and regally glide into port, stately and strong, for loading and unloading.

More than a landmark, this ferry served as sort of a brand for Luddington. Their central parks on the water all had signs throughout that showed the history and impact of the *Badger*. In Chattanooga, the city planners did very much the same thing with the pedestrian bridge over the river.

Shaking off the last vestiges of Covid, we took a short two-hour, thirteen-mile jaunt down to Pentwater. We'd stay there for a couple of days to continue to rest up, reprovision our boat, and let our bodies recoup. It was yet another lovely Michigan town, with stunning waterfront views and beaches. The spell of consecutive days with decent weather was blessed, and we got into a pattern of running in the early mornings, arriving a couple of hours before noon, the checkout time for most marinas. Most places were full, but we were still able to find landing spots.

We kept heading down the lake until we got to Grand Haven. There, we stopped to complete our recovery in advance of a programming conference we'd attend in Colorado. We met several different loopers, including our friends Tim and Martha on *Margin*. This couple departed Traverse Bay only days ago and were starting their loop. Martha took Maggie shopping, and I stayed on board to rest.

The memorable Grand Haven Dancing Waters

At Grand Haven, we saw this interesting light and water show, the famous Dancing Waters. The light show across the river wasn't the Barcelona Magic Fountain of Montjuïc, but it wasn't bad either. We stayed on the bow, dancing like teenagers, with an intense star-field sky above us, perfect late summer air around us, and just enough wind to keep the mosquitos away. I taught a class, our first since the Champlain Canal two months ago.

From there, the waves lay down for us as we cruised down to Holland. We docked the boat for our scheduled maintenance and took a plane trip for the first time since 2020. The experience was strangely disconcerting and emotionally harder than I expected it to be.

We attended a conference called ElixirConf. I taught a class with Frank Hunleth, whom we'd met in Deale earlier. The excellent marina completed our one-thousand-hour service, and while they had the boat out of the water, we had some high-pressure engine hoses replaced to eliminate any potential slow leaks from developing. The staff took great care of us. Just as we were leaving, the alternator went out. Luckily, we were still within sight of the marina. We had to replace it, and the service manager told us that finding the part would take a while.

While there, we befriended Mike and Pam from Holland. The couple thought they might do the Great Loop some day, and we loved meeting the locals to learn about the true nature of a place. The happy couple was eating, with their mini-poodle Piero, at a restaurant called La Playa. One of the best things about the loop was the frequency of surprises. Holland had no right to have a Mexican place this good. Their tacos were better than most places I'd found in my thirty years in Austin. They were nuanced and excellent, with authentic Central American salsas and subtle flavor combinations, with unusual ingredients like jicama and hibiscus. Each bite piqued my curiosity and left me longing for more. We saw the couple several times, and they were generous with their time. They picked us up at the airport after the conference to take us out to one of their favorite places. Then, when it took longer than expected to find an alternator, they drove us to the usual pristine Michigan white-sand, salt-free beach.

Our best Mexican: La Playa in Holland, Michigan

After a week, our alternator came in and we were off. We stopped briefly at St. Joseph for a night. As we went to the marina office to pay, *Masquerade* was on their way to a football party, and they had the snacks to prove it. We had a lovely short conversation with them and silently jotted their names down in a growing mental notebook full of people we'd like to know better.

We jutted out across the last corner of the lake, at one point touching three states in fifteen minutes. When we pulled into the Chicago Yacht Club dock, *Flying Colors* was there waiting for us, thrilling each of us with the serendipitous encounter. Ron helped us tie up, and we paused for a few nights to take in Chicago, the windy city itself.

Indeed, it was. As we took in the city, swells in the lake grew to over ten feet. That didn't matter to us, but we thought about the loopers behind. They'd have to wait out the telltale fall winds in place.

We loved Chicago, appreciating it much more than we thought we would. I wondered about those writing the guides we were reading. Most of them were dismissive of the big cities. I tucked the oddity away into the great junk drawer in my mind and walked with our friends.

We had another group of visitors. Fedrico and Kristen Reinking spent an evening with us, and we also connected once more with Cam and Heather on *Sea Clef*. Oh, the walks we all took together. We walked along a concert celebrating diversity and heard two remarkable bands warm up, two famous acts we would have recognized when we were hip and young. Well, when we were young and *Maggie* was hip. I never was. We walked to Italian markets and outdoor memorial parks and to an architecture water tour. We passed other marinas and miles of outdoor bike paths. Chicago was famous for pizza, seafood, and popcorn. We tasted it all. Chicago in the evening was festive, with light shows and bustling tourists.

The stunning building-side laser show in Chicago

We also let some old fears go. We had six people aboard on our tiny tug. We'd never fed so many loopers at once, being self-conscious about our diet and our smallish boat. Patty and Bill on *Let Time Go Lightly* were gracious guests, and we genuinely enjoyed our time with Ron and Nancy, talking about everything from heart disease to the virtues and fallbacks of catamarans in surf. Later, we had our final guests for this phase of the loop, Federico and Kirsten.

We learned about ourselves and hospitality that day. To us, the best parties were those thrown with the intention to know and be known. On the loop, we had nothing to hide. In our tiny 290 square feet, there was nowhere to do so. In some ways, those docktails and parties were just like dinners at home. Plenty of the people on the loop were lonely, curious, or simply longing for connection. We were reckless with our time and our desire for community.

Just as it was time to go, Lake Michigan blew up. Even close to shore, four- to six-foot seas ravaged the coastline. In the middle of the lake, they were higher. It didn't matter to us. We were tucked safely inside of Chicago's seawall. It's hard to describe the difference that a few days made. When we came in, the boats on mooring balls were laid out like kings on a marble chessboard, masts reflecting like crosses on the surface.

The moorings outside the Chicago Yacht Club

It would take a while for those behind us to get moving again, and we knew the scheduled lock closing over most of the summer would condense over three hundred boats into the same place. It was now or never. We made plans to meet our friends on *Amy Marie* at the Chicago Harbor Lock in the morning. As to *Currently*'s crew, we could see the finish line and were ready to be home.

CHAPTER 39

The Hole

"Gidna hoe!"

We looked at each other, trying to make sense of the thick Cajun accent blaring out of the radio. We had the handheld radio watching channel 16 for pleasure craft, a watch on 13 for commercial craft, like the boat in front of us, and the main channel pointed to 17, our chat channel with our friends Mike and Beth on our buddy boat. They had a twenty-seven-foot blue-and-tan Ranger Tug named *Amy Marie*. They were the very same couple we'd met in Chattanooga and had later seen again in Savannah. Beth, the feisty nurse who had put Mike together after a vicious bike wreck, was also a bit confused about the directions from the tow captain. After a brief pause, we heard her say "Repeat, please?"

"Gidna hoe!"

He said it like a Scotsman in a Home Depot paint-shaking machine speaking through a burger joint's failing drive-through mic. In the narrow commercial river, the speaking captain was on a tug pushing barges three wide, and we could see them scraping the rocks on the port side, taking every inch of the river. We saw a little gap in the row of tugs and barges on our starboard, and then it clicked. We moved to "get in a hole" between the barges. We moved toward an opening, before seeing two disconcertingly life-like spotlights peeking over the top of a barge from a tele-scoping helm station. This arrangement allowed the tugs to fit underneath bridges.

Telescoping bridges to navigate overpasses

"Not dat hoe!"

We saw another tow occupying our target, so duly motivated, we continued down a little further and slipped in behind our buddy boat. A dozen feet or so separated us from tons of aggregate, barley, or whatever was in the barges. Ignoring for a moment the game of live Tetris with barges that wanted to smash us to paste, the rivers were our domain. We knew the radio lingo and understood the commercial shipping craft. Our route home started with 330 or so miles on the Illinois, a few days and 160 miles on the screaming Mississippi, a quick 50-mile run upstream on the Ohio, and finally 450 miles over a week or so on the Tennessee. We'd cross our wake after roughly 200 miles on the Tennessee, and then run another 250 or so home to Chattanooga.

We had a couple of problematic locks between us and home, most notably the Peoria Lock, closed except for a few openings on Wednesday and on weekends. Aside from those logistical issues, we had a massive wall of boats coming down from Chicago, the largest group ever to do the Great Loop. The crowd was condensed by a long lock closure for most of August and a few days of early September. We moved quickly down the river before the wave of boats above us in Chicago could get moving.

Over the next few days, an interesting and unexpected game popped up. With *Amy Marie*, we'd count eagles. Some days, we'd encounter dozens of these lions of the sky. We'd see them flash like golf balls in the treetops, flying overhead, and even standing on the opposite banks. I'd never seen clusters of eagles like this. Like dolphins, eagles gave us a sense of peace and joy.

Our first stop was a tiny marina downstream of Joliet, tying up to cleats that might have been more at home on a doll house than a commercial dock. Score one win for our tugs. Bigger boats would not have fit and would have grounded in the four-foot approach, anyway. Then we moved seventy-five more miles down to the tiny, free Hennipen City Docks, notching another win for Ranger Tugs. Next, we cruised through our third consecutive big day, fifty miles and a lock. We locked through at Peoria and anchored at the bottom.

With a wave of boats behind us, we were catching up to another group ahead. There was no way around it. The next few days would be crowded. Our tugs were perfect to navigate those conditions. If we wanted to, we could slow down and conserve fuel. If we needed to, we could speed up and rip off an eighty-mile day, make a lock, or sneak into a marina before nightfall.

We had another benefit too. We were approaching a set of marinas and town docks that were little more than loosely organized commercial barges, or tie-ups to tugs. The increasingly chaotic docking scenarios would make our short lengths and flexible footprints premium features. One such dock lurked ahead of us, Logsdon Tow Service.

Rafting up at Logsdon Tow Service

There, we tied up to *Aries*, loopers from Atlanta who were in turn tied up to conglomeration of rafted commercial tugs and barges. To access shore, we'd walk through their Defever and then hop through the huge tug and then through a gate and onto a barge, and eventually onto the dock. The marina wasn't for the faint of heart. We were grateful that it was available, but we had to stay alert because of the commercial conditions.

The day before we arrived, a woman slipped and broke her ankle. We didn't know how bad it was at the time. Looking around at the various ropes and rusty fixtures all around knee level, I could see how she fell. In all fairness, I *loved* the stop. Seeing commerce up close was tremendously satisfying. Walking up the gangway to the office upstairs felt like walking home from work after a long week on the river.

The barge operations were helpful in other ways too. Our friends on *Margin* grounded a few nights before. A passing tug offered to help, blasting by in hopes that the commercial tug's wake or prop wash would drive the recreational Nordic Tug off of the bottom. As the tug zoomed by, *Margin* leaned over on her side and then shot up like a cork. Shaken but not stirred, Tim had the presence of mind to gun his engines and drive off of the bottom. Martha had more intense thoughts about the situation, but I'll not print them here.

At Logsdon, we had a regular walk with Mike and Beth and got to know them. He was an engineer, and he thought about the world optimistically, the way I did. They had lived through their share of tragedy but had the most relentlessly positive attitude I'd ever seen. Of all of the people on the loop, they were among the closest to us, and I bet many others felt the same. Their stories resonated with us. We walked through the town, making a beeline to a cantina, where we paid $2.99 each for the best margaritas on the loop. We would have paid four times that.

Great margaritas in Beardstown, Illinois

The rest of the way down the Illinois, we traveled with the same set of boats—*Calypso, Aries, Nibbi Dancer, Stardust, Dancing Bears, Titan,* and more. The last two of those boats were bound for Chattanooga, just as we were. Jerry, on *Titan,* was relocating his boat from the east coast, and we'd seen him at several stops on the way. For the most part, the big collection didn't slow us down very much. With so many pleasure craft descending together, it was better to lock through as one big unit. I'd never met a lockmaster who preferred two smaller lockages to one big one. Once we reached the Mississippi, we could break into smaller groups, based on the limited anchorages and running speed of each vessel. *Amy Marie* had plans to attend a concert in Nashville, so they wanted to run fast, just as we did. Maggie and I had to be back in Chattanooga for a memorial service for my brother, so both tugs would have to push pretty hard to make those appointments.

We pushed our way on down, the flotilla staying together at River Dock Restaurant. That evening, *Calypso*'s skipper played a tune in the restaurant on his trumpet, and the owner's daughter joined in—a delightful side with our excellent dinner. One day later, *Amy Marie* took us on a side trek around the shallow end of an island, where the houses stood on stilts nearly two stories high. I knew exactly what that meant. We'd reached Grafton on the banks of the volatile Mississippi.

We tied up in Grafton, one of those surprises on the loop—an unexpectedly lovely town. My guess was that Grafton was the only Mississippi River town with both a ski lift and wineries all around. *Amy Marie* stayed with us, and we picked up another blue-and-tan Ranger Tug, Brian and Jen on *YOLO*. The three blue-and-tan tugs were all within a few dozen feet of one another on the same dock. We saw a fourth tug pull down the aisle. I shook my head with an emphatic "No" and pointed back into the harbor. Then I broke into a smile, and the new tug's captain saw all of the other tugs and laughed with me. We helped tie *Tern* into her new temporary slip and set out to explore Grafton with Mike and Beth.

While in town, I would teach my final class on the loop. This class was on a typical schedule based on Eastern time, while we were on Central time. I would have to wake up early, but we were used to waking up with the rising sun, and the class would wrap up late afternoon. We'd let some weather pass through, and nothing else was on the schedule. We liked the farmers markets, festivals, live music, and the fish market as well. We picked up some catfish and made outrageously good tacos. Grafton also had an oddity for this part of the country—a ski lift. We couldn't pass up the opportunity to check out the views from the dangling chairs.

The Grafton gondola was a delightful surprise

From the top of the ski lift, we could see the Mississippi stretched out before us. I grew up in Memphis, but the river was wider than I remembered. Once we got under way, the main current would add three to eight miles per hour to our speed. As I wrapped up the last days of our class, we hopped a few miles down to Alton, feeling the pull of mighty muddy waters. The marina there was our second straight unexpectedly nice stop. They had a pool and a nice restaurant with Louisiana-style food. We shuddered as we saw the crowds of loopers who would be competing for the same limited anchorages and docks for space. We were glad we were in our little tug. We were there for a single afternoon, so we topped off the fuel tanks and ordered some groceries.

They left our groceries in a deserted alley

Usually, grocery delivery services were one of the most important provisioning tools on the loop, but occasionally, the drivers have a difficult time finding their drop-off points. The better drivers called ahead, and we would talk them in. Occasionally, a driver couldn't be bothered, and they'd just drop their load wherever they happened to be, like a puppy on a brand-new carpet. In Alton, the marina address was confusing, and our grocery deliver showed up in an alley nearly a mile away from our marina. Maggie and Beth trekked all over town with a marina cart on the great grocery hunt.

On the last day in Alton, I finished my class and we got under way at noon. We were confident that we'd had a landing place when we arrived because we had reservations at Hoppies, a loop institution. On our way downstream, we took an exit to a diversion canal, a must-exit that bypassed a dangerous, rocky set of rapids that were unnavigable at these river levels. In years past, a sailboat had missed the turn and wound up on the rocks. Over several weeks, the boat was on the news. Eventually it sank, but the single-handing captain was rescued.

As we made our way downstream, we exhaled with relief when we saw that the river's wing dams were exposed, the tops peeking out of the water. We'd all read about boaters who hit the dangerous partially submerged structures. Wing dams here were loosely bound rocks that extended from the bank to the channel, angling slightly downstream to push the main body of water in toward the channel in the center of the river. These controversial structures reduced the buildup of sediment in the main channels. They were to be feared, and sometimes they were hard to see.

A typical wing dam from above

When we planned where to anchor, or any other time we left the channel, we needed to know where the wing dams were. We sometimes used Google Maps in satellite mode, identifying the destructive dams, even when submerged, by the telltale thin tan lines.

The closest marina to St. Louis, Hoppies was yet another commercial operation that catered to commercial traffic and was a fuel stop for recreational boaters who needed a bit of extra range. For boats with less range than *Currently*, Hoppies was an essential stop for fuel, but power was iffy and there were no other services. The other reason to stop at Hoppies was a captains' briefing, which offered experienced local knowledge to those making the trip downriver. A long row of rusty barges and metal docks, the floating strip of moorings was in a pretty robust current.

When we got there, we could see how low the Mississippi River was.

We got to town, took a short walk, and met once again with Diedre, our neighbor from Chattanooga. Rick and her daughter joined us for a laid-back dinner. Through the evening, other boats came in. Most of them were couples, but one was an elderly gentleman single-handing a tiny Rosborough. This pocket trawler was shorter than *Currently* and didn't have much power, especially for the Mississippi. Still, we'd seen a variety of craft and weren't worried about him at all. He tied up a few boats down from *Currently* on the end of the dock. He'd be leaving before first light. When we woke up in the morning, he was gone.

So often in this part of the journey, we woke up before sunrise. If even possible, sunrises on the Mississippi were even more beautiful than those elsewhere on the loop. The interplay of the sun and the brown of the river often led to vivid reds. The flat landscapes and the cloud formations so common in September led to explosions of color beautiful enough to make me laugh, even before my first cup of coffee. The photo of us beneath the sunrise at Hoppies in particular was almost too pretty for a Ranger Tug marketing brochure.

Hoppies is a Great Loop institution near St. Louis

From there, we headed downstream for one of the longest travel days of our entire loop—we planned to go 110 miles. As our convoy of *Currently*, *YOLO*, *Titan*, *Margin*, and *Amy Marie* left for the day, we heard a clipped radio message. The Rosborough had lost power and was drifting free in the current. I couldn't imagine drifting free in that river with blind curves almost all the way down, wing dams off to either side, commercial traffic, and massive currents. I looked down at my GPS and noticed several severe bends right where the drifting boat would be. Even worse, the gentleman was single-handing. He'd have to deal with the motor or keep a lookout, but he couldn't do both.

That day, the actions of the loopers in the convoy spoke to me. Mike walked him through troubleshooting the problem, and he was able to start the motor again. *Currently* hung back with *Amy Marie* and *YOLO* to make sure he would be OK. It's a good thing we did, because the tiny boat's motor died again and could not be coaxed back to life.

Amy Marie and *YOLO* closed with the little trawler as she rocketed down the main channel. *Amy Marie* came alongside. Mike and Beth tied the boat up hip to hip, the way I'd seen Sea Tow do it before. Then Mike deftly piloted both boats back to Hoppies. All the while, *YOLO* maintained a lookout on the water and on their GPS. *Currently* sped up to travel with the rest of the convoy and make sure that the two loopers would have a place to anchor, as both would be coming in late.

Throughout the day, we ran down Old Man River, picking up speed as the many tributaries fed water, silt, nitrates, and flying carp into the quickening channel. *Currently's* throttle was running at a speed that would barely give us seven miles per hour in most places, but I glanced down to see our speed rise to fourteen miles per hour. Though the water was low, we were moving like we were on plane. The convoy of boats barely even tried as we wound around bends, passed barge trains, and generally soaked in the experiences from the ancient waterway. Our convoy of half a dozen boats or so started thinning out as *Titan* pulled into a little anchorage to secure space for *Amy Marie*.

Titan was a Lord Nelson Tug, a beautiful wooden tug with classic lines and all of the best features of a classic trawler. Through the rest of the loop, the single-handing Jerry Jones would become increasingly important to us as we got closer to Chattanooga. Eventually, he would end his year's travels in Chattanooga, a short mile's walk from our house on the river.

One hundred ten exhausting miles later, the sun was just touching the horizon as we pulled up into the Little Diversion Canal and joined nine other boats already anchored there. I thought there was no way in the world we would all fit, but they made room. We rafted up to old friends on *Fourth Dimension* and were happy to see them again. *Margin* dropped their hook and made room for *YOLO* to come in later. Both Good Samaritans tucked in just as the sun disappeared beneath the horizon.

A packed Little Diversion Canal anchorage

We had two more days to run before reaching Green Turtle Bay at the top of the Tennessee River, and another couple after that to finish out our loop. With the drama of the Mississippi behind us, our loop felt all but done. We settled in with Kip and Insel on *Fourth Dimension* to talk about the thrill of passing beneath West Point from the water after we'd spent the time touring it together on land.

It struck me that this experience was refreshingly normal on the loop—a day of work and travel, small-group conversations, shared joys and frustrations. We were two generations sharing a moment on a trip full of them. The next step was to find a way to bring more of these encounters home with us and share them.

CHAPTER 40

We Crossed Our Wake

Rivers can be dangerous places. I mentioned the 2021 sailboat that missed its turnoff entering the Chain of Rocks diversion, but other incidents happened too. In August 2022, a month before we were there, a high-performance cruising boat struck a barge near Decatur at night. Three people were killed. Wing dams, too, have their own kinds of risks at all different water levels. At high levels, boats can pass over wing dams and strike them with their keel or prop. At lower levels, boats can get caught in water formations, especially when anchoring beneath dams as the water levels change.

For all of these reasons, many loopers looked upon the rivers with great trepidation. I knew these dangers too, but the past nine months had prepared me well. The closer we got to home, the more we knew how to protect ourselves from the challenges each day brought to us. As we left Little Diversion Channel, the current continued to boost us while the miles flew by.

Ahead of us, Jerry on *Titan* was letting the tugs know about our convoy. Maggie communicated with the locks, calling in advance so that we could time our arrival to lock through without disrupting commercial traffic. Both of these roles were acquired skills. Jerry had some skill on the VHF due to his days as a captain and pilot. When he saw approaching traffic, he'd ask which side we should use to pass by. If the tug responded "one whistle," we'd pass by on the right, keeping the tug on our left. If they said "two whistles," we'd pass on the left side, keeping the tug on our right. Since the Mississippi meandered around curves and islands, sometimes it would take a while for all of the pleasure craft to squeeze through. At first, Jerry would tell the approaching tugs about his boat and the one or two boats closest to him, but as time wore on, he'd pass on more information about the loopers trailing far behind. As we pressed on, he became a very good group leader.

Working with the locks, too, was an acquired skill. We'd have to communicate often enough to tell the lock exactly when we'd arrive but not so often as to annoy them. By keeping most communication to one vessel, we kept the lockmasters happy. They would have one or two big lockages in a day instead of five or six little ones. Maggie perfected exactly the right tone, engaging and warm but not overly chatty. This was a skill cultivated over the first five thousand miles of the loop, and the Army Corps of Engineers working the locks appreciated our professionalism.

We turned the corner onto the Ohio with mixed emotions. We were one step closer to home, but we also had to leave behind the fast current at our stern to head upstream into the mighty Ohio. We had a two-hour run to the lone lock on the Ohio. We had to wait a couple of hours for some commercial traffic, but eventually the chamber cleared and the horn at the base of the lock and the green light announced the chamber's readiness. We crept in, boat by boat. Those boats against a wall tied up against floating bollards. In this huge lock, there were bollards for everyone.

We floated slowly to the top, the horn sounded, and the gates opened. The group in the lock broke into smaller groups so we'd all be able to find room. Anchorages on the Ohio and Mississippi tended to be smaller. *Currently* anchored with *Titan, Amy Marie, YOLO, Margin,* and a few other boats at the Grand Chain Reach anchorage, a half day's travel from Paducah. The last of the busiest commercial locks were behind us. Through the end of our voyage, we could expect locks with a much healthier percentage of recreational craft mixed in. Mentally, I calculated four hundred miles from home, and two hundred from crossing our wake.

The river was pretty industrial and the anchorage nondescript, but it felt oddly homelike to me. The eagles and herons reminded me of the many days we'd spent on our pontoon boat. I smiled wistfully, remembering a day with strange clarity. We were cruising downriver toward a beautiful gorge, when our two bored kids asked their bird-watching parents to just go on without pausing to watch yet one more eagle. Maggie and I sat on the bow, the scene peaceful, with each boat a private little island in a tiny sea.

The next day marked a short run to Paducah, with high winds and waves. Tensions were high, and the Paducah city dock had room only on the landward side. Sustained winds were up around fifteen miles per hour, with gusts much higher. The fuel docks were downstream and tied to a floating pier. On the channel side, most boats could tie up right beside the river channel. On the landward side, conditions were a bit dicier because those boats had to navigate past an extremely shallow area at the end of the dock in wind and growing waves. We expected each boat to enter the landward side of the dock and then move toward the fuel dock to leave room for the following vessels. That's not what happened.

Jerry on *Titan* went in first. To our surprise, he tied up on the end of the inside dock. I knew I would have to steer around him where it was shallow, and I knew the wind was blowing toward the land. With the stress of the moment, I simply erupted.

At some level, I understood. If I was single-handing, I might have done the same thing. He'd have to leave early the next day. Still, I rationalized that nothing prevented

A packed Peducah Municipal Marina

him from walking his boat down to the end of the dock, leaving space for others who wanted to park there. Indeed, other boaters offered to help him do so. I completely lost my mind. I yelled over the VHF. Maggie lost her composure and yelled over the front of the bow. The folks all along the dock stared, dumbfounded at the scene playing out before them. All of this predictably led Jerry to dig in. Eventually, it became clear that he wasn't going to move, and I was going to have to dock the boat.

I could see my future landing playing out in slow motion, laid out before me like Picket's disastrous charge at Gettysburg. We were going to ground the boat, and then probably drown and die. I nosed the boat into gear, pointed to the opening, pointed the boat around *Titan*, and the wind promptly blew me into the shallows. I verified mentally that we'd in fact paid our Boat U.S. tow insurance. Just as I could see the muddy cream kick up in the water behind us, the winds mercifully let us go. Our bow came around, my thrusters finally responded, and we pulled the rest of the way in.

I didn't talk to Jerry for a good hour or so. Eventually, level heads prevailed. Jerry moved his boat, and another boat called *Perch* tucked right in where he had been. Kim, the president of the AGLCA, traveled on a beautiful cruiser with her partner Michael. Though they had twin screws, it took three of us to wrestle that big boat into the slip.

The thing about this encounter that stands out to me is that I still have tremendous affection for Jerry, with his larger-than-life stories and his constant invitations for friendship and great Scotch. He is competent, kind, and one of the most interesting characters we met. We walk by his boat docked near us in Chattanooga two to three times a week, keeping an eye on things and dropping in when we can. When he comes to Chattanooga for the boat, despite our yelling at him over the radio and across a dock packed with people, he still invites us over. The loop brings out the best and the worst, but in the end the ties that bind us are stronger than our mistakes or the nasty things we say when we're docking.

Indeed, that evening, Jerry led some of the loopers out to a bar to get some good Kentucky bourbon, while the rest went to a quilting museum. I chose Jerry and his stories. I may have chosen poorly. The quilts in the pictures that came back were so intricate and detailed that I thought the quilts must be photographs. One of them, the Port of Cassis by Lenore Crawford, struck a chord after our time on the loop.

The next day, we in *Currently* pulled out first, making sure to scout the depths out eight feet beside *Titan* so he'd have a pretty good idea of where the bottom was at any given area.

I don't remember exactly where we were, but while we were somewhere near the Ohio, Hurricane Ian made landfall at Cayo Costa Island as a Category 4 storm, right where we'd had the magical dinghy ride with Peg and Craig on *Dream Weaver* to the Tunnel of Love. Every looper knew someone who was impacted, and we were no exception. We spent the next few days texting the new friends we'd accumulated over the past year. Some of them who had a boat no longer had a home dock. Others had tied up in Florida for the off season and lost their boats. Still others

A quilt from the Peducah Quilting Museum

lost their livelihood, or favorite vacation spot, or had damaged homes. We'd been to many of those places, and seeing them destroyed on CNN felt tragically close to home.

As we left, we lined up behind Jerry. I can't remember exactly how many boats there were. Maybe four of us started together, and by the time we reached Bradley Lock at the top of the Tennessee River, there were two or three more. We didn't have to wait too long to lock through. We slipped right into the lock, tied up, and rose up to Green Turtle Bay.

The resort on Turtle Bay is in Kentucky on the famous Land Between the Lakes. It's a massive marina and a common place for wake crossings and boat sales for the loop. Indeed, several different boats crossed their wake there. Among them were boats we knew, the Kadey Krogen *Uncle Wiggly* and the little Nordic tug called *Green Eyes*. There, we would say goodbye to *Amy Marie*. After their trip to

Nashville they'd cross their wake where the Tenn-Tom intersects the Tennessee, just as we would in a few days.

We picked up one more passenger, Nickole Moore, wife of Sam Moore, who crossed the Gulf with us. The stop felt a bit like the breaking up of the Fellowship of the Ring. Some of us would wait for a while there. Others would head up the Cumberland River to Nashville. Still more would go one more stop down the river and meet at the Rendezvous in Paris Landing, Tennessee. Others would just continue down the loop. A few more would come up to Chattanooga, but only *Titan* would travel on our schedule.

Nickole joins *Currently* on the home stretch

Green Turtle Bay offered time to rest from the grueling pace we'd maintained on the river systems. Beth and Martha on *Amy Marie* and *Margin* would walk with Maggie, taking advantage of the kitschy tourist attractions in town. They cut loose and enjoyed one another as now-familiar friends do.

The next few days, we'd have lots of time to reflect. A couple of the days we'd spend with Nickole. Maggie cruised down to Paris Landing, alone with our guest on *Currently*, while I drove our guest's car down to the next stop. The next day, I drove *Currently* with Nickole, while Maggie took the car. We had a robust chop a foot high, rare turbulence on this river. This part of the river was mostly straight, and it ran with the wind. Some strategically placed turns wouldn't let the fetch get too far out of hand, so Nickole and I settled down to catch up and listen to some podcasts.

For Maggie and me, the loop was a voyage of self-discovery. We wanted to understand more about our country, especially the attitudes that destroyed community and trust before substantive relationships could even get started. *The Holy Post* by Phil Vischer—from *VeggieTales* fame—and Sky Jethani taught us about the impact of politics on the church. The e-book *Braiding Sweetgrass* by Robin Wall Kimmerer helped us understand the Native American perspective of stewardship of the land. Jemar Tisby's *People Who Don't Ask Questions* podcast helped us put words to ideas about systemic racism. Nickole and Sam were important to us because we explored many of the same issues back in Chattanooga, so it was a great time to reflect on and explore with her what we'd learned. In the morning, we said goodbye and headed back into a glassy Tennessee River.

Now that we had time to appreciate it, we absolutely fell in love with the Tennessee River all over again. The cliffs, quaint towns, lovely and inexpensive marinas, and familiar wildlife dotted the banks. The birds of prey cried out their pain, while the turkey and deer would hide on the banks while we passed. We'd pass the occasional barge train, but the channel was more than wide enough to accommodate us.

That afternoon, we pulled back into Grand Harbor, the marina where we'd spent that miserable night in freezing temperatures nine months ago. Under changed leadership, the marina provided every experience the previous one didn't. Oh, and we crossed our wake, becoming one of just a few thousand people who had ever sailed all of the way around America's Great Loop. Over 500 people started the loop in 2022, and fewer than 140 finished it.

Even so, the experience of crossing our wake was strangely anticlimactic, almost depressingly so. We had left the great crowds behind, with the mad scramble for common resources, but also the camaraderie of huge gatherings for docktails. The loop was closed, and it was almost as if a jigsaw had carved out this nice, neat hole, leaving a piece of myself to fall out. We were *done* but not yet *home*. Still, we dutifully pulled down our white burgee and hung the gold one. I can still see my face in that picture and notice something missing.

Hanging *Currently*'s gold burgee

One other Great Loop couple came in later, Jen and Brian on *YOLO*, who would be soon closing their own loop. We sat at a dark, lonely table together in front of some condos, and had our own docktails. It was exactly what we both needed. Like us, Jen and Brian planned to sell their boat, *YOLO*. We told stories together, we laughed, and sometimes just sat in silence. It was one of the few times that there were no beginners. We didn't have to sell the loop, and that was a great comfort in this particular moment.

Over time, the magnitude of what we accomplished *did* sink in. I pulled out my notebook computer and opened the map, reminiscing. All of the people and places pinged around in my mind, memories already fading. I thought, too, about the pep talk that Ron on *Flying Colors* gave us, about all of the challenges we'd experienced along the circuit, and the wildly different skills we developed to deal with them. I thought about the six-foot waves in Decatur, only days away from there, our crossing into saltwater in Mobile, and the crossing of the great Gulf of Mexico alone. Wistfully, I was back in Tampa Bay with Mike, and he was alive again, rocking and smiling.

My thoughts headed up the Atlantic coast to the storm in Carolina Beach, the run in the fog with Alexa and Frank, and the crossing of the Jersey coast with *Long Recess*. I thought about Barnegat Inlet, our successful passage, and the boat that sank there. I smiled as I thought about our experience on the canals and the unexpected beauty we found with Brian in Burlington. My heart went to Montreal with my daughter Kayla and Alex, thinking he'd bought a ring and they'd be engaged soon.

Then I suffered hardship again as my finger wandered through the dots of the Rideau, the Trent-Severn, and the Great Lakes, where we'd gotten Covid twice each, and where Emmy had died in the lock. Then I looked at the dots along the rivers, barely believing we'd spent less than a month there.

The last few days of our trip were like that. We'd sit content in each other's presence, occasionally breaking the stillness with a memory or a plan. We picked up *Titan* once again in Florence and stayed with Jerry the rest of the way, through Steenson Hollow, wonderful new city docks at the restaurants and shops of Guntersville, and the quiet Riverwalk Marina. We stopped at Goosepond and reunited briefly with Beth and Mike when they drove from Nashville to meet us for a farewell dinner. We took one last stop at a tiny county park called Shellmound. The place had two little docks. One was deep enough for both *Currently* and *Titan*, so we pulled up and tied off and decorated our boat for our arrival. We had a special guest waiting for us.

Homebound from Shellmound

My sister, Cheryl, and I embraced, and maybe I cried a little, but she was all smiles. She'd been under tremendous pressure with Mike's death and the demands of her young business. Appropriately, she'd cruise the final half day with us. We walked around, we drank a few cocktails, and then we put up some decorative flags. It was a more anxious moment than any of us cared to admit. Homecomings are sometimes hard. We'd been struggling when we left home, and the loop let us leave our troubles behind for a while. What would be waiting for us with our return?

Having moved to Chattanooga in 2017, we were still relative newcomers. Many of the people on the trip told us it would be hard to come home, and we'd not be able to pick up where we left off. Friendships took time and commitment, and the investments in time and energy we'd been making were mostly with loopers, not the landbound. Would our short relationships survive the time we'd been away? Maggie was deeply concerned about our arrival, and some of her angst was rubbing off on me. For Cheryl's benefit, raising the stream of decorative signal flags on *Currently* was a festive event, but the emotions were forced and stilted.

Our last morning on the loop, we cast off, pulling in behind *Titan*. We planned to switch positions when we got close to home, and we tried to let go of our expectations about our return. We meandered our way upstream, reading from the Tennessee River guidebook as we went, tourists for one more day. We passed the abandoned Hales Bar Dam, and the shaky marina that had grown up there. We picked our way by Raccoon Mountain, the bizarre place where TVA pumped water to a reservoir on the top of a hill only to generate power with it. Surprisingly, the place made money because rates were higher at some times than others. We navigated around the spinning Southern Belle from Chattanooga, the paddleboat taking tourists down the river to see the fall colors rage through the gorge.

Cheryl and Maggie were nibbling on treats and tidying our boat up. I had my comforting Currently Crew mug, filled with fresh coffee from the Michigan shore. I kidded myself that after the loop, the reception at home wouldn't matter. The trip itself should be its own reward, but I didn't quite believe it. We invited a dozen families or so but hadn't heard from most people.

Back on Nickajack with Cheryl

As we worked our way up, we passed the place where we first stayed in Chattanooga while we waited for contractors to finish the last few details of our new house. We passed Baylor High School on the port, then a wedding venue and Lookout Mountain on the starboard. *Titan* gave way, and we pulled up and around them to cover the last two miles.

As we slid up the glassy river with the Alstom crane, we knew we were close. Cameron Harbor with our docks, parks, and home were right around the bend. Right about then, we saw ten people or so in the park next to our house, right beneath a thirty-foot-high sculpture full of primary colors, like a freeze-frame of an exploding children's museum. I honked my horn to acknowledge them, and they cheered. Then Cheryl and Maggie went out to the bow to take in the moment. *Titan* honked behind us. As we pulled along the first few blocks of the development, a dozen or so more people gathered in a clearing, near the metal infrastructure from the site's history in iron production.

We slowed down to idle speed to let the people from the park briskly walk next to us to cover the last quarter mile to the docks. We could see residents up on the balconies, cheering. Once loading docks, the decks overlooking our dock had people too, and they were cheering. I honked *Currently*'s horn, *Titan* honked, the tugs across the river honked in reply, and I think I may have even heard the *Southern Bell* honk too. Had Jerry called ahead by radio?

Blessedly, our landing was picture perfect. Richard, the first mentee from our Elixir Chatt program and current Google employee, was there with our neighbor Dan to catch lines. Pat and Steve, who had given us the advice to go, and go now, were on the docks. So many were there, blurring the lines between friend and neighbor, stretching across the nine months of time. I looked at Maggie and she was smiling, a little moist but holding up remarkably well. We were remembered. We were loved.

We were home.

Coming home

CHAPTER 41

Harder than Hangdog Inlet

From the moment I pulled into our dock in Chattanooga, one word jumped into my brain and wouldn't leave. Loop. That word seemed to imply that I would jump onto the circuit, circle around once, and things would be the same when we got back. I could instinctively feel the fallacy. The things around me were mostly the same, much like the feeling of walking into my office the first thing in the morning. The beige dock, the tows rumbling across the river, and the condos lined up like sentinels along the Tennessee Riverwalk. All clicked into place as the neurons in my brain fired in recognition.

Surprisingly, the dock was fundamentally different because *we* were different. I recognized the features of the dock I'd never spotted before and could instantly tell that these solid cleats would hold in a stubborn blow or raging current. I knew that the poles guiding the floating dock were higher than they might be in other places because of the river's flood potential, because I'd seen such features in so many other places.

We circulated through the party like manatees next to the freshwater inlet in Miami. We drank in all of the unexpected hospitality, and it was more emotional than we expected, just as Ron had told us it would be. This was a rite of passage, and our friends and neighbors cared enough about us to share it. After ten minutes or so, Maggie headed back into *Currently*, allegedly to give tours. I knew the truth. She didn't want to feel too deeply in the crowd lest the first tear sneak out, and I understood. The known introverts followed, glad to have the fiberglass shield against emotion overflow, leaving me to face the waves of people alone.

I circled around the party, filling champagne cups and keeping the growing number of corks awkwardly in my left hand because my pockets were full. I led folks in one last looper toast about good ships and friendships, the words finally sinking in. I hugged our neighbors that had made a special effort to take care of us while we were gone, and my first tear leaked out. It seems I'd become a crier on the voyage.

Over time, the party wound down. Richard volunteered to take us upstream to Cheryl's car. Like me, he was an awkward person on the best of days, and full-on nerd on the rest. He usually had metaphorical corks in his hands too. He was in his Tesla and loved to show it off.

It is a heady thing to be with three people I'd known through life-changing experiences. My mentoring program had offered a place for Richard to grow as he made the transition from the floor at Amazon to technical infrastructure at Google. His experience was a brutal one, but it eventually bore fruit and led to the friendship between our families. I think I might have needed Richard's success more than he did. It gave purpose and meaning to my life. I thought about his parents, Rick and Diedre, whom we'd been able to see both at Hoppies and Amelia Island.

Then I looked at Cheryl. She was clearly not in the mood for conversation. She'd been through a lot, and not just the Tesla. Maggie was one of her best friends. Her social vortex was a lifeline to Cheryl when we moved to Chattanooga. Though she'd lived there for years before we showed up, we'd found community much more readily than she had. Cheryl adopted our friends as her own, and I was thrilled for it. When we left, she never complained and always asked what we needed. Our returning was good for her soul.

It took us forty minutes to reach Shellmound after covering the same distance by river in six hours. In the end, we survived Richard's wrong turns and aggressive acceleration. Richard smiled, obliviously unaware of the close encounter his upholstery had with Cheryl's collection of bile, champagne, and vegan snack food. Driving back to Chattanooga, Cheryl and I had a lovely conversation about how much we missed each other, but mostly we made the kind of small talk that covers emotions packed away for later conversation. We'd put off Mike's memorial service for another day.

Cheryl disappeared to get food, and I walked into an empty house. It was much smaller than the house we'd sold in Austin, but today it just felt impossibly huge. I didn't know how we'd ever adjust to something so vast again. Absentmindedly, I shuffled my feet because Emmy was deaf and near blind, but she wasn't there. I couldn't bring myself to record videos, because I usually closed with "From Bruce, and the dog on the floor. This is Groxio Learning." It's an embarrassing bit of writer's block, but there it is.

The cavernous space was unnaturally clean. Our guests had done a wonderful job and left an immaculate home for us. Well, that's not quite true. They left an immaculate *house* for us. Even the spice labels all faced the front of the spice pantry. The baseboards were scrubbed. I looked at our furniture, where other people had sat for six months, including our massive couch. It was the creature comfort we looked forward to the most.

I looked around for Maggie, but she was gone. I knew where she was without calling her. I strolled back toward *Currently*, waving casually to stunned neighbors that couldn't quite stitch together the idea that we'd been gone in the short time it took to pass by. I mumbled something unprintable as I saw the open marina gate, noting it had been left open again. Then I scanned for *Currently* and found her in the unfamiliar slip, our home slip. She sat high and proud in blue with tan-and-white trim with the splash of faded red, almost iconic in our circles. The cheap signal banners probably said something about black plague, but we didn't know, so we didn't care. I walked down the ramp to find Maggie.

My wife was on the boat, but not quite where I expected her to be. She was still, just overwhelmed with the idea of home. Maybe it was the mundane, the big spaces, or the growing to-do lists. Maybe it was something bigger, like the alien feeling of being somewhere that didn't quite fit anymore. Whatever it was, she was mostly lying down on the bed but had one foot on the ground, much like a drunk college student would be, but Maggie wasn't drunk. She'd barely had a sip from her aluminum coffee cup turned champagne glass. The river was flat so there was no hint of motion, and certainly nothing a serious sailor couldn't handle. She just wasn't grounded. I instinctively knew it because I wasn't either. In time, we would be.

We talked about nothing and everything before I wandered back to the cockpit and then hopped onto the dock. As I walked back to the house along the homogeneous houses along the riverfront, I thought back to Ron's conversation back in Baie Fine. I felt almost like a stranger in my own skin because it didn't seem possible that Maggie and I had completed this great adventure. Six thousand miles flew by in my mind in a blur, from the frigid rivers to thousands of miles of coastline to canals to the Great Lakes and home. Before I knew it, I was at that cavernous building I used to call home.

Over the next several days, we had guests come in. My sister lived with us briefly. She'd just sold one home and closed on another but hadn't gone through the busywork of moving one final time. Providing a landing place for a few days was the least we could do, and it would ease *our* transition from nightly docktails to nights full of our big white couch and nothing. She didn't stay long, despite our assurances that she could.

Once Cheryl left, an Austin friend stopped in for a few days, another Austin couple who was passing through visited, Maggie's sister also came for a visit, and so on. Over our first two weeks home, we had just two nights alone as we worked through the first of the lengthy visitor backlog due to Covid 19 and our voyage. We were in a tourist town, parents of college kids, and people wanted to come! We'd been away for only nine months, but Covid-19 put the brakes on most visitors. In some ways, working our hospitality muscles back into shape was a good distraction.

We also had a wave of Great Loopers stopping through. Because many of them were watching the aftermath of Hurricane Ian, they wanted to linger in the river systems while Florida recovered as much as it could. After traversing the ICW through that area, I knew the strategy made sense. Florida would need time to rebuild infrastructure, dredge the ICW, and assess resources for local boats, let alone transient space.

The steady trickle of promising Chattanooga visits and reports of chaos in Florida after Ian led to rumors worming their way back to the fleet. The trickle turned into a flood. One evening, we decided to have a couple of friends over, Al and Arlene on *Arion*. They would come to town, and we knew them well enough to let them see the chaos that had rapidly dismantled our house as we moved back in. That list grew to include *Masquerade*, then *Sea Clef*, and then *Margin*. The list kept growing, including *Dancing Bears*, *Out of the Blue*, *Endeavor*, *True North*, and so on.

When all was said and done, not a half a week had passed, and we weren't yet moved back into our place from the boat and the plethora of storage units my sister had secured when the demands of our tenants and realtors had changed. We still had to prepare for a party of just under twenty people. Since we were coming off of Covid-19 and a year in a tiny space, we had not thrown a dinner party in a good long while.

The tonic was exactly what we needed. Touching base with Al and Arlene, our buddy boat who didn't leave us in the middle of the remote Canadian wilderness, was soothing and grounding. It sounds cheesy when I say it—that we were in the middle of the most beautiful place with the nicest people we'd ever met, but that's very much the way we felt about our time with them in Canada. We had been afraid of what might come to pass. With friends, we were able to relax and take in the places. Even through the fog of disease and loss, the memories will last forever.

While at the party, I had a conversation with Gee on *True North*. As they prepared for their loop, she had spent some time learning about the cruising community. Her experience had not been a pleasant one. She felt alone and afraid, experiencing racism or misogyny, or both in many instances, from other boaters. Once she had plugged into the Great Loop community, racist remarks and glances disappeared. We talked about the *Currently Away* project. I told her that the loop was a place to find and interact with people "not like me." She looked at me with confusion, as this *white man* talked to the *Asian woman*, and must have thought "These people are all like you!"

In truth, I didn't have a precise answer to the question, What does "not like me" mean? We promised we would check in again and that I would express her thanks to the welcoming Great Loop community. I would also present the idea that gender and racial diversity in boating in the United States still has a long way to come. I thought about her conversation for weeks after we had it. Truthfully, as a white man who tries to open doors for underrepresented programmers, I still think about it from time to time. So here's to you, Gee.

Near the end of the party, the crowd thinned out a bit. Al and Arlene stood up to go, but we held them for a while. The couple were aficionados of Port wine. They'd spent a bit of time in Portugal and had grown fond of sampling and even collecting it. We had an unopened bottle that was twenty years old and offered to share it with them. The six or so people who remained around our circle all tried a little of the Port, and it was excellent. We said our goodbyes and took them back to their boat, less than a mile away, feeling better about the transition.

After a few days of being home, we contemplated doing something harder than Hangdog Channel and more nefarious than the New Jersey Shore. We stepped on a scale. Loopers joke that they need three community support groups when they get home: marriage counseling to recover from docking with a spouse, Alcoholics Anonymous for surviving daily docktails, and Weight Watchers to recover from food too good, too accessible, and too plentiful.

For us, the burden was a little greater than it would be for most others because of my heart issues. A number on the scale could be merely vanity, or it could be a life-or-death symptom of a greater problem. My weight wasn't great, but it would come down. Bloodwork came back with the excellent news that the plant-based diet was working, even after a little added fish. The small variance could be rectified with exercise and by doubling down on the diet, especially in the areas of fried foods and snacks.

For Maggie, the news was decidedly worse. She'd picked up a few pounds but also had some bad blood-work numbers for the first time in her life. We learned that plant-based junk food wasn't any better than just plain old junk food. In truth, we always knew it, but this news hit her particularly hard. To someone that thrives on connection and hospitality, dietary restrictions feel like broken connections to the past and the erosion of comfort. Just when we thought we needed to take a break and decide what a new kind of plant-based, alcohol-free hospitality looked like, *Pivot* popped up on Nebo. When I started the loop, I wouldn't have thought having social media stars over would be a good move for this time. I would have been wrong, because they were the exactly the right people at the right time.

Jen and Elliot are lovely people. Their humility and sense of purpose spoke to me deeply—they are gentle souls who view travel the way we do. Their voyages are integral parts of their lives, each voyage making the world a little smaller. Like Maggie, they thrive on connections across cultures and community. We talked about Elliot's dreams as an entrepreneur, our plans for *Currently Away*, and the struggles of life on the liquid road. They were also some of the first people we hosted at home after the loop with our seriously restricted diets.

Maggie made the bold decision to learn to entertain with excellent food that happened to be plant-based. The theory was well and good. In practice, we'd have to sacrifice many a guest on the altar of culinary apprenticeship. The first meal was surprisingly good. Elliot was particularly captivated by the smokey, tangy cashew cream sauce, and even asked for the recipe. Then, for the first time since her doctor's appointment, I heard the sound I'd been longing for—Maggie laughed.

The first squadron of loopers plowed on through, the wakes of the big trawlers making a pleasant hiss on the rocks below our house. The greater wave of loopers continued. We had a few more people over and made time for lunches and dinners. *Sea Clef* lingered with *Out of the Blue* for a little while, *Margin* treated us to a lovely dinner, we took some walks with Jerry from *Titan*, and so on. We met

The video bloggers share a dinner

new friends who knew our old friends. *Sojourn* had run with the Longs on *Long Recess* for a while along the Atlantic ICW. Mark and Cinda Boomershine, on *SEAShine*, another video blogging couple, came with Jen and Elliot. We all laughed as the Boomershines talked with their kids over handheld VHF. It was a charming and beautiful glimpse of a young family taking on the same adventure we were but in a profoundly different way. We reprised the earlier veggie taco dinner, and everyone left satiated.

Currently still had one more task on her arrival list. She needed to host a memorial for Mike's family and two sons. In late October the young men arrived for the weekend. We met at Cheryl's office the next morning. We told stories, had a few words, and then left to board *Currently*.

I stabilized the boat as my surprisingly nimble father and my brother's wobbly sons climbed aboard. Mikey and Kenny had come aboard for a meal in Panama City and Norfolk, respectively, but neither had joined us underway. Mike's true remains would be buried at sea because of his Navy status, but we had a few small tins of rose petals to sprinkle overboard. Sometimes, people with autism have a hard time releasing emotion constructively, but after many months Kenny broke down and cried what he called tears of joy. Finally, his brother did the same. Instead of being across the country, I was there to put my arms around them for comfort and release.

Mike's memorial

We headed downstream from Chattanooga and passed the *Belle* as she made her fall-color rounds. The trees were borderline spectacular in places, but never quite as bright as the first autumn we spent in town. *Currently* rounded the tip of Williams Island near Baylor. Maggie took the helm while Mike's sons, brother, and father all sprinkled his symbolic remains into the river. The petals drifted with the current, holding a coherent shape as they swirled down the river alongside *Currently* as we cried, and laughed, and danced. Ever so slowly, the cloud of Mike's memory drifted, swirled, and thinned until he was gone.

Gone too were people who passed while we were on the trip or soon after we returned. Shortly after we returned, we lost Steve Garrison, who had helped us prepare. It was his wife, Pat, who had told us to go immediately rather than waiting two years. In November, just after we returned, we lost Pastor Ben Ferguson, whom we had listened to underway on some Sundays as he invited us to be more than we were, even as his cancer consumed him. We thought of Emmy, the constant blonde puddle of love on the floor. And, of course, Mike.

To me, the grief of these passings of ones we loved so dearly is something that won't ever go away, at least not in the same way as that swirl of rose petals did. Rather, I think I absorb it into my soul, that emptiness, and with it the joy of those relationships. Maybe they all become part of Bruce Allan Tate.

This great life adventure is like that too. We'll absorb it and it will become us. The loop marks me as surely as our white, now golden, burgee. Like my grief, it has become a part of me. We know the value of green and red buoys: truth matters and infrastructure matters.

The loop also reminded us never to stop being curious. It challenged us to dream big, even audaciously. It relentlessly drove us to more docktails, this time around our dinner table, with other curious people. I know that same curiosity will transcend differences between us by reminding us to keep asking about the people underneath layers of politics and religion.

Big life events can't help but change us. I know I was changed when my mother died, when each plane flew into the world trade center, when each of our daughters was born, when Maggie said "Yes"…, and when she told me she was reading *The Great Loop Experience*, a book about a personal journey by boat.

Bibliography

[GH14]   Captain George and Patricia Hospodar. *The Great Loop Experience*. Atlantic Publishing Group, Inc, 1405 SW 5th Avenue, Ocala, FL 34471, Paperback, 2014.

[Hop20]   Rob Hopkins. *From What Is to What If*. Chelsea Green Publishing, West Wing, Somerset House, Strand, London WC2R 1LA, Paperback, 2020.

[Wri19]   Capt. John Wright. *The Looper's Companion Guide*. CreateSpace Independent Publishing Platform, 4900 Lacross Rd, North Charleston, SC 29406, Paperback, 2019.

The Pragmatic Bookshelf

The Pragmatic Bookshelf is a small independent publisher. We're lucky to be able to publish books that we love, written by authors we consider friends.

We publish deeply technical books written by software developers for software developers. Recently we've expanded our catalog to include titles covering the history of software development, along with issues regarding health and well being.

Please visit us at *https://pragprog.com*.

Printed in the USA
CPSIA information can be obtained
at www.ICGtesting.com
JSHW011704080224
56878JS00003B/3